Diamond

Urban and Industrial Environments
series editor: Robert Gottlieb, Henry R. Luce Professor of Urban and Environmental Policy, Occidental College

For a list of the books in this series, see page 295.

Diamond

A Struggle for Environmental Justice in Louisiana's Chemical Corridor

Steve Lerner

The MIT Press
Cambridge, Massachusetts
London, England

Set in Sabon by The MIT Press. Printed (on recycled paper) and bound in the United States of America.

Library of Congress Cataloging-in-Publication Data

Lerner, Steve, 1946–
Diamond : a struggle for environmental justice in Louisiana's chemical corridor / Steve Lerner.
p. cm. — (Urban and industrial environments)
Includes bibliographical references and index.
ISBN 0-262-12273-1 (alk. paper)
1. Environmental justice—Louisiana—Diamond. 2. Chemical plants—Environmental aspects—Louisiana—Diamond. I. Title. II. Series.
GE235.L8L47 2004 2005
363.7'009763'33—dc22   2004049912

10 9 8 7 6 5 4 3 2

in memory of Leroy Jones and Helen Washington, who lost their lives in a fire on the fenceline in Diamond

Contents

Foreword

Numerous studies have documented that African-Americans and other people of color in the United States are disproportionately impacted by environmental hazards. In the real world, all communities are not created equal. If a community happens to be poor, black, or located on the "wrong side of the tracks," it receives less protection than affluent white suburbs.

In this book, Steve Lerner chronicles an African-American community's struggle against environmental racism. Diamond, a tiny community in Norco, Louisiana, typifies a population under siege from chemical assaults. Clearly, racism influenced local land use, the siting of industrial facilities, the enforcement of environmental regulations, and where the Diamond residents live, work, play, and go to school.

Diamond uncovers a seamy and seldom-told side of the petrochemical industry. The Diamond residents, many of whom can trace their roots to descendants of slaves who assembled small parcels of land from the old Diamond Plantation and passed it on to subsequent generations, fought for decades to be relocated away from the sprawling Royal Dutch/Shell petrochemical plants. The Diamond community is sandwiched between the Shell/Motiva refinery and the Shell Chemical plant. Some residents' property lines are only 9 feet from the fenceline with Shell Chemical.

Dozens of small rural black communities, like Diamond, are on fencelines with chemical, nuclear, and petrochemical plants in Louisiana's Mississippi River Chemical Corridor—an area dubbed "Cancer Alley." Many of these all-black communities survived the challenges of the post-slavery plantation and the "Jim Crow" era but have not survived the toxic chemical assault of nearby polluting industries. Toxic chemical assaults are not new for the Diamond community residents, who live in constant fear of toxic spills, explosions, and routine pollution from nearby chemical plants.

Before the "9/11" terrorist attack, Diamond residents experienced a form of "toxic terror" 24 hours a day and seven days a week. When (not if) chemical accidents occur, government and industry officials instruct residents to "shelter in place." In reality, locked doors and closed windows do not block the chemical assault on the nearby communities.

For decades, Margie Richard, her Diamond neighbors, and the Concerned Citizens of Norco complained about the foul odors, booming noise, perpetual light, and flaring from the Shell refinery. And for decades, Shell refused to buy them out and relocate the community. Ms. Richard took her struggle to congressional hearings in Washington, to the United Nations Human Rights Commission in Geneva, and to the Netherlands (home of the Royal Dutch/Shell Group).

In June 2002, victory finally came when the Concerned Citizens of Norco and their allies forced Shell to agree to a buyout that allowed residents to relocate from the chemical facilities. In April 2004, Margie Richard was awarded the prestigious Goldman Environmental Prize for her valiant and courageous actions.

Diamond provides a unique in-depth analysis of the day-to-day struggle of a fenceline community's pursuit of justice. The book is an important addition to the expanding literature on environmental justice in that it captures the "voices" and "spirit" of the community in detail so that the reader gets a sense of the conditions under which fenceline residents live and a real understanding of why they fight for relocation.

Robert D. Bullard, Director
Environmental Justice Resource Center
Clark Atlanta University

Preface

Every book has a story about how it came to be written. This one is in your hands because my brother, Michael Lerner, invited me to Louisiana to meet Margie Richard, a woman who lived in a trailer on the fenceline with two giant Royal Dutch/Shell petrochemical plants. Richard was part of a group of residents in the small African-American community of Diamond who were protesting emissions from the plants that they were convinced were destroying their health. They were demanding to be relocated at Shell's expense. It was a classic environmental justice struggle pitting a small, relatively powerless community against the resources of a giant multinational corporation.

Since 1976 I have worked with my brother at Commonweal, a nonprofit health and environmental research institute in Bolinas, California. He became involved with the residents of Diamond because he thought their demands for relocation were reasonable and he wanted to alert people he knew in the philanthropic community to the struggle. He also opened up a back-channel dialogue with some of the top officials at Royal Dutch/Shell in an effort to help shape a solution to the confrontation that would work both for Shell officials and for local residents.

When my brother asked me to come to Diamond, the initial idea was that I would conduct a series of interviews with residents and record an oral history of what their lives had been like on the fenceline with the Shell petrochemical plants. I conducted more than two dozen interviews and posted them on the Internet. In the process, I met a number of environmental justice activists, from many different walks of life, who had converged on this obscure community on the banks of the Mississippi in St. Charles Parish. Fascinated by their stories, I began to interview them to find out what had drawn them to this struggle and what help they had been able to provide the residents of Diamond.

It did not take long to discover that Diamond was a subdivision of Norco, Louisiana, and that the two communities, though adjacent, were segregated. I crossed the color line and interviewed white residents in Norco who claimed that pollution from the Shell plants was not bad and that many of them were living to a ripe old age. Residents of Diamond were just complaining about pollution in an effort to squeeze money out of Shell, some of them charged.

To round out the story I also interviewed officials at Shell. They told me that their facilities were not hurting anyone's health, how they were improving the operation of their plants to reduce emissions, and why they were reluctant to buy out and relocate all the residents of Diamond.

In the end, I had hundreds of hours of interviews on tape and a wide variety of perspectives on the grassroots campaign by Diamond residents to be relocated. What had started out as an oral history of the people of Diamond became a broader story about a struggle for environmental justice.

Acknowledgments

This book was made possible by financial support from Carl Anthony, director of the Ford Foundation's Sustainable Metropolitan Communities Initiative, by administrative support from Commonweal, and by editorial support from Clay Morgan at The MIT Press. Carl Nagin provided valuable editorial guidance.

The residents of Diamond generously opened up their homes and spent hours telling me their stories and the history of their community. Margie Richard (former president of Concerned Citizens of Norco) was unstinting in her help on this project, as were many other residents, including Josephine Bering, Deloris Brown, Larry Brown, Janie Campbell, Iris Carter, Carolyn Cole, Devaliant Christopher Cole, Milton Cole, Audrey Eugene, Lois Gales, Lorita Jenkins, Gaynel Johnson, Brent Mashia, Wendy Mashia, Lois Parquet, Dorothy Pedescleaux, Ernestine Roberts, Delwyn Smith, Jenny Taylor, Devon Washington, and Dewayne Washington.

Special thanks are due to Anne Rolfes (director of the Louisiana Bucket Brigade), who introduced me to the residents of Diamond and to many activists in the nonprofit world who supported their struggle for relocation.

Several residents of Norco were also good enough to tell me about their lives in the community adjacent to Diamond and the Shell plants. Among them were Clarisse Webb (chairperson, Shell River Road Museum), Sal Digirolamo (president, Norco Civic Association), and Constable Milton Cambre.

David Brignac, Shell Chemical's spokesman in Norco, patiently explained the history of the relationship between Shell and its residential neighbors in Diamond.

Many environmental justice advocates and experts on environmental contamination also helped place in perspective the conditions that residents on the fenceline in Diamond faced. Among them were Adam Babich (director, Tulane Environmental Law Clinic), Robert Bullard (director, Environmental Justice Resource Center, Clark Atlanta University), Gary Cohen (executive director, Environmental Health Fund), Jack Doyle (author of *Riding the Dragon: Royal Dutch/Shell and the Fossil Fire*), Monique Harden (former staff attorney, EarthJustice Legal Defense Fund), Denny Larson (coordinator, Refinery Reform Campaign), Vernice Miller-Travis (a former program officer at the Ford Foundation who worked on brownfields issues at the Natural Resources Defense Council), Marylee Orr (director, Louisiana Environmental Action Network), Damu Smith (former director of the Southern Community Labor Conference for Environmental and Economic Justice and organizer for Greenpeace), Wilma Subra (president, Subra Company), Robert Thomas (director, Center for Environmental Communications, Loyola University), Peter Warshall (former editor of the *Whole Earth Review*), Maura Wood (Louisiana Delta Chapter, Sierra Club), and Beverly Wright (executive director, Deep South Center for Environmental Justice).

Diamond

Introduction

Josephine Bering, 87 years old,[1] can be found most days in her living room, sitting in a comfortable armchair next to her fish tank. She lives in Diamond, an African-American community 25 miles west of New Orleans on the banks of the Mississippi. Her house is located three streets from the fenceline with a Shell Chemical plant. The day I met her, she was wearing a white and green plaid dress and white socks. One of her many grandchildren slept on the couch while two others played in a back room. Outside and inside her home, the air was permeated with a smell that one would expect to encounter in a closed storage closet filled with industrial-strength cleansers.

Bering lived on the fenceline with the chemical plant for more than 60 years. Her late father polished floors and cut grass at the plant. A few years ago, in recognition of her father's long service, Shell officials helped Bering fix up her house. But when she suggested that it would be better to move her away from the fenceline and the health problems she associated with the fumes from their plants, Don Baker, a Shell official, replied "Repair is one thing; relocation is another."

That was not a good enough for Bering. "I want to get out of here for the sake of my health," she said. Her sister, also a resident of Diamond, died at 43 of what Bering describes as "phlegm on her lungs." The doctors told her that it came from living near the chemical plant and the refinery. "She suffered with that a long time," Bering remembered. Like her sister, Bering had respiratory problems and was "short-winded." Her asthma improved only when she left the area. She described the air around Diamond as smelling like ammonia or bleach. "It works on me terrible," she said. Asthma also afflicted one of her grandsons; when he stayed with her, she had to hook him up to a "a breathing machine."

Then there were the unexplained allergies and skin problems that ran in the family. Bering attributed the cracked and discolored skin on her wrists to the chemicals coming from the adjacent Shell plant. To underscore the severity of this problem, she called in one of her granddaughters from the bedroom and told the gangly adolescent "Show the man your arms." Reluctantly, the 14-year-old girl stretched out her arms. "It is like that all over her body," volunteered Bering, whose sister was similarly afflicted.

"I don't have enough money to get out of here, so I have to just stay and suffer with it," Bering said. "All Shell has to do is buy people out and let them go. Just give us enough to get out of here. If they would move me out of here and relocate me, I would surely be happy."

Josephine Bering and the other residents of Diamond are not alone in their predicament. In small towns and cities across the United States, fenceline residents are routinely exposed to high levels of toxic chemicals. Who are these Americans who live on the fenceline in such close proximity with heavy industry? Several studies show that poor and minority populations are disproportionately likely to live near hazardous waste sites and "locally unwanted land uses."

"Black communities became the dumping grounds for various types of unpopular facilities including toxic wastes, dangerous chemicals, paper mills, and other polluting industries," according Robert Bullard, who directs the Environmental Justice Resource Center at Clark Atlanta University.[2]

Some fenceline residents were displaced from their previous homes so sites could be cleared for the construction of industrial facilities and subsequently found cheap land on which to rebuild near the new plants. Others arrived later, drawn to the area when pollution lowered property values to the point where they were affordable to the poor. But whatever brought them to these locations, it is clear today that those who now live in the shadows of these plants are burdened by high-level exposure to toxic, highly flammable, explosive chemicals.

How did this geographic segregation come about? According to Vernice Miller-Travis, an environmental justice advocate from New York, the location of minority residents along the fencelines with toxic industries in Diamond and in similarly situated communities did not happen by chance; it is a result of poor land use decisions made decades ago.

A decision was somehow made, consciously or not, that Diamond would be what Miller-Travis called "a sacrifice zone." Its residents would suffer exposure to a disproportionate burden of toxic chemical releases from plants so that other Americans could benefit from the artificially low prices of goods made in these plants. The decision," Travis-Miller noted, "takes us back to the question of who is valuable."

Permission to locate a new industrial facility adjacent to an existing residential area is often sold to the community in terms of the jobs it will create. But this tradeoff, Miller-Travis explained, is viewed by the environmental justice community as a kind of "economic blackmail." Industry comes into a destitute place such as Diamond and offers jobs and economic investment in return for a site for highly polluting facilities (petrochemical plants, incinerators, cement plants). "It is a heinous thing to ask people to do, but it happens all the time," Miller-Travis asserted. In essence, people are offered a choice between jobs and a shorter life, she continued. That fenceline residents get very few jobs in these facilities exacerbates the distrust that builds up between the industries and their residential neighbors.

Diamond is surrounded by heavy industry because of a long history of racially biased land-use planning in the United States, Miller-Travis charged. The situation in Diamond is more the rule than the exception for communities of color, she continued. In white communities, zoning protects residential areas from industrial development. In communities of color, any kind of development is often permitted, including a mix of residential and industrial uses, and as a result the health of residents is compromised.

Today a growing number of environmental justice activists are calling attention to the harm done by the geographic concentration and economic isolation of low-income and minority citizens in rural pockets, inner suburbs, and central-city ghettos. The clustering of poor and minority residents along fencelines with industries infamous for their emissions of toxic chemicals is just one of the forms this "spatial segregation" takes.

A close look at the history of the fenceline community in Diamond provides evidence that the environmental regulatory regime in the United States is not stringent enough in its emissions standards, in its enforcement of existing regulations, or in the scope of its monitoring programs to protect the health of people who live next door to "hot spots" of pollution.

No federal regulations currently exist that require residential communities to be a safe distance from highly toxic and explosive plants. Furthermore, monitoring of the air in fenceline communities is often nonexistent, and large releases of toxic chemicals from adjacent plants are commonplace. Regulatory policing of violations of air permit is sporadic at best and often results in a minimal fine or none at all.

Common sense would dictate that at a minimum there should be health surveys in communities adjacent to the most toxic industries, but such surveys remain rare. There are no consistent records of the level of toxins in the air fenceline residents breathe, nor is there good medical information about what harm the intense pollution may be doing to their health. As a result of these regulatory inadequacies, an unknown number of Americans—possibly hundreds of thousands—suffer from respiratory problems and other health effects associated with unreasonably high toxic exposures.

Not only has the U.S. government's regulatory apparatus been less than effective at protecting the health of fenceline residents; the largest and best-funded environmental organizations have been slow to lobby on behalf of Americans who live next to giant industrial plants. The fight for relocation in Diamond should have been recognized early on as one of the front lines of the environmental movement. However, that did not occur, and much work remains to be done to convince large environmental organizations that it is in their interest to support the struggles of fenceline communities.

The reluctance of large environmental organizations to adopt fenceline struggles has had two important consequences: first, it has deprived fenceline residents of the considerable lobbying talents and resources that the largest environmental groups can bring to bear; second, it has robbed the environmental movement of political support from a segment of the population that is highly motivated to see that releases from large chemical plants are controlled. Any political consultant hired by the environmental community worth his or her salt would point out that there are legions of Americans who live adjacent to locally unwanted land uses, and that if this constituency were intelligently organized it would swell the ranks and increase the clout of the environmental movement. Thus far, however, no such effort has been undertaken on a large scale. The likely reason for this is that many environmental activists have yet to see the connection between the preservation of wilderness and the cleaning up of heavily contaminated poor communities, despite the fact that the decontamination of brownfield sites in many parts of the country already provides living space for many Americans who might otherwise live in an area that was previously farmland, rangeland, or forest. Furthermore, if Congress ever sees the wisdom of tightening environmental regulation to the point where people can safely live in close proximity to industrial facilities, the need to build on open space will diminish. Finally, if buffer zones around potentially toxic industrial facilities were to be required, they could be used as sites for light industry or for new swathes of green space.

Curiously, traditional environmental groups have been slow to take up this cause. It is not that environmentalists are racist, Miller-Travis observed; rather, they are culturally isolated. "They just don't get it yet," she said. As a result, at many environmental gatherings there are no people of color represented, and the environmental interests of low-income people of color are never raised. This leads to an impoverished environmental agenda that is not relevant to as many segments of society as it could reach. As a consequence, the environmental movement remains only a fraction as powerful as it could be, and it remains on the fringe politically.

The residents of Diamond, who are more heavily impacted by pollution than other segments of the society, should be seen as the front line of the environmental movement. Among them are some grassroots resident-activists who have taken on some of the world's largest industrial companies and have demonstrated great perseverance. Diamond residents grew up in a toxic environment never knowing what it was like to live beyond the reach of air pollutants, yet despite this deprivation they continued to believe that better environmental conditions were worth struggling for, Miller-Travis noted. In the most basic sense, these are heroes in the struggle for environmental quality who deserve to be backed by the full power of the environmental movement, she argued.

Environmental injustices, such as the one evident in Diamond, are also civil rights issues. By highlighting the disproportionate toxic burden that some poor and minority communities endure, environmental justice activists have effectively opened a new front in the long struggle for civil rights. As Representative John Conyers has observed, they have raised questions of fairness: Do all Americans have a right to live and work in a healthy environment? Is it fair that we expose poor and minority citizens to a disproportionate burden of toxic chemicals?

Old-line civil rights organizations have been slow to get behind efforts to organize and protect the health of fenceline communities that are disproportionately made up of people of color.[3] The lack of initiative shown by some of the best-known civil rights groups is all the more surprising insofar as the organizing being done by environmental justice groups in fenceline communities has the potential to reinvigorate the civil rights movement. Instead it has been left up to grassroots groups of residents of heavily impacted communities and their allies in the environmental justice movement to take on some of the world's largest chemical and petrochemical companies. Despite a lack of resources and technical assistance, some fenceline communities are beginning to make their plight known, not only in the United States but also internationally. And despite tremendous odds a few of them are prevailing in their campaigns to be relocated.

I

Diamond

1

The Diamond Story

Diamond is not a place where most people would choose to live. Located in the heart of the "chemical corridor" between the mouth of the Mississippi River and Baton Rouge, the four streets of this subdivision are hard up against fencelines with a Shell Chemical plant and the huge Shell/Motiva oil refinery.[1] Residents here have long breathed the fumes from these two plants, suffered illnesses they attributed to toxic exposures, and mourned neighbors and friends killed by explosions at these facilities

The view from the homes in Diamond is of heavy industry at work. There are catalytic cracking towers, stacks topped by flares burning off excess gas, huge oil and gasoline storage tanks, giant processing units where oil and its derivatives are turned into a wide variety of useful chemicals, and a Rube Goldberg maze of oversized pipes. The clanking and crashing of railroad cars coupling and uncoupling can be deafening, and the eerie sight of the superstructures of gargantuan oil tankers soundlessly moving up the Mississippi to dock and unload their crude oil completes the industrial landscape.

The streams of chemicals pouring out of the plants in the vast, sprawling Shell/Motiva Norco Complex are used in factories around the United States. Truly, these two mammoth plants are part of the front end of the system that has forged the American lifestyle by making products cheap and convenient. One cannot help but be in awe of the ingenuity, tenacity, and hard work that built these technological behemoths.

What seemed an incongruous sight, however, was a small residential community sandwiched between these two giant plants. The terrible cost of introducing heavy industry into a residential neighborhood soon became apparent. In the homes of Diamond residents there were many signs that this was not a healthy place to live. On many days the plant stank. Shell officials said that the smell was not dangerous and was caused by an organic digester unit that became backed up and gave off a rotten odor as millions of micro-organisms died. They were working on a solution to the problem, they said. But on some days the smell emanating from the plants had a toxic bouquet. Not infrequently, there was an acrid, metallic odor than caused headaches, sinus problems, and stinging eyes. There were even days, residents and visitors reported, when they could actually see a chemical fog swirling around their legs and seeping through the cracks into the houses.

And while it was notoriously difficult to prove that there existed a causal link between the toxic chemical released from the plant and the health of neighboring residents, inside the homes of Diamond residents were a disturbing number of children with asthma; young adults with severe respiratory, allergic, and unusual skin problems; and older people whose breathing had to be aided with oxygen tanks.

Then there was the history of periodic explosions. A 1973 explosion took the lives of two Diamond residents. A 1988 explosion that killed seven Shell workers blew out windows and doors and brought down sheetrock ceilings in many homes. Diamond was evacuated in the middle of the night. Many homes required extensive reconstruction.

If it was so poisonous and dangerous to live there, why didn't the residents of Diamond just move? The answer was that few of those who lived in Diamond stayed because they wanted to. Given an opportunity to sell their homes and move they would do so, but without getting decent prices for their homes they could not afford to leave. Living next to the Shell plants had not only been bad for their health, they said; it also had been lethal to property values. As the chemical and oil plants expanded to an area just across the street, residents who wanted to sell their homes and relocate could not find buyers who were foolish enough to want to purchase their homes. In other words, they were stuck: they could not bear living where they were because of the bad air, but they could not afford to move elsewhere.

Faced with this dilemma, a small group of Diamond residents decided to organize and demand that Shell give them enough money for their homes so that they could relocate elsewhere in St. Charles Parish,[2] away from the fumes and the danger of explosion. They began picketing the Shell facilities, seeking face-to-face meetings with Shell officials, and talking to the press. One 80-year-old woman who joined the picket lines told me that she just wanted to be relocated so she could live the rest of her life in peace: "I would

go. I'm not particular [about the replacement house] as long as it is not raining in there and the plumbing and floors is good. I am not a picky person.
I am just looking to get away. I just want to be gone."

If this were a script for a Hollywood movie, I could stick with a simplistic
story line: a group of neighbors living near two petrochemical plants
become sick of breathing toxic fumes and decide to organize a relocation
campaign. But reality is rarely as neat as a simple plot. The fact was that not
everyone in the vicinity of these two Shell plants agreed that a relocation
program was warranted. Tellingly, opinion on the subject was divided along
racial lines. Those who lobbied long and hard for relocation lived in
Diamond, where all the residents were black. Their community was separated from the adjacent white community of Norco by a wooded strip of
land and railroad tracks. And many of those on the white side of Norco
dismissed these complaints, arguing that the town was a great place to live
where they and their neighbors were healthy and lived to a ripe old age.
Diamond residents who claimed that the plants were making them sick
were either lying or at the very least exaggerating the problem in order to
make a buck, some of them said.

There was also the perspective of Shell officials in Norco, at Shell's
Louisiana headquarters in New Orleans, at Shell's national headquarters
in Houston, and at Shell's international headquarters in London and The
Hague. They vehemently denied that their facilities were hazardous to the
health of their neighbors. They contended that their plants were meeting
regulatory standards, that they were permitted to operate by federal and
state regulatory agencies, and that their emissions were harming no one.
But Diamond residents who had to breathe the fumes from these facilities
daily held a very different view of the facts. They laughed at Shell's assertion that the emissions were harmless.

Some Diamond residents traced their history on the land back to plantation days. Their story started during the days of slavery, when many of
their ancestors worked the sugarcane fields of the Trepagnier Plantation
that subsequently became the Diamond Plantation, Belltown, and finally
the Diamond subdivision of Norco. After the Civil War, when the plantation was abandoned by its owners, many of the freed slaves continued to
occupy their old slave cottages; others moved into the plantation house. In
1916, when Shell Oil began to build its refinery near this African-American

enclave, some of the residents hoped they would find employment at the new facility. Few of them were hired, however, and most of those who did find employment at Shell were relegated to menial jobs.

When Royal Dutch/Shell purchased the land that the freed slaves lived on in the early 1950s and began to build the Shell Chemical plant, residents were forced to move off the land they had worked for decades. They tore down their homes and rebuilt them a quarter of a mile away on what became the fenceline with the giant Shell refinery and the adjacent chemical plant. Again there was renewed hope that they would find employment in the vast new facility that was being built on their doorstep; again, however, they found themselves on the receiving end of the fumes from the plant but with few of the jobs.

Over the years the plant expanded ever closer to their homes. In the mid 1970s, unable to sell their homes for a reasonable price and move elsewhere, a small group of Diamond women began to organize protests and to demand that Shell buy them out. In the late 1980s, as the grassroots movement (led by a tenacious local schoolteacher named Margie Richard) gathered steam, people outside of the parish began to hear of this David-and-Goliath struggle between the world's third-largest petrochemical company and a tiny black community on its fenceline. Over time, Norco became a "poster child" for environmental racism and environmental justice activists, and toxics activists began to provide support for the struggle.

Shell officials denied that their plants were causing illness and pointed out that there were more white people in Norco than there were blacks in Diamond and that the former had few complaints about living next to their plants. But the plight of Diamond residents on their fenceline continued to receive sympathetic treatment from the press, and the pressure built on Shell to relocate them.

2

Early Days

Nearly 200 years ago, Diamond was at the epicenter of the largest slave rebellion in U.S. history. At the time Louisiana one of the worst places to be a slave. Slaves arrived by the thousands at the port of Algiers after a harrowing ocean voyage during which it was routine for a third of them to die. In Algiers slaves were "seasoned" or "broken" through the deliberate use of whipping and other forms of torture. Recalcitrant slaves were whipped until they were docile enough to be useful in the sugarcane and tobacco fields and in the plantation houses. Then they were sold to plantations up and down the Mississippi. Many of them were destined for the river parishes of Louisiana, where they cleared swamps, built levees, and worked the fields. This was brutal labor under onerous conditions, and many died young. Elsewhere in the country, slaves were cautioned by their masters that if they were not obedient they would be sold to a plantation in Louisiana.

From the air-conditioned comfort of present-day Louisiana, it is easy to forget that some 300 years ago the state was still up for grabs. The French claimed it for King Louis XIV in 1682. (Until then, the population had been mostly Native American, with a smattering of Spaniards.) The French made a game effort to make a living off this mosquito-infested malarial delta but likely would have starved to death had it not been for the Native Americans who helped supply the settlers and taught them how to live off the land. This coexistence ended in 1729 when Natchez warriors attacked the French fort at Rosalie, killing 237 and capturing 50 white women and 300 black slaves. The Natchez were subsequently exterminated by the French.

Under these unsettled conditions it was hard to convince immigrants to move to Louisiana. The French turned to John Law, a Scot, to convince settlers to come to Louisiana Territory, but the project turned into a financial disaster. In 1720, after Law's abortive attempt to develop the area, two dozen German families fleeing war and occupation in their homeland moved into St. Charles Parish. In 1721 there were 177 African slaves in Louisiana and 177 whites. By 1860 the slave population had risen to 326,700 and the total population in the lower Mississippi to 708,000. To help control the slaves, the French administration (and later the Spanish one) tried to attract white settlers by promising Europeans, particularly the families of military officers, large estates in exchange for moving to the region. In this fashion the plantation system was established.

Pierre Trepagnier arrived from Canada in the 1740s. Trepagnier was the beneficiary of one of the first land grants made by the king, who, subsequently established 16 plantations in St. Charles Parish. By 1790 Trepagnier had built a grand plantation home of cypress on the banks of the Mississippi.

From what little is known of this period, it appears that Pierre Trepagnier, who is said to have been susceptible to intrigue, was lured into leaving his home under the pretext of some secret mission trumped up by a couple of impostors who arrived in what appeared to be an official state carriage. Trepagnier was never seen again. Eventually, presuming her husband dead, his wife sold the estate and moved to New Orleans.[1] Pierre Trepagnier's brother, Jean Pierre, remained in the area and built his own plantation— later named Myrtleland, and subsequently the Diamond Plantation—in and around what are now the Diamond and Norco communities.[2]

Life on the unimproved banks of the Mississippi at the beginning of the nineteenth century cannot have been easy. The river was unpredictable and periodically flooded, the weather was sweltering, tropical disease was rampant, and the area was far from secure. Against this one must count the advantages of being granted title to land without cost and having a troop of slaves with which to work the land and make one's fortune. For families such as the Trepagniers, this was a rare opportunity to improve their economic standing and join the Southern aristocracy.

Some slaves in the river parishes were growing defiant, and a number of them ran away from the plantations and set up camp on islands of dry land deep in the swamps. These runaway slaves, known as maroons, would sally forth from their marshy hideouts to steal from travelers and raid plantations for tools, arms, and food. In 1747, maroons and Choctaw Indians attacked plantations in the river parishes. Those who were caught were hanged or burned alive. During the American Revolutionary War there were more small-scale revolts. In 1792, some 40 slaves were convicted of planning to rebel and were executed.

Meanwhile, Louisiana was changing hands as quickly as small-denomination currency. In 1762 France ceded it to Spain. In 1800 Spain sold it back to France. In 1803, in an effort to raise money for a war with Britain, Napoleon Bonaparte sold France's claim to Louisiana to the United States in a 565-million-acre deal that came to be known as the Louisiana Purchase.

In 1804, word of a successful slave revolt in Haiti gave the slaves and maroons of Louisiana hope and the plantation owners cause for alarm. Napoleon Bonaparte had dispatched 43,000 of his best troops to Haiti in an effort to put down the revolt there. They had been promptly defeated, many of them killed or subjected to the same tortures that the slaves had suffered. On January 1, 1804, Jean Jacques Desalines, one of the former slaves who led the revolt, declared Haiti independent.

The slave revolts in Louisiana around that time were relatively small. In 1791 and 1795 slave revolts at Pointe Coupe were forcefully put down, with 31 conspirators flogged and 23 hanged. By 1811, however, the slaves of the river parishes of Louisiana had become bold enough to launch what some historians have described as the largest slave revolt in the history of the United States. What later became the community of Diamond/Norco was at the heart of this revolt. At the time, the population of New Orleans was estimated at 11,000 slaves, 8,000 whites, and 6,000 free people of color. With these numbers, the insurrectionists calculated, they could rally the slaves in the river parishes to march on New Orleans and take over the city, which was enclosed in walled fortifications with four gates of entry. They counted on aid from conspirators in the city who planned to raid the armory and pass the weapons out. With most of the federal garrison away fighting the Spanish in Florida, the timing seemed auspicious.

Leaders of the plantation slaves and maroons met in the swamps near Maupas to plan their strategy. At sundown on January 8, 1811, according to the Marxist historian Albert Thrasher, "the slave mutiny was launched at the Andry plantation located some 36 miles above the city [of New Orleans]."[3] Armed with only a few weapons and a variety of agricultural tools, some 500 slaves began their march on New Orleans. They marched in orderly units, carrying flags and beating drums, following their officers and their leader, Charles Deslandes. The next day, having covered 6 miles, they arrived at the plantation of Jean François, son of the widow Elizabeth Jean Barre Trepagnier.

According to Thrasher, Jean François Trepagnier owned a young slave named Gustav and treated him like a pet dog, keeping him under the table at mealtimes and feeding him scraps.[4] Trepagnier promised to emancipate Gustav when he came of age, but when Gustav turned 21 and asked his master for his freedom he was put off: "Maybe later . . . we'll have to see." Unsatisfied with this response, Gustav ran off and joined a maroon community until the revolt began. Then he returned and hacked his master to pieces.[5]

In the end, the poorly armed slaves proved no match for the firepower of federal troops and their plantation posse. Planters organized militiamen and vigilantes to hunt down the rebel slaves. They were soon reinforced by U.S. Army troops from Baton Rouge and New Orleans. The Free Black Militia also offered its services to help put down the rebellion, and one of its companies was accepted. The slave attack on the arsenal in New Orleans failed, and the 500 insurrectionists marching on New Orleans never received arms. The decisive battle in the slave revolt occurred 18 miles outside New Orleans at Michael Fortier's sugar works, where the slaves were defeated by concentrated cannon fire. A mopping-up operation captured 16 of them. Sixty-six were reported to have been killed in the fighting or executed on the spot, though reports of the discovery of more bodies trickled in later. Only two white combatants were killed.[6]

Executions of convicted rebels took place outside St. Louis Cathedral at the Place d'Armes in downtown New Orleans. A number of slaves from the Trepagnier Plantations were tried and executed.[7] Most of those convicted of insurrection were shot or hanged. Their heads were cut off and stuck on poles along River Road near the plantations from whence they had come.

This ugly chapter in American history, not taught in schools, was passed on from one generation to the next as oral history in the river parishes. The African American History Alliance in New Orleans commemorates the event every year by retracing the route of the rebel slaves. The memory of this uprising is still very much alive in the Diamond community because the Trepagnier Plantation, which was at the heart of the revolt, was subsequently renamed the Diamond Plantation, and many of the descendants of surviving slaves stayed in the area. "The biggest slave rebellion [in U.S. history] was right here," a present-day resident of Diamond observed. "They cut off their heads and put them on sticks in front of the plantation right down on Washington Street where we live."[8] This painful image, which remains a raw wound in the minds of Diamond residents, helped form the context of their struggles with Royal Dutch/Shell.

Belltown

Margie Richard sat at her kitchen table staring at a faded photograph of some smartly dressed men taken around the time of her birth, 61 years ago. Sunlight flooded in through the kitchen window, glinting off the clean white-tile floor, as Richard told the story of her family, the Eugenes, who had deep roots in this Louisiana river parish. She was a member of the fourth generation of her family to live there. Some of her ancestors had taken part in the slave revolt of 1811, a chapter of her family's history she recalled with pride.

The sepia-colored photo Richard held in her hands was of the leaders of Stonewall Chapter 76, a Masonic Lodge that drew its membership from the African-American population in a three-parish area near Belltown, where Shell Chemical would later build its facilities. Her father, Theodore Eugene, captured in the photograph, was elected secretary of the chapter because he had two years of college at Xavier University before his father died and he had to abandon his studies to take over the farm. When Richard later asked her father whether this abrupt end to his studies had angered him, his response was succinct and muted: "Perhaps." That was all he said about it. But that one word contained a world of missed opportunities and spoke volumes about what it meant to grow up black in the river parishes of Louisiana in the 1930s.

For those who knew Richard's family history, it was not surprising in the least that she was selected by Diamond residents to lead their struggle against Royal Dutch/Shell, the world's fourth-largest corporation. Richard seemed an unlikely candidate for such a battle. But despite her small stature, she was a remarkably determined woman who rarely flinched from speaking her mind. She had taught school for nearly 30 years, and her family had a long tradition of leadership in the community.

Asked how she got the gumption to take on Royal Dutch/Shell, Richard did not talk about herself. Instead she recounted the history of her family and of her community and cited her religious faith. Asked about the struggle to relocate her people away from the fenceline with a highly polluting refinery and chemical plant, she skipped decades back in time to explain how it came about. "We ain't where we should be, but neither are we where we used to be," she said. Her grandfather was a farmer who owned 15 acres of Belltown, an area that encompassed the lands and houses of the old Trepagnier Plantation. At harvest time he employed local residents to prepare produce for sale before he trucked it to the French Market in New Orleans and elsewhere. He sold corn, lettuce, and other vegetables, mustard greens, dairy products, chicken, beef, and pork. Farming on the fertile alluvial soil, carried down and deposited over the ages by the Mississippi River, was profitable. "The cantaloupes and watermelons were the sweetest," Richard recalled. "All the vegetables were just prime. . . . I remember the bell peppers and the green beans. Everything was real good." It was a big operation and a good living, she said

During the same period, Richard's mother worked at a restaurant on the white side of Norco. The front door bore a sign saying "whites only." There was a window on the side where blacks could buy take-out. Since she was in charge of the kitchen, Richard's mother took full advantage of this segregated arrangement, dishing out 13 shrimp on a loaf for the white customers and 32 shrimp on a loaf to black customers at the window. Richard could take a super-loaded sandwich home and make short shrimp po' boys for the whole family. "Hah," her mother rejoiced. "They [the whites] think they got us, but we are going to make it."

In 1953 Shell Chemical purchased the Belltown land for $109,000 as a site for a chemical plant. Richard's grandfather and father lost the use of the land and had to move.[9] Her grandfather was paid a portion of the $90 his family got in exchange for being evicted. Fortunately, he had set aside some money from his farm business. He was able to buy six lots in Diamond on what would become the fenceline with the chemical plant. Other descendants of freed slaves were not as fortunate. Those who did not own land and lived in "the Big Store" (previously the plantation's central building) were paid little or nothing to move. Some of them, however, eventually scraped together enough money to buy lots in Diamond.

Richard's father purchased two lots in Diamond from his father. He did it officially, seeing to it that all the paperwork was in order. He was elected secretary of the Oddfellows, an African-American organization that was informally involved in looking after the interests of community at the time. "They were sharp," Richard recalled, and among their accomplishments was the building of a school in Diamond. Her father also handled the paperwork for a lot of people in town and taught adult education classes.

Richard's cousin, Audrey Eugene, remembers picking lilies out of waterholes and sitting under the huge oaks that graced the Big Yard until Shell cut most of them down to build its plant. Eugene, 63, lived on Bethune Street in Diamond in a handsome white-brick house with blue trim and tiled floors. With six children, nineteen grandchildren, and six great-grandchildren, she lived in Diamond long enough to see great changes. She recalled that her parent's house was rolled down the hill from Belltown to Diamond when Shell bought up the old Trepagnier Plantation. She was about 10 years old when the eviction took place. "I can remember as a little girl in the morning we would go over there [to the farm] and clean shallots," she recalled. "They would get them out of the field and the ladies would sit there and we would clean them, wash them, and bunch them and then they would take them to market. I can remember all kind of vegetables we cleaned and got ready for market."

Belltown consisted of the Big Store, the Big Yard, and three "lanes" (dirt roads) lined with old slave quarters. One photo shows the laundry of freed slaves strung along the verandah of the Big Store. That building, occupied by a number of families, gradually became a focal point for evening gatherings at which the residents would cook outdoors and tell stories. Margie Richard's uncle George Eugene, 81, remembered the Big Store: "On Saturdays they would have a house supper and make big pots of jambalaya and gumbo and sit around laughing and talking and that's how they used to get along." On Fridays, when someone needed money for their rent, they would have a fish fry and sell fish or kill a chicken and sell fried chicken. "People didn't stay up too late, because they had to get up at four o'clock to cut sugarcane and stuff," he added. The children would play games with a broomstick bat and a ball made from a can, run around in the swamp, pull sugarcane off the railroad cars, and eat cucumbers and tomatoes out of the surrounding fields. Eugene later opened a small restaurant called The Chicken Coop before landing a job in Destrehan handling corn for animal fodder.[10]

Other Diamond residents also have vivid memories of the old days in Belltown. Deloris Brown, 72, who lives hard up against the railroad tracks that feed into the Shell Chemical plant, remembered a muddy street which ran down through Belltown to River Road, residents with gardens and farm animals, and pecan trees on the land where the chemical factory was eventually built. "My sisters," she recalls, "were still over there in Belltown when they sold the Diamond plantation. The owners gave the people the houses [they were living in] but they sold the land to Shell. [Residents of Belltown] tore down the houses and took the materials with them." When the trains laden with Shell products passed, the whole house shook and it was hard to hear what was being said.

Another resident of Diamond, Delwyn Smith, 51, explained that her family had moved to Diamond from Belltown. Smith's mother, grandmother, aunts, and uncles all had lived there. Her grandparents' house had had one big room, with a curtained-off area for sleeping. A big tin tub was available for bathing, and there was an outhouse. For food storage there was an icebox .

Many of the men who lived in Belltown and worked at jobs outside the community had gardens to supplement their wages. "My grandfather had one of the neatest gardens over there," Smith said. "He was known for his beautiful garden." In addition to raising vegetables, he kept horses and chickens. Occasionally four or five families would share in the expense of buying and slaughtering a cow and then divide up the meat, Smith remembered.

In those days, with segregation, Jim Crow practices, and very limited opportunities, life was not easy for African-Americans. But former Belltown residents said that there was always enough to eat and that people shared. They were able to survive because the community was tight-knit, and that sense of community survived the relocation to Diamond.

The eviction of African-American families from Belltown was part of a broad societal transition that took place across the nation as the economy developed from its agrarian base to a subsequent industrial stage. But in Diamond (as elsewhere in the South) there was a racial factor that made the transition even more brutal than it was elsewhere in the nation. Since many of the residents of Belltown were sharecroppers who did not own formal title to the land, they were vulnerable to being intimidated by white businessmen and local officials into selling the land on which their families had lived for generations for almost nothing.

No written historical record explains why the residents of Belltown moved to Diamond, not elsewhere, when they were forced off their land by

Shell. However, oral history suggests that they were given no other option. Richard's parents, for example, told her that they moved to Diamond because that was the deal they were offered by the white land owners and because the land in Diamond was cheap. It was also close enough so the residents of Belltown could all move to it and stay together as a community. Further, there was no obvious alternative to the proffered land in Diamond, and it is not clear that the black residents of Belltown would have found it easy to locate other land in the parish where they were all welcome.

There was also the promise of jobs. "From what my daddy and older relatives said," Richard noted, "all they were focused on was that there were going to be jobs coming in and people needed jobs. But they had no idea what chemicals were going to be processed [by the new plant that would be their neighbor]. They were just happy that industry was coming in because it meant upward mobility for the town . . . they thought."

From all accounts it seems clear that black land owners were not given the option of holding on to their land. The forces behind Shell's purchase of Belltown were too strong for them to fight at the time. Richard's father told her that "the Man came around and made us a contract." It was a proposal he could not refuse. He was told when he would have to move out, how much he would be paid, and where he could move.

The sale of Belltown to Shell was a turning point in the lives of the residents. When they were forced off the land, they lost their self-sufficiency and their capacity to grow and market their own food. Had they been permitted to continue to farm the land, their quality of life might have been markedly better than it was after industry took over the area. For example, Margie Richard's grandfather, George Eugene Sr., owned his own land and would have been able to make money off the cultivation of his fields. In addition, the property was intrinsically valuable because it was elevated and so it never flooded. Located just 25 miles from New Orleans, the land would have appreciated considerably over the years. Had he been able to hold on to it, Eugene might have lived to be quite a wealthy man.

Instead, this fertile land was purchased by oil and chemical companies, which transformed the river parishes into one of the most polluted regions in the nation. The people who lived there, among them the residents of Diamond, came to suffer the consequences. Had her father and grandfather known how industry was going to transform the landscape, Margie Richard conjectured, they would have said "Don't bring the [chemical] facility, because farming is our livelihood."

When Shell officials are confronted with this version of history and are accused of having evicted an African-American community from plantation buildings and slave quarters in order to build a chemical plant, they argue that very few Belltown residents were displaced. "The photos from 1953 show very few structures on this property," said Shell spokesman David Brignac. Norco, he said, "has grown up pretty much around our plants. It is pretty doubtful that Norco would be a town today if Shell wouldn't have come here."

Diamond resident Audrey Eugene begs to differ with Brignac's account of Belltown's history: "We were here first. We were just run off [and told to] get over there. [We were told by Shell] 'We are going to put this [chemical plant] here whether you like it or not.' . . . The big corporations . . . you can't win with them."

Many other Diamond residents confirm that they once lived in Belltown, or that their parents or their grandparents did. For example, Lois Gales is just a generation away from Belltown: "My mom moved to Diamond from Belltown. . . . [Shell] moved my parents from over there. They were forced to move. . . . I had an aunt who lived up there who I went to visit. I can still see the house in the back. They had a fire and a cousin of ours died there. My aunt had a house on a little street that was well laid out."

Beverly Wright, executive director of the Deep South Center for Environmental Justice at Xavier University, provides the historical context for Audrey Eugene's and Lois Gales's stories about the eviction of their parents and grandparents: the forced removal of African-American families from Belltown to Diamond "is not an uncommon story for black communities along the river. . . . Some families were moved two or three times"—not just by industries moving in, but also by the Army Corps of Engineers, which moved whole communities when they built the levees and the Bonnet Carre Spillway, Wright noted. "They moved where they were told to move," Wright said bluntly, "and the decision about where they were going to be moved was made by others . . . not by them."

What is striking is that there are two apparently contradictory versions of history: the black stories about life in Belltown and the forced exodus to Diamond, and the white stories of the town's growing up around the Shell plant. Certainly it is possible that, although there were a limited number of houses in Belltown when the construction of the chemical plant began, all those homes were occupied and there were many families living in the old plantation house. Similarly, it is clearly true that over time, after Shell built its refinery in 1916, numerous white workers moved to the area and built homes next to the plant. But these two histories of Norco and Diamond were never integrated, because the two communities remained geographically segregated. A wooded area separated the white and the black sides of town.

What is clear, said Denny Larson, coordinator of the Refinery Reform Campaign, is that the first instance of environmental injustice in this story took place when Shell Chemical pushed the Belltown sharecroppers off their land and built a chemical plant on it. Shell "put these people in harm's way" by sandwiching them between the refinery and the chemical plant, Larson asserted.

Shell Comes Ashore

The land occupied by the former Trepagnier Plantation, now known as the Diamond subdivision of Norco, has changed names a number of times over the years. In the late 1700s it was designated on maps as a site of French-owned plantations. Subsequently it came to be known as the German Coast as the above-mentioned German families moved into the area, providing a new ingredient to the gumbo of racial and ethnic groups. Later the area was renamed Sellers after a wealthy family who settled there. Local lore recounts that one of the descendants of this family, Thomas Joseph Sellers, was orphaned at a young age and worked as an assistant cashier—a "mud clerk"—on riverboats with Samuel Clemens, who later adopted the pen name Mark Twain.

Life in Sellers and elsewhere in St. Charles Parish began to change dramatically in 1911. Until then the land had been valuable primarily because it contained rich soil that was ideal for agriculture. But now Sellers, Belltown, and the other settlements in the river parishes had another allure. The area was a perfect location to bring oil ashore for storage, refining, and trans-shipment. The old Trepagnier and Good Hope Plantation grounds were desirable locales for a refinery because they were adjacent to the oil-rich Gulf of Mexico, they were on the Mississippi (the great artery of U.S. commerce), and they were far enough upriver so that oil tankers could dock there and find shelter from tropical storms. By geographic happenstance, Belltown was suddenly in the crosshairs of Big Oil.

The suitability of the river parishes for an oil refinery did not escape the notice of Richard Airey, an agent for Henri Deterding, head of the Royal Dutch/Shell Group, who had been dispatched to Louisiana to purchase properties so that the company could get a toehold in the lucrative American oil market. In 1911 Airey purchased 366 acres of sugarcane fields for $21,000 at the Good Hope Plantation. The plan was to use the land, located adjacent to Belltown, for a marine petroleum terminal. On these grounds he built the New Orleans Refining Company (NORCO), which was really a proxy company for Royal Dutch/Shell.[11] In 1920 the NORCO refinery began processing Mexican crude oil into asphalt. In 1929 the Shell Petroleum Company purchased the NORCO refinery. By then, a company town had begun to take shape around the sprawling facility. Postmistress Lillie Schexnaildre officially changed the town's name from Sellers to Norco.

In the early 1950s, when the refinery was pumping out 75,000 barrels of oil a day, Shell wanted to build a plant to produce intermediate chemical feedstocks for a variety of industries. To this end, Shell purchased Belltown in 1953. By industrial mitosis, the facility was split into two distinct entities: the refinery (a part of the Shell Oil Products Company) and the Shell Chemical Company.

Over the years, both companies in the Norco Manufacturing Complex grew. By 1995 Shell Oil was refining 300,000 barrels of oil a day into automotive gasoline, aviation fuel, and heating oil. Shell Oil was also piping product to the Shell Chemical plant, where it was turned into intermediate chemical products that would eventually be used to produce "antifreeze, tires, plastic food containers, trash bags, laundry detergent, cosmetics, adhesives, coatings, furniture, and tennis shoes." By 1998 this complex of facilities employed 1,400 employees, who were paid $80 million annually in wages; the companies also paid more that $30 million annually in sales and property taxes.[12]

Jim Crow in Diamond

The former residents of Belltown, who had been displaced by Shell's purchase of their land in 1953, relocated to the new Diamond subdivision of Norco, where they had to adjust to no longer being able to make a living as farmers. They also had to come to terms with living between two giant petrochemical companies and in a starkly segregated community.

Diamond, just a stone's throw from Belltown, was framed on the south by the Mississippi River levee and on the north by railroad tracks that led into the Shell Chemical plant. On its west side, starting from the fenceline, Diamond's four streets ran parallel to the Shell Chemical plant. Washington Street, at the west end, was immediately adjacent to the chemical plant. Beyond the Shell Chemical plant was the Bonnet Carre Spillway, a wide depression in the landscape separated from the Mississippi by huge mechanical gates that can be lifted to divert river water during periods when flooding threatened New Orleans.

While administratively Diamond was a subdivision of Norco, social reality had little to do with jurisdictional lines on a map. On the ground one could literally point to the racial divide between Diamond and Norco. On the east side of Diamond was a strip of densely wooded land, known as the Gaspard Line, that neatly separated the black and white communities. On one side of the line, Norco was 98 percent white; on the other, Diamond was 100 percent black.

Diamond was often described in press accounts as "poor," but this depiction hardly captured a more complex reality. In fact Diamond was a mixed-income African-American community with deep roots going back to the days of slavery. It was also a tight-knit community where everyone knew everyone else and a remarkable number of residents were related by blood or marriage. The homes varied greatly in quality. Though many were modest, and there were numerous abandoned and boarded-up homes and trailers, these were often adjacent to solidly built and well-maintained homes occupied by middle-class families whose college-educated breadwinners held jobs in the surrounding communities. Diamond also boasted a high percentage of home ownership. This said, there were numerous Diamond residents who were just scraping by economically. Many were elderly and were living on welfare or a modest pension. In order to provide poor relatives with places to live, there were often creative rental arrangements in which a sister, a brother-in-law, or a cousin was permitted to park a trailer on the back of a lot.

Racially, the community remained isolated. "When we grew up we were sheltered," recalled Diamond resident Lois Gales. "The only time we went past First Street or the Gaspard line my dad took us in the car and we were going to New Orleans. We never went into the other side of Norco into the white area. We just always were here in this community [of Diamond]. This was our life. We weren't welcome over there [on the white side of town]. As a family, we hardly associated with whites at all. So there were two towns. My mama would go down to pay utility bills. You only went there to pay utilities or to Loupe's [a store], but that was later. When we grew up there was hardly no association [between whites and blacks] at all. It was naive of me but I hardly knew they [whites] existed. [Laughs]. Our school was here; we went to church here. . . . When I graduated from Bethune I went right on to Xavier [University in New Orleans]."

Margie Richard had painful memories of the racial divide between Diamond and Norco. When she was growing up in Diamond, Norco's only public movie theater (located where the Dollar Store now stands) was segregated. "On Sundays, if you put on your Sunday best, you could go to the [movie] show, but you better not get that dress dirty," she recalled. The faucet outside [the theater] said "coloreds only," and after the faucet had been used a few times the dirt beneath it turned to mud. This created a dilemma for Richard and her friends: it was hot and they wanted a drink of water but they did not want to get their Sunday dresses and shoes muddy. "The faucet inside the show was nice and cool, and they had one man collecting tickets, so we always went in all at one time, ordered popcorn, and when he turned his back to get the popcorn we would drink from the white faucet because we didn't want to get our dress dirty." To this day Richard is proud of the strategy that she and her young friends devised to circumvent the segregation rules.

Richard was also exposed to the larger civil rights movement as a very young child. She recalled distinctly when her father and mother took her and her sister to a clothing store on Apple Street in Norco and purchased white blouses and navy skirts for them. They then went into New Orleans for what Richard thought would be a train ride—an exciting prospect for Richard, who had never been on a train. When they arrived, however, Richard was disappointed to find only a single Pullman car to explore. Inside the "Freedom Train" were civil rights displays and artifacts. "Dad," she asked, "when are we going to ride the real train?" Her father (who was acquainted with Ralph Abernathy, Martin Luther King Jr., Andrew Young, Israel Augustine, and other movers and shakers in the civil rights movement) told her to be quiet and read the documents that were on display.

Meanwhile, other strategies for fighting Jim Crow in Norco were being devised. While the girls were sneaking drinks at the water fountain reserved for whites, the boys had their own brand of protest. In those days blacks were made to sit upstairs in the balcony of the theater, where it was stifling hot owing to the absence of air conditioning. "They put us up top, but we used to throw stuff down [on the whites in the seats below]," recalled Devon Washington, 47. As a result, black patrons were soon moved out of the balcony and made to sit in the front rows. That was a victory of sorts.

Diamond children were also required to sit in the back of the school bus, residents recalled. Devon Washington, now a burley refinery worker with two adolescent sons, recalled that in the early days of school desegregation he and a few friends were bused under a voluntary integration program from the black Bethune school in Diamond to the white school in Norco. "The bus driver picked the blacks up the first morning and told us we were going to load from the rear," and that way all the black students were in the back of the bus. Then in the afternoon, when the bus picked the students up at school and some of the white students were in the front of the line, the black students still went to the back of the bus. By that time, Washington explained, "we were trained already from the morning to load from the rear."

For years, Mary Bethune High School was the focal point of Diamond. The school was immediately adjacent to the Shell Chemical plant. (Just how dangerous this location was later became apparent when the roof of a Shell Chemical gas storage tank blew off and flew over the fence into the recreation yard.) Children played within sight of the chemical plant and were occasionally forced inside because the air was so bad. "Every now and then we had to evacuate [because of accidental releases from the plant]," Devon Washington recalled, "but . . . it seemed normal. It wasn't until I got older that I realized how dangerous it was. . . . It was pretty rough.

For a while after the black children of Diamond were integrated into the white school in Norco, Mary Bethune High School was used only for recreation and an after-school program. Later, population pressure in the parish built to the point where it was illogical to leave the school empty. Reoccupying the school, however, would have required busing white students into black Diamond. Mysteriously, the school burned in the middle of the night. Many residents suspect that this was no accident. "I was in the last class that graduated from Bethune in 1969," said Diamond resident

Larry Brown. "Then it burned. There is a controversy about that." Power company officials visited the school during the day; then it burned down at 3 o'clock the next morning. "It was totally fishy. . . . I think [the whites] didn't want it to become an integrated school," Brown surmised. Dorothy Pedescleaux, whose husband Ernest taught industrial arts at Mary Bethune High School, also thinks it was burned for racial reasons: "I think really it was burned down because of integration. . . . Whites didn't want their babies coming here."

Apart from the school, the other major presence in the community was the Shell refinery, which employed large numbers of residents of white Norco and played a significant part in setting the tone for how race relations would be handled in town. For years Shell officials hosted what they called "plant day," with entertainment for the children, mechanical rides, and a picnic. This was part of running a company town, and residents saw it as one of the perquisites of living next to heavy industry. Here was an opportunity for the whole community to gather across racial lines and get to know one another. However, that is not the way Shell chose to run things. Instead they sponsored two plant days: one for the white residents and one for African-Americans. Clarisse Webb, chairperson of Shell's museum at the Motiva refinery in Norco, insists that there was a separate plant day for blacks because that is what they wanted. But former Diamond resident Margie Richard remembered plant days differently: "No sir. . . . African-Americans had no choice."

3

Dangerous Neighbor

On a beautiful summer day in 1973, a Shell Chemical pipeline sprang a leak, eyewitnesses report. The pipe ran parallel to Washington Street in Diamond, which forms the fenceline between the industrial facility and the residential community. Diamond residents saw a white cloud of gas snake down the street. Dorothy Pedescleaux recalled telling some young men "You see that white stuff coming down the street? I bet it's going to be a fire." Just down the street, Leroy Jones, 16, was cutting grass at the home of Helen Washington, an elderly woman, who was indoors taking a nap. Jones had taken a break from his chore and was chatting with some friends who had stopped on their bike rounds of the neighborhood. After they left, Jones pulled the cord to start the lawnmower. A spark from the engine ignited the gas that had leaked out of the Shell pipeline, residents conjectured. The ensuing explosion scorched Leroy Jones and burned Helen Washington's house down. Badly burned, Jones stumbled around in shock, clutching his eyes. "When emergency workers arrived they wrapped [Jones's] blistered body in a baby quilt that a neighbor had hung out to dry," neighbors reported.[1] Jones died a few days later in the hospital. Helen Washington died immediately, burned up in her own home.

Larry Brown described the day Helen Washington and Leroy Jones died as one of the most traumatic in his life. He recalled a fog-like gas escaping from the Shell pipe and said he called out a warning to Leroy Jones not to start the lawnmower. "When he cranked it there was a big BOOM . . . a big flame . . . and I saw him crumple and claw his eyes," Brown recalled. Then one of the grandsons of Helen Washington ran into the burning house and pulled his grandmother out. "She was burned," Brown said. "I couldn't look at it. I just left. I'm trying to think how to put it: seeing someone burn . . . that is a horrible feeling to watch . . . another human being. I saw it,

I smelled it, I still feel the stink of that flesh. . . . I ran for my life. I feel bad that I ran and didn't try to help. I didn't know what was going to happen [blow up] next."

Delwyn Smith, 51, remembered the bodies of Washington and Jones being carried to her mother's property: "They brought them over there and set them under mamma's oak tree right in the front yard."

Two boys on motorbikes had just passed when the explosion erupted. One of them was Devaliant Christopher Cole, 13 at the time. Cole remembered riding with a friend that day past a young man messing with a lawnmower. When they were about two blocks past him there was a loud explosion. "I looked back and WHOOF . . . just like a big old fireball . . . and it kept burning for awhile," Cole recalled. "It looked like a flamethrower. A big flame just shot across the street. It tore the house down . . . everything all at one time. . . . I never saw anything like that in my life."

The horror of death by fire rippled through the close-knit community. "I'm sorry in a way that I went over to see because it is forever etched in my memory. The fireball was like a rolling ball of fire through the street, and that lady and that little boy burned," said Audrey Eugene. Later Shell put a little sign up near the pipes saying that they were hazardous.

Ernestine Roberts, 52, was watching TV when the explosion occurred. She recalls: "We just started running. When we got there . . . the whole house was just flat. There was a lot of hollering and screaming going on because in a small town everyone knows everyone."

The fatal accident changed the way residents of Diamond viewed living next to Shell's facilities. "That [explosion] made quite a difference," recalled Lois Gales, who was in Diamond that day, pregnant with her first son. Suddenly she realized that accidents from the plant could reach out across the fenceline and take lives. It was at that moment that Gales realized "it was kind of dangerous living here."

Part of the fear this accident engendered had to do with the fact that no one was sure what was going to blow up next. "I just couldn't stop screaming," said Lois Parquet, who was afraid at the time that a pipeline near her house would burst next. "Who is to say what is under my property? . . . You don't know the danger that lies underground. . . . It was their time then, but it could be our time next. . . ."

Fear that there would be additional explosions continued to trouble some residents for years. "When the explosion happened I was under the line hanging up clothes," recalled 72-year-old Deloris Brown. "My nerves were just shattered when those people died. I went out in the street and looked at the flames and everything. . . . I was shook up. Other people got over it [the accident] right quick but I will never get over it." Jenny Taylor, 61, has the same problem: "After that first big explosion you really haven't been yourself since because if trains hit too hard [coupling and uncoupling] you think one of them plants blowed up."

When asked how much the victims' families were paid in compensation, Shell officials say they have no record of it. But Diamond residents are unanimous in recalling that the relatives of Helen Washington were paid $3,000 for her burned house and land, and that Ruth Jones, Leroy's mother, was paid $500.[2] This compares poorly with a multi-million-dollar settlement Shell made with the families of two boys who were killed in a pipeline explosion in Canada.

Not only are there no records of the two fatalities that occurred in Diamond in 1973; there is also no mention of the event in Shell's Norco Museum. When questioned about the incident, curator Clarisse Webb did not know the details. Indeed, she asked if it had anything to do with Shell. Residents of Diamond, however, recall the incident well. "I think I heard they gave [Ruth Jones] $500, but, being elderly, she didn't know [that she deserved more], poor thing," Wendy Mashia said, adding that Shell had been "messing over people" for years. Gaynel Johnson also finds the minimal compensation for the deaths on Washington Street troubling: "You [Shell] could have given her [Ruth Jones] a check every month, and you could have bought her a home. But [instead] this lady was on rent until she died." Margie Richard goes even further, arguing that Shell should have offered to relocate the whole neighborhood after the explosion in 1973, when it became clear that living there was unsafe.

Monique Harden, formerly an attorney for the EarthJustice Legal Defense Fund, is also incensed about how Shell handled the deaths of Jones and Washington. "This horrendous tragedy in 1973 shows how little the lives of African-American residents in the Diamond community meant to Shell at the time. It is beyond an insult. The company doesn't feel sorry for what happened. It doesn't feel sorry for the loss of lives. It doesn't value the people and what they meant to the community or their families or survivors."

Providing some historical context for how it could have happened that the families of Leroy Jones and Helen Washington were compensated so minimally by Shell, Beverly Wright said: "It speaks, in the deep South, to the race issue and the extent to which African-Americans have been disenfranchised and have had no political power or support. That made it possible for people to devalue them and know that they were not going to be challenged."

While noting that there are no company records about what compensation was provided to victims of the accident in 1973, Shell spokesman David Brignac said he understands that the minimal compensation residents say was provided by Shell spoke powerfully to them about how their lives were valued by the company at the time. "We would do vastly differently today than what you describe people say we did back in 1973," he continued. "If [the minimal compensation] is a sore point and it is something that people are hanging onto, I agree that it is something we should do something about."

The Big Bang

The "big bang" in Diamond was not a cosmic event that occurred light years away; it was right next door. At 3:40 A.M. on May 4, 1988, a catalytic cracking unit at the Shell refinery blew up, killing seven Shell workers and injuring 48 other people (some workers, some residents). The explosion spewed 159 million pounds of toxic chemicals into the air, caused widespread property damage, and required the evacuation of 4,500 people.

Corrosion in a pipeline eight inches in diameter permitted 20,000 pounds of C-3 hydrocarbons to escape. A vapor cloud formed and then ignited. The explosion toppled a 16-story-tall fractionator. Debris from the explosion was found 5 miles away, and structural damage to homes and businesses radiated out a mile from the point of the explosion. The blast could be heard 25 miles away in New Orleans, where it set off burglar alarms. The east wall of the Norco Coop Supermarket on Fourth Street was blown off, and the ceiling of Bill's Dollar Store partially collapsed. After the explosion, a fire burned for 8 hours at the refinery before it was brought under control. A black film covered homes and cars in surrounding towns. The governor declared a state of emergency in Norco and St. Charles Parish.[3]

"The night the explosion happened, . . . I actually thought it was a nuclear bomb that had hit our area . . . that we were being invaded by another country," said Larry Brown, 51, as he sat in his house next to his parents' burned-out tavern. "At that particular time I was here with my parents. The explosion knocked me out of bed, and it scared the hell out of me because all I saw was flashes and everything falling down. . . . I ran outside, which was stupid, and I saw fire shooting 150 feet in the air. So I told my parents that it was time for us to go. At that time my father had both of his legs amputated because of poor circulation, so I got him and my mother together in the car and we got out. The police were in town with the mikes on their cars open telling everyone to evacuate. We went out through the spillway. . . . If the spillway had been full I hate to even think what would have happened, because it was real crowded on the road. It was a [traffic] jam with everyone trying to get out."

Brown had been a member of the crew Shell had hired to clean up after the explosion. One of the Shell workers killed was a friend of Brown's, and they found his foot about eight blocks away from the site of the explosion, Brown said. Brown quit the cleanup job when he was instructed to pick up material covered in asbestos. Told that there was no reason to believe the material was dangerous since it had not been tested, Brown said "I don't care if you tested it or not. I'm not going to be here." And he left. "They didn't have proper equipment to work with asbestos," he observed. Brown suspects that many residents were exposed to airborne asbestos when they returned home from the evacuation. "We later came to find that there was enough asbestos in the air that we shouldn't have been let back in for a week. . . . But you won't find that in their [Shell's] files," he charged.

Just as most people who were alive at the time remember where they were when Martin Luther King Jr. and John F. Kennedy were assassinated, everyone in Diamond remembers where he or she was when the catalytic cracking unit at the Shell refinery blew up. And each of them has a very personal way of describing the noise it made.

Delwyn Smith recalled that she had just gotten out of bed to get a glass of water and had returned to bed when the explosion hit. "BAAATUNG. . . . I thought it was a plane had crashed," recalled Smith, who noted that Diamond was in the flight path of nearby New Orleans Airport. All the windows in Smith's house were blown out, and the door was broken and hanging from the top hinge. Smith needed to buy gas to get out of town. "It was like chaos. . . . People were out there crying . . . like my aunt whose husband had just had open-heart surgery." The explosion made Smith realize that "it was not really safe here [in Diamond] at all."

Just how terrifying this explosion was to small children is best described by Ernestine Roberts, 52, who recalled lying in bed listening to Shell's industrial cacophony that night: "Shell had been roaring all night, but it was a different kind of roar. I could hear the difference and you knew something was going to happen. You could feel that something was going to happen. So I lay in bed and it was making this sound, making this sound, making this sound . . . and you get to know the sounds . . . but this was a different sound. I got up bedroom and headed for the kitchen and then all of a sudden BOOOOOM. It knocked me off my feet. I went running to the door, and all I could see was fire. I ran back in here to get my son. I was calling for him and he is not answering me. And all I could see was fire through the windows. And I am calling for him, I can't find him, I am looking in all the closets, I can't find him. . . . Now I am panicking. . . . I can't find him. Finally when I did find him he was under the bed. And I couldn't get him out because he was holding on to the box springs so I am telling him 'Come out, come out.' And he is not crying. He is just holding on and I cannot get him out. And I am pulling and trying to get him out. . . . And finally I pull him out and grab him up in a blanket. . . . And we just run. . . . "

Others were also terrified by the explosion. "That was just scary, scary, scary," say Deloris Brown, 72. "I just ran out through the back. . . . I just prayed I wouldn't cut my feet [on all the broken glass] . . . but I was running the wrong way. . . . The explosions worry me the most . . . and the odor. You hear a noise and you think: I wonder what is happening in Norco. I am afraid of the explosion and that anytime it might be something."

Many residents have not slept well since the explosion. "We slept in our clothes for a long time," said Jenny Taylor. "Tell you the truth I still have my clothes laid out on a chair so I can jump into them. . . . We don't know what they [the plants] are going to do, so you can't ever really be relaxed."

Many people decided to move out of Diamond. "It tore up the neighborhood so bad. You had people that rebuilt their house but you had a lot of people who didn't," recalled Devaliant Christopher Cole. Some just left. Boarded-up homes gave the community a damaged and bedraggled look and brought real estate values down.

Ever since 1988, Devaliant Cole has been waiting for the next accident. "Even now, with the train nearby and the train cars pushing and slamming, I jump up," he said. And when he drives home in the evening and sees smoke rising over Norco, he wonders what has happened.

After the explosion, some Diamond residents just wanted to get out of town. Audrey Eugene spoke with Shell officials about selling her home. "I was ready to leave. . . . You know when something like that happens you don't rest well. It is just too much. You sleep with your shoes right there by your bed, so while it happened in 1988 it didn't go away. . . . I don't have the means to just leave here without selling. . . . I didn't cause this problem. . . . If the land is important to them, let them have it as long as they compensate me what is fair," said Eugene.

Commenting on the safety record of the Shell/Motiva complex, Shell spokesman David Brignac said he was "confident that our safety record is going to improve and continue to improve." Shell had a strong safety program in place, not only for the benefit of the community but also for its own workers, he noted. Shell officials took the attitude that accidents don't just happen but rather have a preventable cause. A lot of time and money was spent on safety, he added. "Regrettably, we have had significant incidents," Brignac conceded, referring to the explosions in 1973 and 1988. The 1988 explosion was last major incident, and since then there have been improvements in safety procedures. Despite these improvements, Brignac is careful not to overpromise. "I can't tell residents that we will never have a big event [again]," he said. "So I don't know how to deal with that fear. I don't have a good answer."

"I Feel Like I'm in a Hole"

"I made 80," said Janie Campbell when asked her age. She said it with no small amount of pride. Many of her friends who lived in the same heavily polluted neighborhood in Diamond died prematurely, she claimed. And, while she cannot prove it, Campbell attributes their early illnesses and deaths to fumes from the adjacent Shell petrochemical plants located just three short blocks from her front door. "Everybody that I knew they died of the cancer. And they all have their breathing machine. A lady died day before yesterday, and she had a big old breathing tank she had to travel with all the time because she couldn't breathe. Another young girl she died also," she said. Giving substance to Campbell's suspicions was a long history of air pollution violations by the neighboring refinery and chemical plant. The air in and outside her home had a biting metallic taste.

Forty years ago, Campbell moved to her home in Diamond, arriving in St. Charles Parish with a sick husband and seven children. She chose Diamond because she found a house there that cost $4,500 and buying it meant that she could own her own home instead of paying rent. The house was cheap because it was located right on the fenceline with Shell's chemical plant and refinery. Shortly after she arrived, her husband, a laborer for Louisiana Power and Gas, died from a stroke. To feed her family, Campbell took a job first as a janitor at Shell's refinery and later as a maid working in the home of a white family in Norco until age 70, when chronic health problems forced her to retire.

Born with poor eyesight, Campbell subsequently developed diabetes, an irregular heartbeat, and a cyst on her spine. She also has arthritis and is often short of breath. "Sometimes I can make do for myself and sometimes I can't," she explained. Though most of her children had left Diamond, one daughter, Mary, lived a few blocks away; that daughter checked on her mother, prepared her meals, did her shopping, and drove her to the doctor.

Explosions at the Shell plants in 1973 and 1988 left Campbell with a bad case of what she called "nerves." During the earlier incident she was sitting on her porch when, as she described it, "something blowed up at the chemical plant and it killed the old lady [Helen Washington] and the little boy [Leroy Jones] who was in the yard. It was like the fire [from the explosion] was coming over my house." Campbell became hysterical. "The funniest part is that every time the kids would start yelling and screaming I would tell them to shut up but then I would start screaming. But it wasn't really funny," she allowed. Hearing about the explosion, one of her sons-in-law came with a dump truck to evacuate her and the kids. The bed of the dump truck was so high that normally Campbell would have been unable to climb into it, but not this time. "I was so frightened that nothing was too high for me to get in," she said.

Campbell found that she did not get over her fright. The home she was working in as a maid had a squeaky faucet, and when the owner of the house turned it on Campbell thought there was another explosion: "I went running down the hall hollering and screaming that [the plant] blowed up again." It got so bad that her employer told her she had to see a doctor. Sent to a mental health clinic, Campbell told the doctor "My nerves are bad, but I don't think I'm crazy." "Janie," he said, "you aren't crazy. You just need some pills."

The 1988 explosion "picked my house off the pillars and dropped it back down," Janie Campbell recalled. "It was . . . just like going through hell. And since that time I don't sleep, I sleep light and if the house creaks I wake and if the trains hit connecting with each other I sit up in bed and say to myself 'Well, that is just the train.' So it is just scary and I have to live on nerve pills and I think that is just horrible to have to live on nerve pills to keep together at night. I just shake because there is too much pressure. I'm frightened."

Campbell is still worried that the refinery or the chemical plant might blow up again, and that she would be left behind in the confusion or the evacuation routes might be cut. She counts it a blessing that during the last big explosion the spillway was not full and Diamond residents were able to escape across it. But if the spillway is full during the next explosion she does not know how she will get out. She cannot drive or swim. "I feel like I am in a hole," she said. "Have you ever seen a hole way down and there is no way for you to come out? Well, I feel like I am in a hole. I'm in a hole with nowhere to go. I'm surrounded. The [railroad] track is there, the river is there, you don't know when an accident is going to happen and the spillway could be full of water. And I can't swim it and I can't walk it, and I can't go through it in a car because it [the water] is so high. . . . Where am I going to go? I just wish I could get away from here before I die so I could have peace of mind and sleep one night in peace without being afraid that the plant is going to blow up." Campbell was acutely aware of how close the plants are to her: "It is not like they are ten miles away. They are right here. And the odors. . . . It is just horrible. And now and then [the plants make loud noises like] VROOM, VROOM, like something they are trying to keep from blowing up. It [the gas] wants to blow up, and it is trying to escape from something. And when they have the flares coming out of the top, it makes a noise like something that is too full and it is trying to escape . . . the pressure. And you don't know if it is going to explode. You don't know what it is going to do. Nobody knows but the good Lord." Shell officials told her the plant was not going to blow up but, as she pointed out, they had not anticipated that the catalytic cracking plant would blow up in 1988. In fact, after the 1990 Clean Air Act required chemical companies to prepare a "worst-case scenario" map of vulnerable areas around their plants it became clear that Diamond was within three overlapping vulnerable zones.

Campbell prays to God that Shell officials will move her so she can have a few years of peace. "My [government] check is $525 a month," she noted. "You can't move on that, and nobody ain't going to buy here in Norco because everybody is afraid [of living near the plants]. I can't sell my house to nobody. Nobody don't want it."

Like many of her neighbors, Campbell would prefer to leave town rather than fight Shell. "I would go," she insisted, as long as Shell paid enough for her house that she could relocate in a safe area. "I'm not particular as long as it is a decent place. . . . I am not a picky person. . . . I just want to get away from here. I am looking just to get away. I just want to be gone. . . . People want to get away from here so bad. They are desperate because they know what they have been going through here and they don't want to raise up children here in this mess."

Unfair Deal

Residents of Diamond harbored deep resentment about the way they were compensated for damage done to their homes by the blast in 1988. In the aftermath of the disaster, there was a widespread sense that Shell played the black community cheap. One accusation that surfaces repeatedly was that Shell sent adjusters out into Diamond immediately after the explosion and offered homeowners $1,000 checks to cover the damages.

Many Diamond residents accepted a small instant payment rather than wait for a larger settlement, said Devon Washington. "We have black people who look at the money and grab it. A lot of people on the [white] side of the track didn't do that," he continued. Instead of taking the proffered $1,000 they held out for a settlement of $40,000 to $50,000, he added. Shell made $1,000 deals with 1,100 people in all. "Why would they have done that at a time when they knew people were shaken up?" asked Margie Richard, who accepted the on-the-spot payment. "I think Shell . . . took advantage of people in shock," said Deonne DuBarry, an attorney who represented Norco plaintiffs in 1993.[4]

"I truly think that Shell thinks that all black people are crazy and don't have any sense," said Ernestine Roberts. Shell adjusters first offered her $5,000 for the repair of her home; she kicked him out and called Shell and told them to send someone else. The walls of the house were warped from the explosion, she explained. When two more adjusters made minimal offers, Roberts sent them packing too. Eventually she had an independent assessor estimate the damage. By holding out, she got three and a half times what Shell had originally offered.

About her home, Roberts said "It was here for me in the beginning before Shell blew me up. I was living in it fine. It may not have been a mansion but it was mine. I worked for it and paid for it. I put everything into it and I wanted it the way it was." Roberts, a college graduate who was turned down for a job at Shell, now works in a department store.

Many other Diamond residents did not know how to bargain with Shell over compensation for their damage, Roberts noted: "In Diamond the people definitely had the wool pulled over their eyes. . . . I would say the majority [of residents] got enough to put in new windows and doors, maybe buy new carpeting and put the ceiling back, but literally that was it."

Shell eventually paid out $172 million in damages to some 17,000 claimants for the 1988 explosion.[5] There was a widespread sense that many people who did not live in the area and were not significantly affected by the explosion piggybacked on legitimate claims, reducing the amount of money that went to those who had suffered real damages.

A number of Diamond residents complained that the white residents of Norco received a better deal from Shell than they did. As proof of this they pointed to the fact that some unoccupied, run-down homes on Apple Street on the white side of town were completely rebuilt while many of the African-American residents were afforded only superficial repairs that did not address some of the structural damage their homes suffered. "There were a lot of houses on Apple Street that were falling down [before the explosion]. They were in really bad shape until that happened. After it happened they just renovated everything . . . the whole nine yards . . . and we got $5,000. It was definitely unequal treatment," said Diamond resident Devaliant Cole.

Another memory of the immediate aftermath of the explosion still rankles, said Diamond resident Larry Brown. Shell sent truckloads of plywood into Norco soon after the explosion. Residents used the plywood to board up their windows and doors until repairs could be done. Unfortunately, the availability of these supplies was not made known to some of the residents of Diamond. By the time they heard about it, two or three days later, there was nothing left for them. "Some of the white guys took enough lumber to build a new house," Brown claimed.

Not only do Diamond residents feel they were not as handsomely compensated as the white residents of Norco; they also bridle at the fact that, once they won their class-action lawsuit for damage from the explosion, the payments they had received from Shell to cover the costs of repairing their homes were deducted from the settlement.

The experiences described above created a trust gap. Some residents of Diamond found that Shell was sometimes less than straightforward with them. Take, for example, the cutting down of the hackberry shade trees in the yard of Brent and Wendy Mashia. One day they came home and found the trees had been cut down. She thought he had done it and he thought she had done it, but in bed that evening they figured out that neither of them had done it. This left them outraged: someone had come onto their property in broad daylight and cut down their trees without their permission. The Mashias live in a property that is right next to a Shell pipeline. It is so close to the pipeline that Shell would not even let them put up a fence to hide it from view; Shell personnel said the fenceposts might interfere with the pipeline. They are also close to Brent's mother, Deloris Brown, who also lives adjacent to the pipeline. She was paid $200 to allow her trees to be cut down so that the roots would not impinge on the pipeline. Logic suggested that Shell also cut down the trees on the Mashia property for similar reasons, but Shell officials denied it. Asked if perhaps a subcontractor working for Shell cut down the trees, Brent Mashia responded "Maybe so." Clearly he had his suspicions about who cut down his trees without his permission—after all, who but Shell had an interest in seeing that the trees were cut? But when you live next to a company worth billions of dollars you do not call them liars lightly. Unwilling to push the matter further, the Mashias let it rest.

"A Flying Saucer"

The rupture of the Shell pipeline that killed two Diamond residents in 1973 and the 1988 explosion at the refinery that killed seven Shell workers and did widespread damage throughout the community were not the only explosions that breached Diamond's fenceline. On February 10, 1998, at 6 P.M., overpressure in the alkyl chloride service at the Shell Chemical plant blew the iron roof off a massive storage tank. The metal roof of the tank vaulted over the Washington Street fenceline and buried itself in the middle of a playground at the former site of Mary Bethune High School.[6]

Gaynel Johnson remembered the incident vividly: "I thought it was a flying saucer. I was coming out of my door to go to my daughter's place in the back and suddenly BOOOOM. I'm standing on the steps and I feel this vibration. . . . I had never seen a flying saucer before but this thing went GNNNNNGNNNNG." When she ran over to see where it had hit she found it had dug a waist-deep hole in the playground. Some kids who had been playing basketball there had run away. If it had gone a bit farther it would have landed on one of the houses, Johnson noted.

"If there had been children in the playground someone would have been killed," observed Carolyn Cole. Since Diamond residents are closer to the fenceline than those in the rest of Norco they are especially vulnerable to these kinds of accidents, she observed. Audrey Eugene fears for the children: "From what I hear, the substance that was in the tank got too hot and it blew, and that big heavy thing leapt off the tank and flew through the air and came over in the school yard and dug a crater. Now if you had a bunch of children there when that happened it would have been very tragic. And Shell is telling me that they are going to put a playground there where my children can play. No. Nope. It is too dangerous over there. I tell my grandchildren they don't need to play over there."

4

Air Assault

In addition to the danger from explosions at the neighboring refinery and chemical plant, residents of Diamond complained they were daily exposed to large volumes of chemicals that escaped the facilities and wafted across the fenceline into their community. There is considerable evidence to back up this assertion. Diamond residents lived in the heart of one of the most highly polluted areas in the United States, known as "Cancer Alley" or "the chemical corridor"—a heavily industrialized 80-mile stretch of land between the mouth of the Mississippi and Baton Rouge. Within this "chemical corridor" are 156 industrial facilities, which emit 129 million pounds of toxins a year—about a sixteenth of the total volume released in the United States and "nearly twice as much as the next largest concentration of toxic releases, in southeast Texas."[1]

Refineries like the one in Norco release 75 percent of their Toxic Release Inventory chemicals into the air because of the "high percentage of volatile organic compounds (VOCs) in refinery emissions," according to one report.[2] Air emissions take place in almost all stages of the refining process, the report continued, and not all the emissions are reported. In a survey of 17 refineries, the EPA found a valve leak rate of 5.0 percent—nearly four times the leak rate of 1.3 percent that refineries reported. "Based on their monitoring results the EPA estimates that petroleum refineries emit 80 million pounds of unreported VOCs every year." Texas, Louisiana, and California top the list of most unreported fugitive emissions.[3]

Diamond residents reported seeing and experiencing such pollution first-hand. Some days the air in Diamond made their eyes sting and played havoc with their sinuses, residents said, and the air often had an acrid smell that brought on coughing and a headache. Occasionally the pollution became so thick that residents reported seeing gases collect near the ground. Usually, however, the fumes were invisible. Residents were reminded of how Shell's pollution was affecting them with every breath. "It burns my eyes and throat," said Diamond resident Brent Mashia. "It is so strong sometimes it just comes inside. You get accustomed to it and you figure that is just the way life is supposed to be. You stop complaining because nobody is going to listen anyways."

Life on the fenceline in Diamond was not normal. Residents lived in a strange, upside-down world in which the nights were lit up so brightly by flares that street lights were often unnecessary. Noises from the plants continued through the night, creating a cacophony of clanking railway cars, loud public address systems, roaring flares, and hissing release valves. Residents said they became accustomed to these noises and to the stench. That they could tolerate the odors did not mean, however, that they were not affected by the chemicals. In fact, some residents became hypersensitive to them through repeated exposure.

Ernestine Roberts reported that on some nights she had to go into the bathroom and put a wet towel over her head so she could breathe. "Sometimes," she said, "it will give you a headache that you wouldn't believe. It's like whatever they are putting out is the pure chemical itself. It is like [here she clapped her hands] it is right up on you." To reduce her exposure, Roberts turned her air conditioning off at night, but fumes seeped in through the ducts, she said. Two of Roberts's three children were asthmatic while growing up in Diamond but not after they left home, she claimed.

Roberts's neighbor across the street had trouble breathing when the fumes from the plant were bad at night. Sometimes her children called Roberts to come help her with her breathing treatments. "It gets to the point where she can barely breathe and at some times we have to call the ambulance to give her treatments because what we are doing is not working," Roberts explained.

There is a shortage of objective data on the health of Diamond residents, but one health survey of 47 households in Diamond, carried out by the Deep South Center for Environmental Justice at Xavier University, revealed that 42 percent of those polled reported respiratory ailments, 35 percent of children reported asthma and only 22 percent of residents said they were in good or excellent health.[4]

The fact that Diamond's residents had to live with air that they felt was not fit to breathe made many of them furious. "I have been sucking up

Shell's shit for fifty years," Larry Brown asserted. As evidence of the harm done to him he held up his arms, blackened by a skin disease that he and one of his sons suffer. "I done had this since I was 15 years old. I went to several dermatologists. I cover it with salve. It is not cancerous, but where the hell did it come from? I know it came from these plants. I have been to so many doctors and no one can explain anything. They don't even have a name for it. How the hell can they name it when they don't know what it is? It itches, burns, and scales. If I don't keep it moisturized it cracks up. . . ." Brown is convinced that many of the health problems his family suffered are due to pollution from Shell. "My mother died of cancer. I attribute that to the plant too. My father died of liver cancer. . . . I still say cancer is cancer and this is Cancer Alley."

Despite Shell's reassurances that its facilities meet state and federal regulations, everyone I met in Diamond was convinced that there were enough emissions from the Shell plants to make the air hazardous to breathe. Diamond residents are almost unanimous in contending that the regulatory bodies do not monitor the Shell facilities on a regular enough basis to catch Shell polluting. Many of Shell's releases take place under cover of darkness, they added. "It is worse at night than during the day," Devon Washington said. "That is when Shell does its dirty work. . . . At night nobody is around but me, and they don't care about me. . . . The odor is just ridiculous. . . . Sometimes I got nauseated when they had a chlorine leak over there about four years ago."

Community residents were also skeptical about the determination of federal and state regulators to protect them. Regulation of oil and chemical plants in Louisiana was notoriously lax, and the governor instructed environmental and health officials in the state not to create problems for big industry, noted several environmental activists. Some politicians believe this leniency was needed to lure big industry to the area in an effort to create jobs and increase tax revenues in one of the poorest states in the nation. But environmental activists argued that the choice between jobs or toxic air was a false choice and that it was possible to have both a livable environment and reasonable work. Agreeing to allow a toxic industry to operate in a community so that jobs would be available to some of the residents was self-defeating because it caused illness, lowered property values, and frightens away tourists and business development, environmentalists argued.

While the debate about jobs versus the environment was going on in Norco and other fenceline communities, many residents of Diamond remained dubious about Shell's claims that there was no air-pollution problem. "Shell comes out with this jive about how they are cutting down emitting this toxin," said Larry Brown. "That is a whole lot of crap. Soon as it gets foggy or a little bit of rain, they dump it."

Brown often found himself arguing with Shell workers who claimed it was safe to work there and live near the plant. "Do you think they [Shell officials] let you know exactly what they are dumping?" he asked. "They aren't telling you nothing. They are a company . . . and they are going to cover their behind any way they can . . . from all angles." Brown was further convinced that Shell ignored the problems of Diamond residents "because we are a minority and we are few." After 35 years watching Shell officials deal with his community, Brown had come to distrust them: "They come up with more rhetoric and bullshit than anyone I know in my lifetime. . . . They have so many devious ways they can do things: and they can hurt you in so many different ways. It is a crying shame."

Leaks and Upsets

Diamond residents and Shell officials disagreed sharply about the quality of the air in Norco. Shell officials maintained that they were meeting federal and state regulatory standards and that as a result they were permitted to continue to operate their facilities. Diamond residents insisted they were inhaling fumes that were causing them a wide variety of respiratory diseases and other illnesses. Furthermore, there had been no effective monitoring of the air they breathed, they pointed out.

Although Shell officials dismissed reports of pollution-induced disease as unsubstantiated and anecdotal, there exists a substantial compilation of statistics drawn from Shell documents and regulatory reports. Those statistics suggest that there was good reason to believe that the air in Norco and Diamond may not always have met regulatory standards and that residents of the area were most likely exposed to more toxins than average Americans. This is not terribly surprising from a commonsense perspective. If you live next to two giant industrial plants—one a refinery and the other a chemical plant—chances are that you are going to be exposed to a certain amount of chronic leakage and accidental emissions. After all, the

Shell/Motiva Norco Complex was a huge industrial facility with 2,275 employees. Ships, trains, and truckloads of explosive, flammable, and highly toxic products were loaded and unloaded every day. In the process there were numerous releases. It was the volume of those reported releases, however, that gave one pause about the wisdom of permitting people to live next to these facilities.

In 1999, according to Wilma Subra, a chemist who works as a consultant to fenceline communities such as Diamond, the eight facilities in and around Norco emitted a total of 930 tons of toxic chemicals into the air, 900 tons (1.8 million pounds) of which were released into the air. In 1997, according to another report, the Shell Chemical plant and the Motiva refinery in Norco released 2 million pounds of toxic chemicals into the air.[5]

The Shell/Motiva Norco Complex was rising to the top of the list of major regional sources of air pollution. In 1998, the Shell Chemical plant and the Motiva refinery were responsible for half of all toxic air emissions released in St. Charles Parish.[6] And the Shell/Motiva Complex was also the second-largest emitter of toxic chemicals in Louisiana, releasing more recognized carcinogens into the air than any other refinery complex in the state.[7] Shell officials conceded that the report of 2 million pounds of releases was correct but insisted that the comparisons made with other refineries were "like comparing apples with oranges" because they compared integrated petrochemical complexes with stand-alone refineries. "The fair comparison would be to break out our number into a Shell Company number and a separate Motiva refinery number," they pointed out.

Despite these qualifying words from Shell, it could not have been comforting to the residents of Diamond to learn that the Shell Chemical plant, immediately adjacent to their homes, produced epichlorohydrin, methyl ethyl ketone, allyl chloride, specialty resins, hydrochloric acid, and secondary butyl alcohol. According to Wilma Subra, these chemicals were known to cause a variety of diseases, including decreased fertility in males; lung, liver, kidney, and nervous-system damage; lung cancer; irritation of nose and throat; coughing; shortness of breath; possible developmental malformations; dizziness; light-headedness; headaches; nausea; blurred vision; and skin allergies.[8]

Shell officials noted that the only chemicals the Shell Chemical plant either produced or used were methyl ethyl ketone and hydrochloric acid. "The other chemicals listed are for Resolution Performance Products," they

asserted. (Resolution Performance Products is a chemical company adjacent to the Shell Chemical plant.) However, a number of informed observers
saw this as a distinction without a difference. Shell deliberately spun off
Resolution Performance Products but continued to hold a financial stake in
it, send products to it, and use Shell employees to run it, they argued.

Shell Chemical alone released 332 tons of toxic air emissions in 1997,
254 tons in 1998, and 300 tons in 1999, Subra wrote. On average more
than half of these emissions were "fugitive emissions" from leaks in valves
and pumps which were released closer to the ground than those pouring
out of the plant's stacks.[9] Shell claimed that emissions from its chemical
plant in Norco were reduced 35 percent since 1998 and that a significant
capital investment program would decrease emissions further.[10]

Of further concern to Diamond residents was the fact that Shell's Norco
facilities had a long history of frequent accidental releases. (The corporate
euphemism is "upsets.") From January through March of 1998, Shell
reported 27 accidental releases to the Louisiana Department of Environmental Quality (LDEQ)—an average of one incident every three days,
Subra observed.[11] From January 1990 through September 2000, Shell's
Norco facilities reported releasing 1.15 million pounds of chemicals during
341 "events" in which unanticipated releases occurred. These events
included 33 releases of benzene, a known human carcinogen, Subra
reported.[12] Shell officials conceded that "1998 was a bad year" but said
that the amount of benzene released during the 33 releases was "likely very
low and would not have resulted in benzene concentrations in the community above ambient air standards." In the company's defense, Shell officials
further noted that they were upgrading their instrumentation to prevent
operational upsets.

The Shell Norco facility was identified as one of eleven facilities in Texas
and Louisiana that were responsible for half of the accidental releases of
chemicals into the air between 1994 and 1998. The EPA invited Shell officials to participate in a voluntary initiative to reduce the number of accidental releases as an alternative to an enforcement order, said Wilma Subra.
To avoid the enforcement action, company officials agreed to voluntarily
decrease episodic releases by 50 percent by 2003. Shell had made good
progress, the company reported, and had reduced these incidents at its
Norco facilities from 20 in 1999 to 14 in 2001. It aimed to have ten or fewer
incidents in 2002, a company website stated.[13]

Flares

In addition to fugitive and accidental releases, there were also emissions caused by the Shell Oil's refinery's (now Motiva's) penchant for flaring. Flaring involves the burning off of gases at the top of one of the refineries many stacks or chimneys. Understanding flares requires a brief explanation.

When crude oil is refined, its sulfur content has to be removed by a sulfur-recovery plant. The elemental sulfur recovered through this process can be diverted and sold. In addition to producing a saleable product, the sulfur-recovery plant also acts as a pollution-control device. Reducing the sulfur content in the processed fuels limits the amount of waste gases, such as hydrogen sulfide and sulfur dioxide, released directly into the air. Both of these chemicals are potentially harmful. Hydrogen sulfide is a highly toxic gas that smells like rotten eggs; short-term exposure to high concentrations of it "may result in reduced lung function accompanied by such symptoms as wheezing, chest tightness, or shortness of breath in asthmatic children and adults." All these symptoms were reported by Diamond residents. Furthermore, long-term exposure to sulfur dioxide could lead to respiratory illness and aggravation of existing cardiovascular disease.[14]

When upsets in the refining process occurred, waste gases were burned off in a flare. Regulators recognized that flaring in emergencies was a good practice because it prevented fires and explosions and "converts noxious and odorous gases released in emergencies to less hazardous and less objectionable emissions."[15] Flaring, however, released a great deal of sulfur dioxide into the air and should be used only in real emergencies that could not be anticipated or prevented, the EPA stated, because more sulfur dioxide could be release in one day of flaring than was released normally during an entire year when the sulfur-recovery plant was in proper operation. Frequent flaring was not due to malfunctions but rather was a failure to anticipate fluctuations in the amount of sulfur in the feedstock or a failure to provide a sulfur-recovery system with adequate capacity. When plant operators dumped waste gases to a flare instead of using the sulfur-recovery plant in non-emergency situations, they were violating air-pollution regulations, EPA regulators warned.

Flaring was a common event in Diamond, and residents often saw large fires at the top of refinery chimneys emitting dark plumes into the air. The flares at Motiva and Shell Chemical were sometimes so large that they lit up the night sky and made it possible for Diamond residents to read after dark without turning on a light. "I will be in my house sometimes with all the lights off at night and when that flare comes on a couple of times I think my house is on fire," reported 27-year-old Diamond resident Catina Hill.[16]

According to Denny Larson, coordinator of the Refinery Reform Campaign, operators running units at full capacity were faced with a choice: they could shut a unit down when unwanted by-products built up, or they could keep it running and burn off the unwanted gases in a flare. Since plant operators were under pressure to meet production schedules, they often flared off the gases, arguing that the toxic gases would be burned up in the process. Unfortunately, Larson noted, no flare is 100 percent efficient, and inevitably large volumes of pollutants escaped during flaring.

Though Motiva officials claimed that flaring was the safest way to handle "upsets" and that none of the releases posed a health threat, in fact flaring could be quite harmful both to the environment and to the health of adjacent residential populations, such as those in Diamond and Norco. In addition to creating acid rain, sulfur dioxide was known for impairing breathing and aggravating bronchitis and other respiratory diseases. Residents of Diamond and Norco were exposed to a lot of sulfur dioxide from flaring. During the period 1996–1998, the Motiva refinery emitted 25 tons of sulfur dioxide into the air in ten separate documented releases.[17]

When a refinery went out of whack it could emit huge volumes of air pollutants in a short period. For example, during one nine-day period starting in October 5, 1996, Motiva vented 442,350 pounds of gas into the air adjacent to Norco.[18] The Louisiana Department of Environmental Quality imposed no fines for the releases.

In their own defense, Shell officials claimed that flaring incidents were down significantly in 2001 compared with the year before. "Flaring is an event where chemicals are burned high above the ground to avoid ground-level emergencies. Flaring therefore is necessary for safety considerations, but in the process releases pollutants into the air so we are reducing the number of flaring events," a corporate website explained.[19]

Fines

The flaring, the accidents, and the "upsets" suggested that the Motiva refinery and the Shell Chemical plant were sources of significant pollution that could affect the health of nearby residents. The evidence that these were facilities with real problems was mounting.

A 1990 inspection of Motiva by the EPA uncovered so many violations that it resulted in a $1 million fine. On April 3, 1998, a Louisiana Department of Environmental Quality (LDEQ) inspection team found disconnected pipes, loose bolts, and cracked welds in a unit that had malfunctioned at Motiva. LDEQ slapped the company with a $330,000 fine. In March 2000, Motiva was revealed to have improperly handled the treatment of wastewater. On June 2, 2002, LDEQ and EPA discovered hundreds of violations that caused concern about the lack of monitoring and documentation of monitoring of many of the valves and pumps at the refinery. In a March 2001 settlement with the EPA, Motiva agreed to spend $4.03 million on beneficial environmental improvements at the Norco facility "above and beyond the $500,000 penalty assessed by LDEQ and a $1 million penalty assessed by the EPA."[20] The settlement also included a provision that required Motiva to develop a project with community representatives to set up air monitors in Norco.

Commenting on Motiva's handling of its leak-prevention program, Sam Coleman, director of enforcement for the EPA's Region VI (which covers Texas and Louisiana), said: "They [Motiva officials] had a meeting with us and they said, 'There are no problems.' We looked into it and we found massive problems. That means either that they don't know what is happening in their plant or that they weren't being candid. Neither is good."

There were also questions about whether the expansion of the Motiva refinery had been accompanied by an adequate upgrade in its pollution-control technologies. Under the Clean Air Act of 1977 and subsequent amendments, new power plants and refineries were required to install the "maximum achievable control technologies" to reduce their emissions. However, aging utilities, steel mills, paper plants, coal-fired power plants, and refineries—such as the Motiva refinery in Norco—were exempted from this requirement if they made only marginal improvements in their facilities. But what constituted repair and maintenance of an aging facility, and what constituted a major overhaul and expansion? Some utilities and refineries took advantage of this regulatory loophole by expanding existing facilities instead of building new plants that would require more advanced pollution-control technologies. Under the Clinton administration the EPA went after some of the highest-polluting industries that were expanding their facilities without investing in advanced pollution-control technologies. The Bush administration has taken a different view and is by one account "downright hostile to pursing such investigations."[21]

A recent study by the National Academy of Public Administration found that the New Source Review regulatory program, though it effectively controlled pollution from new facilities, failed to reduce emissions from our oldest and dirtiest factories and power plants. "Contrary to congressional intent," the *Washington Post* reported, "many large, highly polluting facilities have continued to expand their production (and pollution) over the past 25 years without upgrading to cleaner technologies. . . . The result: thousands of premature human deaths and many thousands of additional cases of acute illness and chronic diseases caused by air pollution."[22]

Shell officials disputed the view that their facilities constituted a danger to public health. Shell has a permit to operate its plants from the Louisiana Department of Environmental Quality and is meeting its obligations to operate safely, said David Brignac.

Brignac was particularly adamant when the subject of cancer rates came up. "Cancer in the industrial corridor is no higher than anywhere else in the country," he said. In fact, cancer incidence for black males, black females, and white females was statistically lower than the national average according to studies by the Louisiana Tumor Registry, he continued. A study of Shell employees who worked from 1973 to 1999 showed a lower mortality rate from cancer and other causes than average Americans, Brignac added.[23] Shell employees are statistically healthier than the average American and tend to live longer, he continued. "Cancer Alley" was a misnomer and could be traced to a bitter union dispute in the 1970s, he added. However, no studies had yet been done of respiratory problems among workers or local residents, he conceded.

While they firmly believed that the company was not causing ill health in adjacent communities, Shell officials said they were interested in seeing that health studies were carried out in Norco to prove the point and allay the fears of some local residents. Shell was willing to help pay for these studies but wanted to find a universally credible third party to conduct them. There was no point doing the studies if critics could later argue that they were biased, Brignac pointed out. A search is currently underway for an unimpeachable third party to do the study, he added.

As for Shell's record controlling toxic emissions from the plant, Brignac claimed that the company had done a good job and continued to improve. Emissions from the plant came from four sources: stacks (which released both permitted and illegal emissions), fugitive emissions (leaks from equipment), accidental releases, and flares. The regulatory agencies had standards for the average amount of toxins that could be in the air when it hit the fenceline. There were also rules about reporting accidental releases.

One thing that made it difficult to assess whether Shell was really reducing its toxic air emissions was that the company kept reorganizing itself and selling off units, so that, on paper at least, it no longer was responsible for them. This could make following which company was responsible for emissions more challenging, Wilma Subra noted. While it was true that Shell stopped its deep-well injection of hazardous wastes in 1989 and thus dramatically reduced its land-based and water-based dumping of toxics, its reduction of air pollutants in 2000 "did not show a whole lot of progress," David Brignac conceded. Shell Chemical's emissions went up a little bit and Motiva's went down, Brignac noted, but much of this can be accounted for by "paperwork" transactions over which company is responsible for which equipment. There should be considerable improvements in air emissions data in the future, Brignac predicted.

5

Grievances Mount

Diamond residents could not prove that they were being poisoned by emissions from the neighboring Shell plants, but most of them suspected that the air they breathed would eventually make them sick.

"The fumes [from the Shell plants] are going in your body. If they have a long-term effect on you [or not] I do not know and I don't know about all the toxins that are being let out over there. But I'm quite sure it is nothing good for you," said Audrey Eugene. "I think our family's health has been affected by living next to these plants. It may not be evident now but I can't help but feel maybe later on down the line. . . . The average person who passes away in this community . . . has some kind of breathing disorder. My aunt, we called her Nanna, she used to have breathing difficulties. She passed away now. She lived on Cathy Street. My mom, she had glaucoma and a tumor on her kidney that turned into a cancer. But whenever those fumes are let out here you get to coughing."

Diamond residents reported a plethora of health problems, including an unusually high incidence of asthma in their children. Kalei, the 2-year-old granddaughter of Lorita Jenkins, was one of them. When I went to visit her, Kalei, who suffers from both asthma and sickle-cell anemia, crawled up into her grandmother's lap and went to sleep, breathing sonorously at times. Outside the air had a metallic tang to it that Jenkins said caused Kalei's asthma to act up. "There is always this faulty air. . . . You can smell the odor in you house," said Jenkins, who also had to keep an asthmatic grandson indoors during the summer. Jenkins was not alone in taking such precautionary measures. When their daughter died, Diamond residents Carolyn and Milton Cole took in their three grandchildren. "It is hard for the children," said Carolyn Cole, "because there are the fumes in the air and they can't even go outside. We have to keep them inside."

While Mary Bethune High School was still in operation, children were frequently prohibited from going outside for recess because of poor air quality. Margie Richard, who worked at the school as a physical education teacher, had to send children inside when fumes from the plants were too strong. This proved to be the prudent thing to do in light of a recent study conducted by the University of Southern California and published in the British medical journal *The Lancet*, which provided evidence that children who engaged in active sports inhaled 17 times as much air as those who did not and that they were more likely to develop asthma than those who were not engaged in active sports.[1]

Almost everybody who lived in Diamond went to Mary Bethune High and exercised in the school's playground next to the fenceline, noted Richard. "My mother's brother died of pneumonia and he was under a doctor's care," she said.

Other Diamond residents knew people who had left town because the pollution made breathing difficult. "Gaynel Johnson moved from Diamond to La Place because she couldn't stand it here anymore," recalled Josephine Bering. "Every time Shell put something out [pollution] it would cut her breath and she would have to go to the doctor. So she had to go."

There was also concern about a cancer connection. "I had a sister who died of cancer," said Carolyn Cole. "She never smoked or anything, but I guess she died of the fumes and everything. So many people here have lost a family member from cancer. I don't know definitely that it is because of the plant, but I'm sure of it." But proving it is difficult, Milton Cole noted.

Shell officials have told Diamond residents that they lack evidence to connect their health problems to pollution from Shell's plants, Margie Richard observed. With no health study that could provide statistical verification, the Diamond residents had only anecdotal evidence.

Looking for ways to prove their case after the 1988 explosion, Diamond residents demanded to know where air-monitoring equipment was located in their area. As Margie Richard recalled, they discovered that the only air monitors were across the river in Hahnville.

Many Diamond residents said they did not need proof of Shell's pollution; they experienced it all the time. The pollution was so bad that they could not lead normal lives. "I spend less time outside than I would normally," one resident observed. "I stay inside. This morning I had my back door and front door closed because you don't want to inhale all that stuff but I hate to be locked up in the house: I feel like I'm in prison."

A number of outdoor events have been interrupted or spoiled because of pollution. "Once my son was barbecuing outside and something [from the Shell plants] sprayed on it and we couldn't eat the food," Janie Campbell recalled. "You could see this stuff on the food, and we had to throw it all away. I think [Shell officials] gave us a little [money] for it." Dorothy Pedescleaux also recalled that day: "This white stuff came from Shell. I don't know what it was but it got over everything, the food and everything they had outside." Shell officials came and told them to get rid of the food and the toys that had been exposed.

"I am in fear all the time," said Audrey Eugene. "All the time something is escaping [from the plant]. On average everybody who expires in this community it is some type of respiratory problem or some type of sickness or some type of cancer. . . . So if the land is so important to them [Shell] let them have it but make sure that they compensate me fair. . . . I think everybody needs to get out of here."

Cause for Complaint

Iris Carter was running late. It was a chilly winter evening when she pulled up to her trailer on East Street in Diamond. Carter, 51, was coming home from her full-time job at an Early Head Start center, where she worked with eight children, three of them infants. She had been doing this kind of work for 15 years and would soon graduate from Delgado College with a degree in Early Childhood Development. After graduation she planned to pursue a degree in Special Education.

An arthritic knee caused Carter to limp up the steps of her trailer; otherwise she seemed exhausted but in high spirits. A deliveryman had left a small package containing a new telephone on her doorstep. As she painfully stooped to pick it up, a white co-worker pulled into the drive and joined her. Indoors the trailer was cold. Carter invited her guest in and went into her bedroom, where she pulled a long, beaded evening gown with matching shoes and a handbag out of her closet. "You're going to look great in this," she said, lending the clothes to her friend.

With her friend gone, Carter settled onto the couch to tell me about her life in Diamond. Her family went way back as residents of the old Diamond,

Belltown, and the Trepagnier Plantation. Though she did not know exactly how far back they went, she could count at least five generations who had lived here on the land.

Carter was very close with her grandmother, who had lived on the open agricultural land known as Belltown before Shell Chemical came in and tore down the old plantation buildings, forcing the African-American residents to move. It was then that Carter's family rebuilt their lives, about a quarter of a mile from their old place in Belltown, at a new location in Diamond, on the fenceline with the new plant.

As a child, Carter explained, she had thought of the chemical plant and the refinery as just there—part of the landscape: "As children we were not aware of the dangers much. We were innocent and ignorant of the facts: we didn't know. We would just play around the plant. We just grew up here. It was home to us." But as she grew older, Carter began to take note of the toxic odors coming from the refinery and chemical plant. She became convinced that Shell's pollution was making her family sick. Before her mother died at the age of 67, Carter took her to a doctor. "She had lived here all her life," Carter said. "She lost a lot of weight and then the function of her body. She couldn't get up and walk any more. When we took her to the clinic at Louisiana State University one of the doctors asked us if we lived near a plant. The doctor said my mom's condition was partly caused by the environment we lived in."

Six months after Carter's mother died, her sister died at 47 of sarcoidosis, a rare disease that a number of Diamond residents contracted.[2] "Her doctor also said her sickness was caused by the environment," Carter said. Her sister took Shell Chemical to court, arguing that pollution from the plant was killing her, but she lost her case. Shell's lawyers, Carter said, "made my sister look small. They talked bad about her. They talked down to her to make them right and us wrong."

Shortly after her sister died, Carter herself started coughing up blood. "It kind of scared me when I started getting sick," she recalled, "and I went to the doctor and he asked me where I lived. He asked if I live near a plant; I didn't tell him that. So when I told him I did he just said 'That is some of your problem right there.'" The doctor suspected that her condition came from her living next to a chemical plant *before* she told him where she lived, Carter noted. To her this constituted important evidence that her problems were caused by pollution from the plant. "I went to Charity Hospital," she said, "and didn't even mention that I was living in a chemical environment, sandwiched between a refinery and a chemical plant. That doctor did not know where I lived. . . . Come on now. . . . I didn't pay him. I was going to Charity Hospital for free. So the finger is pointing back at Shell."

"My mom died," Carter said, "my sister died [and then I got sick], and we were here all the time, breathing this stuff in, not knowing that it was maybe causing our lives to be shortened and causing ill health." Her suspicions were confirmed when her cousin and neighbor Avis Moore died of respiratory disease at a younger age than her sister. "The doctors said that she was in the condition she was in because of the [polluted] air," Carter said. "It doesn't take a rocket scientist to figure out that if all these people are dying and sick in this community. . . .

Carter was clearly angry about the way her family and community had been treated by Shell. "Shell needs to stop lying," she maintained, referring to the stated position of Shell spokesman David Brignac that emissions from their plants were causing harm to no one. "First you need to recognize that you have a problem before you can get a solution. You have to admit that you have a problem. Shell needs to say 'We are the problem and we are making the lives of the residents of Diamond very unhappy.' They want to sit back in their corporate offices in their business suits and point the finger at us and say that we want the easy way out. What a joke."

Carter also did not buy the argument of Shell officials that they were meeting state and federal emissions regulations: "The government is not here every day; they are not monitoring 24 hours a day seven days a week. . . . So Shell can be prepared when the government comes in not to emit the stuff or pollute. . . . I'm not stupid. . . . We know what is going on. . . .We are just sick of being treated like second-class citizens as if we just don't matter."

Carter was equally unimpressed by Shell's argument that everyone who lived in Diamond had moved to this fenceline community knowing full well that they would be living next to industrial facilities: "As far as I know we [the African-American residents of Belltown and Diamond] were here before Shell. My relatives were here before they called this Norco. They called it Diamond or Sellers, Louisiana. Shell found us here and they came and they polluted our air. So who should be leaving or who should be paying for us to leave? Should it be us? The question is 'Who is responsible?' Shell is . . . that is all I am saying, and they should face their responsibility."

A religious woman who went to sleep at night praying that God's angels would protect her and other members of the Diamond community from harm, Carter called on God to judge the behavior of the corporate giant that was her neighbor: "Shell can either do the right thing and God will have mercy on them or they can keep on doing wrong and God will let his wrath fall upon them. . . . Come on now. . . . You can either be a blessing or you can be a curse. They can choose. . . . He says vengeance is His. . . . I don't have to lift a finger."

Few Hires

An extraordinarily small number of Diamond residents worked at Shell—only 3 percent of them, according to Margie Richard, former president of the Concerned Citizens of Norco. In sharp contrast, a large number of white Norco residents currently work, once worked, or have relatives working at Shell.

Despite Shell's poor record of hiring Diamond residents, it was not the case that no one from the community worked there. In the early days—when segregation was still in effect throughout the South and during the Jim Crow era—some Diamond residents were hired to perform menial jobs. "Blacks during that time were no more than janitors at Shell. That's all you could do is janitor," said Diamond resident Devon Washington. Those fortunate enough to be hired by Shell polished floors, mowed lawns, and painted the huge gas storage tanks. Some female residents worked as maids in the homes of white residents on the other side of town. Very few of the black Shell employees hired out of Diamond moved up the ladder to the better-paying jobs, and very few are currently employed by the company.

Janie Campbell, 81, recalled working at Shell in the old days: "Shell has grown a lot since I moved here. When I moved here Shell had houses in that plant. I started working for them because I was very poor. . . . I worked over here at Shell doing janitorial work for a while. What stopped me was that an alarm went off and I thought that Shell was going to blow up and that they had forgotten me back there by myself and I was trying to climb the fence and all that [to escape]. Afterwards I gave them the key back because I couldn't do that no more. So I did housework." When Campbell moved to Diamond, she hoped that proximity to the plant might mean one or more of her five children would end up working there. But none of them were hired. "I felt bad for my kids, because I had some educated boys, but there is nothing you could do about it," she said.

There are now only three current Diamond residents working at Shell, according to Larry Brown. As a result, "when something happens on the white side of town they are taken care of but we are not. We are always the last to hear. . . . Is it because [residents of Norco] are employed by Shell or because they are white? I don't want to be rude about it but that is exactly why," Brown asserted. "Shell officials don't really care about us because we are a minority and we are few."

Without jobs at Shell, Diamond residents had to find work elsewhere. Sometimes they traveled all the way to New Orleans for jobs. Audrey Eugene asserted that "there have been no opportunities for black workers at Shell . . . very few." Unable to get a job at Shell, Eugene's husband Claude did a number of odd jobs until he landed a position with General American Tank and Terminal. Audrey Eugene worked two janitorial jobs—one at the airport from 7 A.M. to 3 P.M. and the other at a school from 4 to 8 P.M.

Many of the workers at Shell are white residents of Norco who are related to one another, Eugene said. "That might be one of the reasons the [white] people don't worry so much about the pollution."

White residents of Norco might be ignoring or accepting the health impact from the pollution "as part of the cost of gainful employment," noted Vernice Miller-Travis, an environmental justice organizer from New York and a former program officer at the Ford Foundation. This was part of a devil's bargain in which poor residents in Louisiana must choose between having a job or living in a contaminated community.

"There are not many [Shell] employees from Diamond. . . . That is a problem and we admit it," David Brignac conceded. In defense of his company, Brignac said that it was hard to find residents who met Shell's stringent qualifications. When Shell advertised for 15 operators, 2,000–3,000 applications came in. Competition for Shell jobs is intense, Brignac pointed out, and many of the applicants are highly qualified. In addition, he noted, when Shell had hired Diamond residents some of them had moved out of the community, and this made it appear as if Shell hired fewer residents out of Diamond than it actually did. But in view of the number of college graduates in Diamond and the number of people with experience in the petrochemical industry and other industrial fields, these excuses seemed thin to many Diamond residents. Clearly, had Shell made it a priority, the company could have identified additional Diamond residents who could have done a variety of jobs at Shell.

"They lie," Ernestine Roberts insisted when asked about Shell's claim that applicants from Diamond who were qualified for Shell jobs couldn't be found. Roberts applied for a job at Shell just after finishing community college. "I am competent, but they gave me the run-around," she said, brushing her hands twice against each other as if cleaning dust off them. Turned down at Shell, she found a job at Dillard's Department Store in the nearby town of Kenner.

Roberts was not alone in faulting Shell for failing to hire some of the more accomplished young people in Diamond. Devaliant Cole sat in his immaculate white-brick house in Diamond wondering why Shell never hired him. Shell could not argue that he was undereducated; Cole had attended Delgado Business College and had a class C insurance license that would equip him to work in Shell's benefits department. "It is not as if I am a stupid person," he said. Nor could company officials claim that he did not have sufficient work experience to handle a job at Shell; at the time, he managed a fast-food restaurant with annual revenues of about $1.7 million. He had 10 years' experience as a unit operator at Colonial Sugar. "So it is not like I can't run a [industrial production] unit. I can definitely run a unit," he pointed out. Cole was particularly irked that he has been rejected for employment at Shell at least three times in view of his grandfather's long service at the company. "My grandfather worked there for 53 years [at Shell]. . . . That has got to count for something.'

Cole's friend Dewayne Washington has also applied numerous times to Shell and has been turned down despite good work experience. He worked at GATX, a neighboring oil company, as an operator loading tanks, barges, and trucks with oil, gasoline, and other petroleum products. When he was laid off from his job during a period when the company was being reorganized, Washington applied for a job at Shell but was turned down. He subsequently found employment working as a federal grain inspector.

Shell gives job applicants tests to see if they measure up to the demands of the job, but Washington pointed out that Shell could have trained him: "Everybody knows that companies hire people and train them. They would rather train you because they want you to learn their way." Besides, the real way you got a job was to know someone who is working at the Shell plant, he continued. If you had a personal contact, they could "walk you right through the door," he claimed. The tests did not really mean much, he added.

A carefully crafted training program could have been designed for Diamond residents who wanted to work at Shell and had completed college or accumulated relevant work experience. Even those who just had a high school degree could have been hired to cut the lawns, clean the facilities, and paint the equipment. But Shell awarded those jobs to subcontractors.

"Why," asked Margie Richard, "couldn't Shell open the door for [Diamond residents] instead of using some kind of strategy saying they didn't pass the test? If a person can cut the grass he is no longer a nobody: he is a skilled grass-cutter," she observed. Devaliant Cole agreed: "I really think even with the contractors, even with the guys cutting grass, there are guys in this neighborhood who can do that."

Shell hires people from all over but not from Diamond, observed Brent Mashia. "I felt that since we are in their neighborhood they ought to hire some of us," he continued. If Mashia got a job at Shell, he observed, it might make him look at the company differently. "But we aren't benefiting anything," he said, while there are people on the other side of the color divide pulling down big salaries. Brent's wife Wendy echoed this sentiment: "You are living here and you are inhaling all of this stuff and they [Shell] won't even give you an opportunity to make some money." Wendy Mashia and a few of her friends applied for jobs at Shell but never received any response. "What is wrong with training us?" she asked. "I'm versatile. But they won't give you the opportunity."

In retrospect, the failure by Shell to hire Diamond residents can be seen as a critical mistake. Shell officials could likely have purchased the allegiance of many Diamond residents by hiring out of community just as they did on the white side of Norco. But because so few Diamond residents were given employment at Shell, many residents were alienated from the company and saw no reason to gloss over the impact of Shell's pollution on their health. This cost Shell dearly both in the amount of money it eventually paid for relocating Diamond residents and in negative publicity.

Dead Flowers

In the early years, shortly after they were evicted from Belltown, some Diamond residents did not experience the Shell Chemical plant as much of a problem. At first the plant was small and far enough away that its presence seemed benign. "In the beginning it [the chemical plant] was pretty low profile," said Diamond resident Jenny Taylor.

Gaynel Johnson agreed with this early perception of the plant being relatively unobtrusive. Johnson, who was taken in by her grandparents in Diamond at age 4, recalled the plant growing as she grew: "Coming up as a little girl, Shell [Chemical] over here was not big at all. No, it was not big. As I growed and growed, the plant growed."

Much of the formal and informal business of this highly religious community was conducted in churches. As the refinery and the chemical plant inched closer to Diamond, the churches became places where residents could voice their complaints about them.

Agriculture also continued to play an important role in Diamond in the early days. Moving from Belltown to Diamond meant that residents gave up large-scale farming, but many did not entirely abandon raising their own food. There were still a good number of vegetable gardens and chicken coops in Diamond in the early days. "My daddy raised chickens here in Diamond in the backyard," recalled Lois Gales. And residents continued to share their produce as they had in Belltown.

Diamond residents have always been good at sharing, Jenny Taylor observed: "The neighbors look out for each other. . . . If one got, then everybody got. That is the way we do it. . . . You come home and someone has always got something on the fire—our house, his house, your house—you always have something to eat," recalled Taylor, who in recent years has worked as an aide to the elderly at the Chateau Living Center.

There was also an informal barter economy that permitted people who did not have much cash to live better than they would have elsewhere. "My father had a garden and he grew food," recalls Devon Washington. "We had chickens and hogs, and we ate all that stuff. . . . You could go down the street and get some greens. . . . There was a lot of trade, you know. There was never no money. They were also fishing out of the river." Now, of course, taking fish out of the river is dangerous, because the river is polluted. Washington said he would no longer eat river-caught fish, although others do. He detected some irony in the fact that, while you could no longer raise hogs in Diamond because environmental regulations prohibited such an odoriferous agricultural operation in a residential area, the neighboring petrochemical plants were permitted to create horrendous odors and pollution.

Over time it became apparent that heavy industry next door to small gardens was an incompatible mix. As the chemical plant and the refinery expanded, Diamond residents began to notice that pollution from the Shell plants was not only affecting their health but also killing their gardens. "I do a little gardening in the springtime, but it don't work good," said Janie Campbell. "I think it is from the pollution. If you plant tomatoes they come out too small, and before they get ripe they are falling off the bushes. The stems die and get brown, and then . . . the tomatoes wither. I love gardening because I was raised with a garden. My father was a gardener because my mother had 11 children. So we ate out of the garden: sweet potatoes, string beans, okra, and all that. But when you do it here. . . . I try to put it close to the house so too much of that stuff [pollution] won't fall on it . . . but still it just wastes away. The stems die and then the tomatoes dry up like prunes. And you are afraid to eat it."

Campbell said she could see evidence of the pollution that is killing her plants on her house: "My roof was a brown roof and now it is black. I'm not up there painting it. Where I patch it you can see the different light color. And my house got spots on it. But I painted it and covered some of the spots . . . like oil spots on the aluminum up at the top . . . like something was sprayed on it. I had to paint the whole house because you couldn't wash it off. And if you leave your car here for a few days it is full of little spots. Oh well. It is part of living here."

Gardeners all over Diamond were experiencing plant loss from Shell's pollution. Some of them, including Delwyn Smith, complained that they had been cut off from their deep agricultural roots. Smith's parents lived in Belltown and grew food there, but they were evicted from that land by Shell and moved to Diamond. Next this farmer's daughter found herself unable to even grow flowers in her back yard because of Shell's operations. "I am a person who loves plants. I noticed that after a period of time the chemical that is going up in the air and falling back down is killing my plants. . . . So I know what this is doing to me and the inside of my body over the years," said Smith.

6

Local Residents Organize

Margie Richard had just returned to Diamond from a brief vacation in 1990 when she heard that a number of her neighbors had gathered to discuss what they should do about the ongoing chemical emissions from the adjacent Shell plants. Richard walked down to the meeting hall to see what was up. When she opened the door, her neighbors immediately told her "We need someone to help us file a lawsuit against Shell. . . . We need a leader. . . . We elect you president."

Fed up with chronic pollution from neighboring Shell facilities and episodic explosions, the senior women of Diamond and a few men decided it was time to organize and see if they could help get their community relocated. They were mostly churchgoing women, many of them members of the Greater Good Hope Baptist Church, and their concern about living next to Shell had finally galvanized them to action. They decided to sue Shell and demand relocation. They understood that to win would require a long struggle and that they needed a strong, energetic resident to lead their crusade. The alacrity with which they chose Richard is understandable. They knew her well from the years she had taught health and physical education at Mary Bethune High School, just across the fenceline from Shell Chemical. She had supervised the children's physical education classes in the open air across from the plant.

"All my life I heard people say that the [Shell] plant was making people sick," Richard recalled. "Half my life I heard people say they wanted to be relocated. . . . My concern had always been there but I hadn't voiced it out fully. . . . I would go to church and listen to people talking and saying that this [Shell] plant is killing us."

Richard accepted the offer to lead the struggle for relocation made by the elder church women of Diamond. "I couldn't turn it down. I thought they

must think a lot of me. So I accepted it not with pride but with compassion
. . . for the need of the people," she said.

Richard and a small group of residents began to organize a group that
would come to be known as Concerned Citizens of Norco. Richard plunged
right into organizing her neighbors. Early on she told the core group of
members that just talking about the problem among themselves was not
going to accomplish anything. "I always believe in going straight to the
source," Richard said. They held weekly meetings in her trailer, in her
mother's house next door, or at one or another of the member's homes.
Richard told them that they should run their meetings according to Robert's
Rules of Order and should elect officers. She also felt it was important that
they come up with a list of their concerns and write them down. Their list
started with a demand for relocation but also included concerns about the
impact of pollution from Shell facilities on their health and longevity. They
wanted access to health care, more community involvement in the decision-
making process, and access to more jobs at Shell. This list became the basis
for the group's Community Organization Focus on a Practical Action Plan,
which called on Shell to relocate all Diamond residents who wanted to
move.

The core of the group was relatively small. It included Margie Richard,
her mother, her father, an aunt, and an uncle. Also involved were Gaynel
Johnson, Hazel Johnson, Doris Pollard, Rosemary Brown, Roberta
Johnson, Percy and Mary Hollins, and Deborah Scott. Later they were
joined by Angela and Thomas Dewey, Josephine Bering, Eloise and Bazille
Williams, and others. None of them would describe themselves as profes-
sional activists or grassroots organizers. They were just neighbors who were
concerned about a common problem: the health impact of Shell's emissions
on their community.

At first they focused on mounting a lawsuit against Shell. Not only were
residents fed up with breathing in Shell's fumes, they also felt that they had
been mistreated during the settlement that followed the explosion at the
plant in 1988. The suit was intensely personal for many Diamond residents
who had relatives or friends who they believed had been made ill or died
because of their long-term exposure to chemical emissions from Shell's chemical plant and refinery. It was this strongly held belief that drove them to take
this drastic action. Richard's sister, for example, died at 43 of sarcoidosis. "In
the end she had no lungs. She was on pure oxygen," Richard recalled. When

she took her sister to the hospital, a doctor asked if they lived next to a chemical plant. "After she died I said to myself that I would do everything I could to relocate [our community] because there were too many people sick. Our children have asthma. I almost lost my daughter at age seven because her lungs collapsed on her. . . . The odors in the air were so bad they were telling me that something was wrong," Richard remembered.

Another Diamond resident, Gaynel Johnson, was motivated to become an active member of Concerned Citizens of Norco by respiratory problems she attributed to Shell. "Gaynel's role was pivotal. . . . She was the lieutenant, the second in charge, the person that Margie relied on and complained to, the person who commiserated with Margie. She provided tactical and emotional support which was crucial especially when Margie was being harassed and doubted by people within her own neighborhood. At that point Margie needed something quite simple: a friend. And Gaynel was that and provided an unwavering belief in the cause," observed Anne Rolfes, founder and director of the Louisiana Bucket Brigade, who worked closely with Diamond residents. Johnson, 52, a big woman with short-cropped hair, round glasses, and an easygoing manner, moved to Diamond 47 years ago when her parents separated. She and six of her brothers and sisters were taken in by their grandparents who lived in Diamond. She was a sickly child and grew up in Diamond suffering from asthma. After high school she married, had children, and settled into Diamond. Her problems with Shell began with the explosion at the refinery in 1988. "I was thrown out of bed and hit my back on the nightstand," she said. The doctors found something pressing against her spine. "They said surgery wasn't going to do no good," Johnson explained. The injury made it difficult for her to walk. Shell paid out $116,000 for the injury, but Johnson's lawyers took $77,000 in fees, leaving her with $34,000.

The back injury slowed Johnson down somewhat, but her real problem was that she was highly sensitive to the chemical pollution coming over the fence from Shell. In the years 1993–2001, when she was living in a rental unit, her respiratory problems flared up often, especially when she went outside. "I couldn't go outside anymore," she said. And even when other people could not detect a smell in the air, her lungs would seize up. "I couldn't breathe. . . . It shortens my wind. . . . My chest would draw up," Johnson said. On a number of occasions she was taken to the emergency room at the hospital, where she was given steroids to loosen her chest. Finally, Johnson decided to move: "It was too much. I couldn't take it any more," she said. She moved to a rented red-brick house in La Place, about 15 miles from Diamond.[1]

Johnson recalled the early protests against Shell: "We marched and we picketed outside Shell. We'd go in the morning and [again] in the evening. It was a small group of us. The only time when we would get the community out was when a new report would come out and then you get a big old group of people who want to be in the [news photo]," recalled Johnson who briefly became the president of CCN after Margie Richard stepped down.

Eventually, a group of residents decided to sue Shell and demand relocation. They selected as an attorney Alan Myles of Thompsonville, a relative of one CCN member.

Preparations for the lawsuit dragged on from 1993 to 1997. A court date was set for the suit to be heard by an African-American judge in New Orleans. This was good news to the plaintiffs because they calculated they would draw a more objective group of jurors in New Orleans than they would in Norco, where they believed many white residents were beholden to Shell. Unfortunately, the judge died the day before their case was to be heard, and the case was transferred back to St. Charles Parish.

When their case for relocation finally did come to trial, in 1997, it proved a disappointment. Shell brought in many witnesses from the white side of Norco who were tied to the company in one way or another. They testified that they experience few problems while living next to the Shell plants. The plaintiffs related hardship stories about the illnesses they suffered while living near the huge industrial facilities, but the jury came back with a verdict in favor of Shell. It was only when the verdict was in that Richards and Johnson learned that, rather than ask for relocation for his clients, their attorney had asked for monetary awards for them. According to Gaynel Johnson, the attorney had made that switch without consulting his clients. Several jurors later told Johnson and a number of other plaintiffs that they would have agreed to the relocation argument but that they did not see how giving residents some money would solve their problems.

For weeks Diamond residents had made their way to the overheated courthouse and listened to oral arguments as the suit dragged on. When the verdict came down against them, the lawyers for the Diamond residents hustled out of the room without a word. "Our attorney hit the elevator so fast and did not tell us anything," Johnson remembered. They "sold us out," she continued. "We were angry. We did everything right. We walked the picket line, we carried signs, and we even had the elderly people in the community sitting in chairs with their signs."

After the failure of the lawsuit, Beverly Wright held workshops on "How to Choose a Lawyer." By then, however, it was too late. The residents had failed to win their lawsuit for relocation, and too much time had elapsed for them to sue Shell for the 1973 explosion that had killed two residents. The legal route to forcing Shell to relocate Diamond residents appeared to be at a dead end.

Although the loss of the lawsuit was a huge setback and caused many residents to feel that it was hopeless to try to fight Shell, not everyone was ready to quit. Janie Campbell, for example, told her son-in-law, who was famous for making delicious pastries, "You make the biscuits [for the protesters] and I will pray, because there is a God." About the legal defeat, Gaynel Johnson said "It made us stronger."

"We cried," Beverly Wright recalled after the failure of the Diamond lawsuit for relocation. Apparently the lawyer wanted to settle. "That's what lawyers do," Wright observed. "He was really a pitiful lawyer . . . someone's relative. The loss was a huge setback. People were very depressed, and it took Margie's faith to get Diamond residents going again." Though disappointed, Richard was undeterred: "They say we lost the lawsuit, but I say we won because it was a cry for help."

After the legal setback, Concerned Citizens of Norco began turning up the pressure on Shell with demonstrations. "I've been working so hard on this relocation," said Janie Campbell. "I was the first one out there [picketing Shell] with little Margie. We would be out there in the hot sun marching. We started picketing [because] so many kids were being sick with all this mess and all this stuff coming from the plant," said Campbell, who started carrying a sign along the fenceline with Shell that read: "WHAT'S THAT SMELL? IT'S JUST SHELL."

Campbell was carrying her sign outside the gates of the Shell Chemical facility when a truck driver entering the plant called out to her, in a mocking voice, "Do you smell something?" Campbell told him she did. "It was the truth: it was nothing that we was making up. It was for real. People would pass by in their cars and yell 'You ought to just go sit down somewhere.' But we never stopped, because we thought it was time."

The protests went on, but to many Diamond residents it appeared as if Shell was going to be able to stonewall the complaints of residents about the pollution and the danger from explosions. "We were trapped. Nothing was being done," Richard remembered

From her days teaching school, Richard had learned to deal with student problems using tough love. If one of her students was acting up she would confront them and try to get to the bottom of what the problem was really about. "If you recognize the problem you can work out a solution but if you ignore the problem it will blow up and cause tremendous chaos," she said. So she decided to practice tough love with Shell: the company had to be forced to recognize the problem it was causing before a solution could be found. "When I met the leadership at Shell I told them that they needed to listen to the people," she said.

As she presented the history of the Diamond community's situation on the fenceline with Shell to various different groups, Richard's thinking crystallized and she began to focus in on Shell's shortcomings in its dealings with the community. First, she jumped all over Shell for being hypocritical with its "Good Neighbor Initiative." If you say you are going to be a good neighbor, then you should be one, she said. Shell should "be true to what they put on paper," she insisted. "If you live next to a multi-billion-dollar industry your town should look good. But let's face it, the buck stops at Apple Street [on the white side of Norco]."

As time went on, other residents of Diamond became increasingly angry about the way they were being treated by Shell, said Ernestine Roberts. At first Margie Richard was the only one who really got involved in the struggle for relocation, but then more people joined in, Roberts continued. "When they [Shell] saw that the black people were going to speak out they came and put in a park," but it was just a couple of swings and a few basketball hoops, Roberts said dismissively. "Shell thinks they can do a little bit and it will silence them [us] up for a little while. But people aren't going to be [silent]."

Margie Richard

Margie Richard's heart for doing battle with Royal Dutch/Shell was tested after her community lost the lawsuit against Shell. At that point a number of Diamond residents gave up all hope for relocation. Some said that they had known all along that they could never win against Shell. But Richard was not so easily dissuaded. "Even though I was hurt and some of the people in the Concerned Citizens of Norco were crying. . . . I told them that now the world knows the crookedness of power tricks." "This relocation struggle has got to be done and it can be done," she told them. Seeing the lawsuit as only one aspect of a larger struggle, Richard redoubled her organizing efforts. "We became smaller [as a group] but stronger," she commented. Optimism in the face of tactical defeats came to be a defining characteristic of Richard's leadership.

Instead of giving up, Richard was determined to expand Concerned Citizens of Norco and mold it into a powerful voice to speak for the community of Diamond. To that end she began what she describes as a "walking, talking, and mentoring" initiative. Members of CCN were assigned to "adopt" people in the community and bring them into the group.

But not everyone was enthusiastic about these efforts. "The negatives started to surface," Richard recalled. People would say "What is she making all that noise about?" They were worried that Shell would retaliate with its considerable resources. Some asked "Who do they think they are, going up against Shell?" Others were even less charitable. "All she wants to do is get in Shell's big pocket," they whispered, intimating that Richard was looking to be bought off. "We were being criticized from every hand from within," she said. "There was a lot of fear about demanding relocation and a lot of holding back."

Even some of the ministers who came into the community on Sundays to preach began to question the wisdom of using the churches as a focal point for organizing a relocation movement. "God never intended to mix religion and politics," they argued. In response, Concerned Citizens of Norco organized a prayer breakfast and invited all the town's preachers to come and sit with them while they described their goals. This served to diffuse some of the concerns about the group's relocation campaign, and it drew in more people. It also touched off a new round of reaching out to other members of the community, specifically on the back two streets of Diamond. "We invited everybody to our meetings and explained the facts on a one-to-one basis. We told people that we were not trying to hurt anyone and asked them if they would want to relocate if they could," Richard said. As a result of these initiatives, CCN began to expand.

The resistance to Richard's organizing efforts only seemed to make her more determined. When people began backing away from a relocation campaign, Richard dug in her heels and started holding weekly meetings in her trailer. "People were saying that we couldn't take on Shell. . . . That is exactly what gave me my drive," she said. When she felt beset by critics, Richard would remember the hard times that her parents and grandparents faced in the past and how they persevered under even more difficult circumstances. She thought about the quiet way her father had successfully lobbied to have a high school built in Diamond. And in her mind she could hear her mother's more outspoken voice urging her to "press on." She also would recall her dying sister telling her "something has got to be done" to move people away from the pollution they were both convinced had made her ill. And she would think about her own daughter suffering night after night from asthma.

Richard's resolve was also strengthened by her religious faith. She had a strong sense that God had put her in a leadership position to help her neighbors, she said. All she had to do was to make sure that her actions came from the right motives. "If you are standing up with the right motive then it has to end in a victory for justice," she said. Her connection with her church and with her Bible college was fortifying. Richard believed that it was important to apply the stories in the Bible to life today. For example, she pondered how Moses' parting of the Red Sea applied to her life and to her efforts as a community leader. In a lighter vein, she claimed that she did not want to be like Moses, who led his people to the brink of the Promised Land but was never permitted to enter into it with them. "Can't I be like Esther?" she asked. Richard's sense of humor helped blunt some of the hard feelings she ran up against, but one gets the sense that it was her Christian faith that kept her from giving up a struggle that lasted more than 10 years. Richard saw her community activism as service. "And what is Christianity if it is not service to your fellow human beings?" she asked.

Again and again Richard sought "biblical backup for what I was doing," she said. She found it from the minister of the church she attended and at the School of Urban Ministries in Gretna, where she went to Bible school at night. There she asked for a conference with the dean of the school because she was worried that maybe she was making mistakes in the struggle with Shell in Diamond. "Look, Margie," the dean told her, "God never said it was going to be easy." And that was all the reassurance she needed to hear. After reading the biblical passages she had been assigned and praying on them, she determined that if you start a struggle you have to be willing to see it through to the end.

While Richard was always "referencing her faith" in her struggle with Shell, she was also getting her feet wet in the political arena. After almost 30 years as a teacher in Diamond and the neighboring town of Destrehan, Richards decided to run for a seat on the school board. When she told her father that she was thinking of running, he encouraged her. Her mother gave her more practical help with a gift of $125 to start her campaign. "I decided to run to shake things up," Richard said. It was her first formal entry into local politics. She carried four precincts but lost by 200 votes. "I lost, but I was a winner in my book," she said.

In the early 1990s, Richard began to speak out publicly about the desire of Diamond residents to relocate away from the toxic fumes from the Shell plants. "My name was ringing everywhere . . . both good and bad," she said. Then in 1994 she was called in by the principal of the school where she worked and was asked what her priorities were. The implication, Richard said, was that she had not been attentive enough to her work at the school and that her work as a community organizer was interfering with her performance as a teacher. Her job was on the line. Richard's response was typically straightforward. "You didn't hire me," she told the principal, "and you can't fire me." Richard was proud of her record as a teacher. "As a physical education teacher I didn't just believe in throwing the ball," she said. Instead she took the broader view of physical education and taught her students about how the systems of the body worked, about good nutrition, about hygiene, and she even included a unit on sex education. Over the decades that she worked in the St. Charles school system Richard received numerous letters from former students thanking her for the positive influence she had on their lives. So when the principal reprimanded her for losing her focus at school, Richard told him that what she did in her free time as a community activist was her business and her freedom to speak out about problems facing her community was a right that was protected by the Constitution.

The source of the pressure to fire her remained a mystery, Richard said. But how that pressure played out was painful. Asked to read the works of a well-known pedagogue and write a report, she refused. "I said no because it was a punishment and it was over the holidays," she recalled. "So I got written up and turned in."

After many meetings and phone calls, Richard was called into a meeting at the school which she knew would lead to a process that would end with her being fired. "They had made up their minds to get rid of me," she said. Rather than go through the motions of a process where the outcome was already determined, Richard quit teaching after 29½ years on the job. Had she buckled under, apologized, and ended her political activities, she might have been able to complete 30 years, she conjectured. Instead she chose to stand on principle, continue her political organizing, and leave the school system. The decision was costly: "If I'd stayed I would have gotten $1,000 a month more" from her pension, she explained. "It cost me $1,000 a month, and that is a big chunk because I work for a living. But God has always provided." Instead of leaving on a sour note, Richard said she called up the principal and told him that he had played a role in arranging it so she could answer a calling to the ministry from God. She held no animosity toward him, she added. Once again, Richard snatched a moral victory from the jaws of a painful temporal defeat.

No longer working full-time at school, Richard began to devote more time to her community activism. She and the other core members of Concerned Citizens of Norco began actively seeking allies. "Anybody who gave us assistance we accepted," she said. Not only did CCN accept help, Richard also made those who joined the struggle feel appreciated. She told them what an important role they were going to play and how they would help deliver the community from its suffering. And despite years of hearing from Shell officials that relocation was not a subject they would negotiate about, Richard remained optimistic, prophesying victory even in the darkest hours of the struggle.

Meanwhile, Richard continued to spread the word about the relocation struggle in Diamond. After reading in the New Orleans *Times-Picayune* that a public meeting of the petroleum sector of the Common Sense Initiative sponsored by the U.S. Environmental Protection Agency was to take place at the Sheraton Hotel in the nearby town of Kenner, she telephoned one of the older women from Diamond, Rosemary Brown, and suggested that they both go to the meeting and tell their stories of what it had been like living on the fenceline with the Shell plants. "The struggle had to go beyond Norco," she said. "Somebody needed to hear us."

At the EPA meeting, Brown told about being forced to move out of Belltown when Shell built its chemical plant and about the growth of Shell's facilities up to the fenceline in Diamond. When it was her turn, Richard described the explosions in 1973 and 1988 and what it was like living with the constant irritant of air pollution. "I told them it was like living next to a ticking time bomb," she recalled. Later they were asked by EPA officials for written copies of their comments to take back to headquarters in Washington, she added.

Richard's and Brown's accounts of life on the fenceline in Diamond were not the only stories recounted that day. There were other residents who described life in towns like Convent and Mossville that are also located next to some of the 160 chemical plants clustered in Louisiana's chemical corridor.[2] "I met all of these people and I said . . . wow . . . because we thought we were all alone," Richards recalled. Suddenly she found that her little group in Diamond was only one of many similar groups facing the problem posed by fenceline toxic hot spots where residents faced a disproportionate exposure to industrial pollution. At the EPA meeting "a door opened," Richard said, and she met Beverly Wright, executive director of the Deep South Center for Environmental Justice at Xavier University. "Wright was the connecting point for our struggle," Richard said, looking back.

Other Relocation Stories

The relocation campaign in Diamond was preceded by a long struggle for environmental justice in other parts of the country and by a number of successful relocation campaigns in Louisiana. Some of the leading resident-activists in Diamond learned about this history and borrowed techniques from previously successful campaigns.

To see the campaign for relocation in Diamond in it historical context, one must look back to 1982, when the environmental justice struggle began in earnest. It was in that year that 414 protesters were arrested for blocking a road in Warren County, North Carolina. They lay across the rural asphalt road in good weather. State policemen wearing helmets with visors stood over them. A convoy of dump trucks idled, waiting for the police to clear the road. The protesters had come to stop the hauling of 6,000 truckloads of PCB-contaminated soil to a hazardous waste dump that had been sited in the predominantly black and economically depressed town of Afton. The decision to build the dump in Afton was a curious one insofar as the town's water table was only 5–10 feet below the surface and residents drew their drinking water from local wells. The likelihood that this water supply would soon be contaminated was high, and other more scientifically suitable locations could have been found.[3]

The Afton protest was one of the first salvos in the battle for environmental justice in the United States. It triggered a U.S. General Accounting Office study of the socio-economic and racial characteristics of communities where hazardous waste landfills were sited in the South, which revealed that three out of four major hazardous waste landfills in the region were located in predominantly poor and black areas. A subsequent study in 1987 by the Commission for Racial Justice found a strong association between where these facilities were located and race.

Seen from this perspective, the struggle in Diamond was not an isolated or highly unusual event, nor was the plight of Diamond residents unique. Nor was the demand by Diamond residents to be relocated away from the harm they were suffering on the fenceline with Shell facilities unprecedented in Louisiana. Other towns in the state's chemical corridor had already been relocated. Beverly Wright wrote about three other such relocation efforts.

First, the town of Morrisonville, just south of Baton Rouge on the banks of the Mississippi, was relocated from land immediately adjacent to a 1,800-acre Dow Chemical plant. Like Diamond, Morrisonville had been founded in the 1870s by freed slaves. The community was to be moved twice. In 1931, the Army Corps of Engineers refused to maintain the levee that protected the town. As a consequence, the residents moved their town a mile and a half west of its original location. In 1959, Dow purchased property in the community, and eventually Dow expanded its facilities right up to the backyards of residents' homes. In 1989, Dow began buying out the residents, paying $50,000–$200,000 to homeowners and $10,000 to renters. Some 250 residents took advantage of the buyout. This was "the first time a plant has attempted to buy out a town near its property line without a lawsuit," Wright observed.

The second case involved residents of Reveilletown, Louisiana, who lived on a fenceline with a Georgia Gulf vinyl chloride plant. Reveilletown was also a community founded by freed slaves in the 1870s. In 1987, 13 residents filed suit when traces of vinyl chloride were found in the blood of local children. The case was settled, and those involved in the suit moved out of town. Some 20 other families sold their properties to the company for $1.2 million, and 12 other families were enticed to move away to a sub-division called New Reveilletown. In 1990, Georgia Gulf completed its pro-gram to move 50 families away from its plant. Now all that remains is 6 acres of pecan and oak trees, Wright reported.

The third town to be moved away from a fenceline with a big industry in the chemical corridor was Sunrise, Louisiana, a community purchased by a freed slave in 1874. By 1970, the community was about half white and half black. In 1979, the Placid Refining Company built a plant in town by buying out most of the white residents. In 1990, the remaining 241 residents, most of them African-Americans, filed suit against the company. Residents were subsequently bought out at prices that would permit them to buy houses of similar size elsewhere, Wright reported.[4]

The relocation of these communities has not come without cost. As Vernice Miller-Travis noted, it is erasing historically important communities: "These were places where people who were newly freed moved off the plantations where they had been cutting sugarcane and picking cotton and started living on the fringes of these places. . . .They represent a moment in history that cannot be recovered. . . . They are being wiped off the face of the earth before anyone can document what it took for these people to exist here." The decision to move out of these historically black communities is a painful one but given the level of pollution in Diamond and Sunrise residents were forced to move in order to survive, Miller-Travis added.

In May 2003, residents of the Myrtle Grove Trailer Park, across the river from Baton Rouge, were forced to relocate when it was revealed that a plume of vinyl chloride had contaminated the water they drank and bathed in. Officials at the Louisiana Department of Health had known about the contamination for years but had failed to notify residents because of "human error," they now contend. Once the announcement was made about the contamination, concern mounted that the high level of miscarriages in this African-American community was caused by exposure to the chemical. The landlord was forced to close the trailer park because of sky-rocketing insurance costs, and mass relocation of residents began. No industrial facility has yet been singled out as the source of the spill, but a nearby Dow Chemical plant that makes vinyl chloride is a prime suspect, state officials said. With no company willing to pick up the relocation costs, the landlord of the trailer park is providing Myrtle Grove residents with $2,000 in moving expenses.[5]

Other similar fenceline problems are not difficult to identify. Sierra Club environmental justice activists work with a number of fenceline communities involved in relocation struggles. For example, in Baltimore the Sierra Club recently supported a long-term effort spearheaded by the residents of Wagner's Point. These residents are determined to move out of the airshed of the some 50 industrial facilities—including chemical manufacturing plants and bulk petroleum storage facilities—that moved into their neighborhood, reported Terry Harris, vice chair of the Sierra Club's Environmental Justice Committee.

Similarities between the situation in Diamond and that in Wagner's Point are striking. Both communities existed more than 100 years ago, before industry moved into the area; each is populated by a small number of extended families; and residents have lived through major explosions at the adjacent facilities and ill health due to exposure from pollutants. "[N]earby monitoring equipment had detected the levels of some cancer-causing chemicals in the air at thirty times a health-based screening level," Terry Harris reported. After a local activist fighting for relocation died of cancer, the campaign she had started gained momentum and the state of Maryland obtained $750,000 from the federal government for relocation costs.[6]

Police Presence

Despite the fact that relocation programs had taken place in other fenceline communities in the chemical corridor, Shell officials were adamant in their unwillingness to fund such a move in Norco. Relocation was not up for negotiation, they insisted.

And when the residents of Diamond gathered to discuss relocation, they often attracted an unwanted guest: the police. For a number of years, every time Concerned Citizens of Norco held a meeting a gaggle of patrol cars would park outside the meeting hall and armed deputies would stand out front watching the crowd. This not only created the sense of living in an armed camp; it also scared off potential participants.

"We had a meeting of people who are not troublemakers," recalled Gaynel Johnson, CCN's former president. "And every time we went to a meeting it looked like the whole police force was there." When a representative of Greenpeace was in town, the police even had the roads blocked, she remembered.

Even as late as the spring of 2001, Shell still refused to hold meetings in Diamond, observed Anne Rolfes. "They refused to come to the community, they just would not do it, which was awful," she said. The police presence was heavy when meetings were held at the school in Norco. "There were four police with their arms crossed greeting the residents," Rolfes remembered. "Any time we would meet in the community there would always be cop cars going back and forth. Any time there were two or more cars at Margie's house there was a police patrol. I was followed in the [Diamond] neighborhood by Shell security. I wasn't doing anything wrong: I was paying visits to people. That was outrageous. . . ."

On February 8, 2001, after a CCN meeting at the elementary school during which four police officers had stood outside the doors of the meeting room, Anne Rolfes wrote a letter to Shell and to the Sheriff's Department complaining that "the police presence had a chilling effect on the meeting and affected the participants ability to fully exercise their right to free speech and their civil rights." The letter was co-signed by the Deep South Center for Environmental Justice, the EarthJustice Legal Defense Fund, and the Delta Chapter of the Sierra Club.

Margie Richard had her own way of dealing with the police standing outside the meeting halls, Rolfes recalled. "Margie didn't bat an eye when she saw them. I felt my heart seize up and I became furious but Margie was far too accustomed to dealing with such situations. As she did in every situation she took charge and disarmed them. She walked right up to the police officers and said to one of them: 'Didn't I teach you?' From that moment he was like a little schoolboy shyly looking down, tracing his feet back and forth in the dirt. They were intimidating no more."

But the police presence probably did discourage some residents from attending community meetings. Shell spokesman David Brignac was finally convinced to attend a meeting of Concerned Citizens of Norco in Diamond. He was told that if he really wanted to understand what the residents of Diamond thought he would have to come to their side of town. When he did come to Diamond, Gaynel Johnson recalled, Margie Richard, then president of CCN, stood up and said to Brignac: "Look at these people. Do they look like criminals so that every time we have a meeting we have to have all these police?" Johnson continued: "We told David 'Can't you see that these [Diamond residents] are not violent people? They just want answers and they just want to be heard.'" After that, Brignac called off the security patrols, and the police stopped monitoring the meetings. The end result of that initial meeting with Brignac in Diamond was very positive, Johnson said: "He was willing to listen He wanted to know about our community. He agreed to come to our community to where the meeting was at. No cops . . . no problems."

It was a mistake to send Shell security people and local deputies to meetings held by Diamond residents, Brignac later admitted. But the decision to do so must be understood in the context of the times, he argued. "Things got real testy early in 1999," he recalled, particularly after a representative of Greenpeace implied that racism was behind the fact that more white residents of Norco had been told about a toxic release from Shell than black residents. "That kind of stuck in the minds of Shell officials that, hey, there is a potential in these meetings for things to really get out of hand. Not that we think Diamond people are criminals. We are worried about some outsider coming in and stirring the crowd and creating some almost like a riot atmosphere," Brignac explained.

The police presence at meetings of Concerned Citizens of Norco continued into early 2000, Brignac recalled. "We had some deputies [at the meeting] and in retrospect that was a mistake" because by that time Shell had demonstrated its willingness to attend meetings and listen to resident concerns and the most militant outside activists were no longer there, he continued.

But the problems with the police did not go away entirely. One day when an official of the Environmental Protection Agency drove Margie Richard down to take her photo standing next to the fenceline where she used to live across from the Shell Chemical plant she was accosted by security guards who said that taking photos of the plant was not permitted. Convincing Shell security personnel and local deputies to keep a low profile required some work, Brignac said. Even without orders, Shell security personnel would hear about a meeting and decide to go. "We had to get our security people to understand that police patrolling around [political meetings in Diamond] is a big issue," said Brignac.

II

Shell and Its Neighbors

A Brief History of Shell

To understand Royal Dutch/Shell's perspective, it is worth briefly stepping back and looking at the company's origins to appreciate how it came to own a huge refinery and chemical plant in the heart of the Mississippi Delta.

Shell was born in the early days of the oil boom and started out in the shadow of John D. Rockefeller's Standard Oil monopoly, which was able to drive many emerging rival oil companies out of business by undercutting their prices and taking over their shares of the market.

Royal Dutch/Shell was the result of a merger in 1907 between the British-based Shell Transport and Trading Company, which pioneered the use of seagoing oil tankers, and the Royal Dutch Petroleum company, which made its fortune developing and exploiting new oil fields in Borneo and Sumatra.

During the Civil War, when some of the slaves from the Trepagnier Plantation were joining Union forces to fight the Confederacy in Louisiana, a British Jew from the East End of London was setting up as a merchant on the docks in that great city. Marcus Samuel was an enterprising fellow who decided to greet ships returning to England from India, Japan, Africa, and the Middle East and offer to buy any trinkets and curios that sailors had collected abroad. Before long, word spread among sailors that they could augment their wages by selling to Samuel. With business thriving, Samuel opened large warehouses on the docks to collect these items and resell them. Among the items he purchased were exotic shells, which he had glued onto wooden jewelry boxes. Those boxes were sold to young women who came to the beach for a holiday.

Marcus Samuel had two sons, Marcus Samuel the younger and Samuel Samuel, both of whom went into business with him. When Marcus Samuel the elder died, his sons took his fortune and expanded their father's import/export business, opening offices in Japan and London.

In the 1890s, the French Rothschild family decided to go into business exploiting the oil fields opening up in Baku in Russia. Needing a partner to help them transport and sell the oil, they turned to Marcus Samuel the younger. After a brief trip to the Caucasus, Marcus Samuel decided that the only way to take on the near monopoly grip that Standard Oil held was to radically reduce oil transportation costs. At the time kerosene was transported in crates of tin containers. Loading the fuel into these relatively small containers, crating them, and loading them onto ships was time consuming, expensive, and inefficient, Samuel argued. It would be much preferable to just pipe the oil into a tanker ship.[1]

But here Samuel ran into a technical problem: the buffeting of the tanker by waves would cause the oil to slosh around. If it all sloshed to one side, it had the potential to capsize the tanker and plunge it to the bottom of the sea. To avert this, Samuel's engineers developed a system of baffles and compartments that would minimize rapid sloshing. The first sign that the technology of shipping oil had undergone a tremendous advance came in 1892. It was in that year that the first modern oil tanker, the *Murex*, was commissioned and sailed from Bangkok through the Suez Canal to West Hartlepool, England. With this voyage the modern era of ocean-going tankers was launched. Marcus Samuel was to name subsequent tankers after other shells—Conch, Elax, Cowrie—memorializing the fact that his father's wealth was partially derived from shells collected by sailors. In this manner Shell Transport was born.

In 1907, Sir Marcus Samuel and Henri Deterding merged the Shell Transport and Trading Company with the Royal Dutch Petroleum Company to create Royal Dutch/Shell. Today Royal Dutch/Shell is the world's third-largest oil company. (The company is 40 percent owned by the Shell Transport and Trading Company and 60 percent owned by Royal Dutch Petroleum.) Deterding then brought Shell ashore in the United States in Washington and Louisiana to take on Standard Oil on its home turf. John D. Rockefeller tried to buy out Royal Dutch/Shell with an offer of $100 million in 1910, but the deal was turned down.[2]

Shell expanded rapidly in the United States as the growing number of automobiles created a surging demand for gasoline. The world wars also created a huge demand not only for gasoline, aviation fuel, and lubricants but also for a host of new chemical products derived from oil. Shell helped meet this demand by expanding into the petrochemical business and producing Perspex for treating bomber and aircraft canopies, toluene for TNT, smokeless explosives, petrogel used in flame throwers, water-repellent agents, de-icing greases, and a host of other products for both military and civilian uses.[3]

Today Royal Dutch/Shell is the tenth-largest multinational corporation in the world, with gross revenues of $150 billion, some 90,000 employees, 25 million customers daily, 50 oil refineries, 58,000 gas stations, and operations in 143 countries. It sold 12,424 barrels of oil a day in 2002. In 2001 company profits amounted to $11 billion. In its relentless search for new oil and natural gas fields, Shell spent $2.7 billion on oil exploration activities in 1998. It employs 15,000 employees in 40 countries looking for oil.[4] Worldwide, Shell produces 3.6 million barrels a day and has a daily production capacity of 4.2 million barrels.[5]

In addition to being a giant oil and gas company, Shell has become the world's seventh-largest chemical company. The company's interest in manipulating hydrocarbons into saleable products dates to 1929, when Shell chemists began to realize that a number of their waste streams could be refashioned for sale. Synthetic nitrogen fertilizer was followed by detergents, solvents, anti-freeze, insecticides, herbicides, fungicides, perfumes, and artificial sweeteners. Shell also produces ethylene and propylene (used in plastics) and methyl ethyl ketone (used in paints and medicines).[6] By the mid 1940s, Shell had a team of 1,000 scientists in the United States working to find new uses for its products.

This enormous industrial undertaking—based on flammable, explosive, and toxics feedstocks—has not occurred without a human and ecological cost. In his critical and carefully documented book *Riding the Dragon: Royal Dutch/Shell and the Fossil Fire*, Jack Doyle recounts Shell's history of toxic releases, accidents, and lawsuits that have dogged this petrochemical giant. He cites, for example, Shell's production of aldrin, dieldrin, and endrin, powerful pesticides that are persistent organic pollutants that bioaccumulate in the tissue of animals and humans. These chemicals were banned by the EPA for most uses in 1974; however; Shell continued to produce them and sell them abroad, Doyle noted. Lawsuits about groundwater contaminated with these chemicals ensued at the Rocky Mountain Arsenal outside Denver and in Brazil.

Shell also became involved in the production of DBCP, a pesticide that turned out to cause, among other things, "severe atrophy and degeneration of testes." Some workers at chemical plants in California and Alabama subsequently found themselves sterile. The chemical also started showing up in 200 water wells in California and in wine. More lawsuits ensued.[7] Further, Shell produced MTBE, a gasoline additive that started showing up in drinking water supplies and was subsequently banned in California.

In addition to these toxics and liability problems, Shell facilities also have a lengthy history of major, even catastrophic accidents. In *Riding the Dragon* Doyle enumerates and provides considerable detail about a number of catastrophic explosions at Shell that caused loss of life, injury, widespread destruction of property, environmental pollution, and large claims for damages. For example, major accidents occurred at the following Shell plants:

Norco, Louisiana, 1988 (7 dead, 48 injured, 4,500 evacuated)

Hamburg, Germany, 1989 (1 dead, 2 injured)

Stanlow, England, 1990 (1 dead, 6 injured)

Berre-L'Etang, France, 1991 (4 injured)

Port Klang, Malaysia, 1992 (13 dead)

Belpre, Ohio, 1994 (3 dead, 1,700 evacuated)

El Isba, Syria, 1995 (5 dead)

Woodbridge, New Jersey, 1996 (200 evacuated)

Deer Park, Texas, 1997 (1,500 claims)

Bintulu, Malaysia, 1997 (12 injured)

Shell officials insist that no accident is unavoidable and that each is caused by a chain reaction of preventable missteps. The focus at Shell is to teach front-line staff how to avoid accidents and how to react to them and the company is proud of its safety record. Large signs at the front gate of Shell plants exhort workers to practice safe chemistry and chronicle the number of days at the plant that have passed without a major accident. Nevertheless, there is an underlying tension between the need to be safe and the need to meet production schedules, and between the need to improve control technologies and the pressure to operate plants profitably. It is in this gray area that state and federal officials are supposed to keep companies from operating unsafely. Unfortunately, a lack of manpower or a lack of political will often keeps regulators from doing their jobs properly.

Do these accidents tend to hurt poor and minority populations more than other people? There is some evidence that they do. A recent *Social Science Quarterly* study reveals that low-income individuals are more likely to be exposed to chemical accidents that cause one injury, death, or an evacuation than are wealthier members of society. "Our results indicate that the acute risk associated with chemical accidents at fixed facilities is greater for individuals living in low-income census blocks, especially when comparisons are made within the counties where the chemical accidents occur," the authors of the report observed.[8]

In recent years there have been two dramatic instances in which Royal Dutch/Shell's claims to be a good environmental steward and to be concerned about the well-being of fenceline communities were called into serious question. The first of these occurred in 1995 when Shell decided to dispose of a North Sea oil storage tank by cutting it up and allowing it to sink to the bottom of the ocean. Environmentalists were aghast. Greenpeace activists boarded the Brent Spar to block its demolition. In their book *When Good Companies Do Bad Things: Responsibility and Risk in an Age of Globalization*, Peter Schwartz and Blair Gibb describe how Shell's efforts to dislodge the Greenpeace activists using water cannons failed and stirred such a storm of controversy that the company backed down and towed the superstructure to Norway for land-based disposal.[9] The second confrontation over Shell's environmental behavior concerned the company's operations in Nigeria. Shell discovered oil in that country in 1956. A joint venture between Shell and the Nigerian government to exploit this oil now pumps some 900,000 barrels a day. The Shell Development Company of Nigeria holds about 30 percent interest in this venture and employs 1,200 workers who build and maintain a network of wells, pumping stations, and pipelines through the mangrove swamps and fertile fields of the Niger Delta.

The exploitation of the Nigerian oil fields ran into conflict with the farming activities of the native Ogoni people who complained that their water, air, and fields were contaminated with oil wastes by Shell's operations. In addition to the everyday pollution and flaring from these operations there have been 4,000 oil spills since operations began there.[10] Shell operations are also responsible for half of the 35 million tons a year of carbon dioxide released through flaring in Nigeria.[11] "Since the beginning of Shell's operations in the Niger Delta, the company has wrecked havoc on the neighboring communities and their environment. Many of its operations and materials are outdated, in poor condition, and would be illegal in other parts of the world," reported a Greenpeace International observer.[12]

Ken Saro-Wiwa, a Nigerian writer and journalist, wrote that after a 1969 blowout of oil equipment in the village of Kegbara Dere "water supplies were poisoned, the air was polluted, farmland devastated," and that he "watched with absolute dismay as indignant citizens found neither succor nor help from Shell."[13] Saro-Wiwa and Ogoni leaders subsequently founded the Movement for the Survival of the Ogoni People on October 2, 1990. By 1993 the pollution from the Shell's oil operations in Nigeria was so far below industry standards that Bopp van Dessel, head of Environmental Studies for Shell in Nigeria, resigned. "They were not meeting their own standards; they were not meeting international standards," he said. "Any Shell site that I saw was polluted. Any terminal that I saw was polluted. It is clear to me that Shell was devastating the area."[14]

On April 28, 1993, according to a chronology put together for Project Underground by Anne Rolfes and Steve Kretzmann, tens of thousands of Ogoni peacefully demonstrated against the bulldozing of cultivated land by a Shell contractor. On August 5 of the same year, 100 Ogoni were killed and 8,000 made homeless in the town of Ka. An effort was mounted to disguise the deaths as a result of a tribal conflict, but soldiers later testified that they were involved in the attack.[15] In all, more than 3,000 Ogoni died from government repression, 30,000 were displaced, and 1,000 fled into exile, according to a World Council of Churches report.[16]

Sara-Wiwa knew that protesting against the oil operation jointly run by Shell and the Nigerian government was dangerous: "When I decided to take the word to the streets, to mobilize the Ogoni people and empower them to protest the devastation of their environment by Shell, and their denigration and dehumanization by Nigerian military dictators, I had no doubt where it could end . . . death."[17] This prophecy proved accurate. Sara-Wiwa and eight other activists were arrested on trumped-up charges, beaten in prison, sentenced to death, and executed.

In his final statement to the Nigerian Military Tribunal that convicted him and ordered his execution Sara-Wiwa said: "I and my colleagues are not the only ones on trial. Shell is here on trial. . . . The Company has, indeed, ducked this particular trial, but its day will surely come . . . for there is no doubt in my mind that the ecological war that the company has waged in the delta will be called to question sooner than later, and the crimes of that war will be duly punished. The crime of the company's dirty war against the Ogoni people will also be punished."[18]

Sara-Wiwa and his colleagues were hanged in the early morning hours of November 10, 1995.

In their book *Where Vultures Feast: Shell, Human Rights, and Oil in the Niger Delta*, the journalists Ike Okonta and Oronto Douglas charge that Nigerian police officers assigned to Shell were paid directly by the company and took their instructions from Shell officials. These same police brutally suppressed peaceful demonstrations "and used financial inducements to divide the community whenever there was an oil spill," residents in local communities allege. Okonta and Douglas also accuse Shell of paying off Lieutenant Colonel Paul Okuntimo, who coordinated attacks on the Ogoni, disguising these assaults as communal clashes between warring tribes. The authors also charge that Shell imported weapons to supply their supernumerary police guards.

Shell officials questioned the accuracy of Okonta and Douglas's book. When Shell was criticized for its share of responsibility for the massacres of the Ogoni people and the hanging of Ken Sara-Wiwa and his colleagues, the company's first reaction was that "a large multinational such as Shell cannot and must not interfere with the affairs of a foreign state."[19] But dismissing their culpability in the Nigerian fiasco did not extinguish the international outcry. Ultimately, the Brent Spar and Nigerian incidents created a tidal wave of bad press for the company.

Reeling from this explosion of criticism, Shell launched a substantial process of corporate self-examination. Schwartz and Gibb write: "Most companies under attack go immediately into defensive mode and stay there. Although defense was part of the Shell reaction, it was, to the company's credit, not all of it. One conclusion the company officials drew from the twin disasters was that they had to revisit their basic planning assumptions in light of public attitudes about the environment and human rights. Another was that they had not been letting enough fresh air into the organization, that they needed a more open dialogue with other stakeholders in their environment—particularly the environmental and human rights NGOs [nongovernment organizations] whose protest had been the strongest. A cautious program of outreach to these groups was initiated in an attempt to build dialogue and prevent, if possible, similar conflicts in the future."[20]

There are indications that at the top executive levels there is a push on to make Royal Dutch/Shell a company known for corporate responsibility. "In May 2000, the Shell Foundation was launched, with an initial bankroll of $30 million to spend on sustainable energy and social investment projects around the world," reports Jack Doyle. The Shell Foundation also gave $7.5 million for a Center for Transport and Environment at the World Resources Institute in Washington, and pledged $3.5 million for a Shell Center for Sustainability at Rice University in Houston.[21] In addition, Shell paid for an extensive television and print advertising campaign that attempted to depict its oil drilling as ecologically responsible and sensitive to the needs of local communities.

In a clear effort to refurbish its environmental profile after the Nigerian and North Sea debacles, Shell was the first major oil company to pull out of the cartel of oil giants that opposed the regulation of pollutants thought to contribute to global warming.[22] Shell, following the lead of British Petroleum, was developing a new vision of itself as "an energy company" and not exclusively "an oil company." Shell is also now investing in wind farms and in the development of an energy-efficient hypercar, although these acquisitions remain peripheral to its holdings of oil, liquefied natural gas, and chemical production facilities. "Despite claiming to be committed to sustainable production, Shell invests in fossil fuel production over renewable resources by a factor of 16, with $10-15 billion a year in capital infrastructure investments to prolong fossil fuel production and climate change and just $200 million per year on renewable resources technology," observed Denny Larson, coordinator of the Refinery Reform Campaign.[23]

In 1998, reversing its previous position that it would not be goaded by NGOs into publishing a social responsibility report, Shell published *Profits and Principles—Does There Have to Be a Choice?* Those involved in the preparation of this publication report that company officials learned that a local problem could bring about national and international criticism, that the company needed to test its assumptions with a variety of constituencies, and that it was important to build bridges with stakeholders at an early stage before problems developed.

Residents of Diamond benefited from this internal transformation going on within Shell as the lessons of the missteps in the Niger Delta and in the North Sea began to make their way down the corporate hierarchy from the executive offices in The Hague, London, and Houston to the plant manager's office in Norco.

Further, Shell's history in Nigeria radicalized a number of people who were to play critical roles in the struggle between Shell and the residents of

Diamond. As Anne Rolfes points out, "doing bad things in one part of the world has consequences elsewhere." Not only was Rolfes radicalized by what she saw in Nigeria; she also notes that the president of Concerned Citizens of Norco, Margie Richard, made a trip to Nigeria, and that what Richard saw there validated her sense that Diamond was being mistreated by Shell. Richard collected samples of water that had been polluted by Shell facilities in the Niger Delta, brought them back to Diamond with her, and eventually took them with her to an international conference in The Hague and held them up for the audience to see as she lectured Shell officials about their misdeeds in Nigeria and Louisiana.

8

A Company Town

White residents of Norco and their African-American neighbors in Diamond tend to have very different views of the quality of life next to the Shell plants. Many whites in Norco are either employees of Shell, former employees, or relatives of current or former employees. It is not much of a stretch to describe the white side of Norco as a company town.

Talk with some Norco residents and they will tell you that they love Norco, that the smell from the plants is not so bad, that a lot of people in town live to a ripe old age, that statistically they are in better-than-average health, and that the explosions at Shell are ancient history. People in Diamond who complain about the pollution are "just out for a buck," some Norco residents claimed.

Mr. Norco

Sal Digirolamo, 73, lives in Norco in a comfortable rambler on Oak Street with wall-to-wall carpet inside and a swing set, palm trees, and bird feeder outside. The blocks surrounding him boast similarly well-kept houses with a high density of statues of the Virgin Mary standing vigil on the lawns. Now retired from Shell after 40 years on the job, Digirolamo has two sons working there. (His other son works at a nuclear power plant.) He is not worried about the danger of explosion or health effects stemming from toxic releases at Shell. "I wouldn't consider myself much of a father if I though they were working at an unsafe place," he explained.

One of seven children, Digirolamo moved to Norco when he was a year old and grew up in an Italian enclave not far from the Shell refinery. He is as close to a civic booster as exists in this company town. He loves Norco and the pleasures of living in a community where you know everyone. "All the kids, we have seen them grow up, we have seen them go out and get married . . . seen everyone becoming grandpas and grandmas," he said. Now president of the Norco Civic Association, he has worked hard to see that all parts of Norco, including Diamond, are represented, he added.

Digirolamo is both thankful and beholden to Shell for providing his family with good employment over the years and for the contributions the company makes to the community. He proudly describes Shell's Providence Fund that puts aside ten percent of their employees' salaries every year. "In 40 years that accumulates to a right little piece of change," he allowed. When he retired he considered moving to another community to build a new home but "where else can you go in the world where you have been living by your neighbors for 50 years," he said, explaining his decision to stay. This love of place and close ties to Shell make Digirolamo a favorite of Shell officials, who frequently direct reporters to him to get the white residents' side of the Norco story. "There is no mayor of Norco but if we had one he would be it," said Shell spokesman David Brignac.

As a booster of Norco, unofficial mayor of its 3,300 residents, and defender of Shell, Digirolamo contested almost every complaint about living next to Shell made by residents of Diamond starting with their claim that they were pushed off their land in Belltown by the oil company. That could only have been the case with a few of the residents, he insisted. Digirolamo said he knows that for a fact because he helped build the Shell Chemical plant from the ground up, and when he started work on it back in 1954 there were only two or three houses on the Belltown property. Confronted with contradictory accounts by large number of Diamond residents who lived in Belltown or whose parents lived there, Digirolamo inflated his estimate first to four or five families and finally to "maybe ten." His memory is also based on some aerial photos he saw of the site where Shell Chemical was to be built, he said.

Margie Richard, past president of Concerned Citizens of Norco, disagreed with Digirolamo's version of history. The descendant of slaves who took part in the revolt of 1811 and the daughter of parents who lived in Belltown, Richard viewed the refineries and chemical plants as recent interlopers. "People around here have a memory problem. We have a rich history that began long before any plants moved in," she asserted.[1]

The discrepancy between the white and black memories about Belltown could be explained by the fact that most of the Belltown residents were probably evicted from the land before Digirolamo and the rest of the Shell crew from Norco arrived to start the construction of the chemical plant. There is also the possibility that during the 1950s, when segregation was still in force, Digirolamo was not very familiar with Belltown and did not know the extent of the settlement there because it would not necessarily have been a place he visited often.

In the old days segregation was a problem in Norco, Digirolamo conceded. "I think it [segregation] was terribly wrong. It [discrimination] was something I never did. It didn't take no laws to make me feel the way I did," Digirolamo said referring to desegregation legislation. "I had friends of mine who were black and came down and sat in that chair," he added. Shell did go through a period when its facilities were segregated, he conceded. "Like when blacks used to work up there and they had to do janitorial work that was the way the country was doing business. If you did business any other way you would probably have gone out of business," he added. The bowling alley, swimming pool, and gym at Shell were segregated, he confirmed. But segregation was everywhere at the time even in the town theater, he explained. "If Shell had done something else the local people probably would have hung them," he added. But later on Shell ended discrimination in its facilities because they realized it was bad for their image, he said. "They disbanded that," he noted.

"I am not going to say that they [African-American residents of Diamond] didn't see hard times. . . . They went through hell," Digirolamo observed. But they were not the only ones. "I am Italian and I caught seven kinds of hell for just being Italian, you know. But we put that on the side and moved forward," he continued. Since then there have been more opportunities for everyone and those who work hard and get a good education do well, he added. "I would like more [Diamond residents] to be hired [at Shell]. But don't you dare hire them if they don't know what they are doing because I want the plant to run and be safe. . . . That operation is a little too complex for a guy who does not have some kind of education and brain up there," he warned. Some people in the community do not take advantage of the educational opportunities and then they show up and demand a job that pays big money. They have to get over their sense of entitlement and realize that a good job requires that you work hard at you education first, he added.

Despite the history of racism, Norco is now one community and includes Diamond, insisted Digirolamo, who hated it when people speak of

Diamond as a separate community. "I agree it would be better if we mingled neighbors and so on," he conceded, but people have the right to live where they want to and with their own kind. If a bunch of Italians decide to live together that is up to them, he continued, and similarly for blacks. Calling the Gaspard property a color line was inaccurate because there were a few African-American and Latino-American households outside of Diamond, he claimed, ignoring the fact that no white families have moved into the many vacant properties in Diamond.

Every year Digirolamo and the 400-member Norco Civic Association put on community events in an effort to cross racial lines, including a Christmas parade, potluck suppers, and renovation work parties. "I keep doing things to unite us so we get closer," he said. Despite these efforts many people in Diamond still say they feel unwelcome on the white side of town. They also have a very different view of how dangerous it is living next to the Shell plants. "It is hard to believe that there are two different groups sitting here saying two different stories about the same conditions," Digirolamo observed.

The divergent views about Shell can be partially explained by the fact that Digirolamo worked at the plant for decades and as a result he knows how safe it is, he asserted. (In the early days a large proportion of Norco residents worked at Shell but that number has gradually shrunk and now there are only about 70 Shell employees living in town, one report calculated.[2]) By contrast, few Diamond residents have been employed by Shell and so they do not know how to interpret the noises and flares that occur on a daily basis, he added.

When he first bought his home in Norco with his wife for $12,000 ($1,500 down) some fifty years ago, Digirolamo was struck by how noisy it was with the trains coupling and uncoupling and the sounds from the plant. In fact, he recalled saying to his wife that perhaps they should have spent the night at the house before they bought it. But before long he became inured to the sounds and smells from the plant. "You don't hear it no more. You just kind of adjust to those kind of things to where it doesn't bother you," he said. He even takes his granddaughter to look at the flares, which he said do not bother him in the least or impinge on his quality of life because he knows that is the safest way for the plants to operate. In fact the noises and smells from the plants are "a slight inconvenience" when compared with the benefits that come from the plant, specifically the wonderful schools funded with taxes from Shell that his children and grand-children have attended.

From working at Shell one learns how important an issue safety is for the company, he continued. Employees take up to an hour preparing for a job in the morning before they go off to do it, he said. And Shell has an interest in keeping their workers safe and healthy because it costs them about $200,000 to train one, he noted. A single mistake can cost them millions, he added.

Even the huge explosion at the Shell refinery in 1988 is seen differently in the Digirolamo household than in those of Diamond residents. "You can't find a safer place than this even with the explosion," he asserted. "We have only had nine fatalities in 80 to 90 years," he pointed out. A salesman who has to do a lot of driving runs greater risks than does someone working at or living next to a Shell plant, he claimed. Despite this staunch defense of Shell's safety record, Digirolamo hinted at how close to home the explosion hit in 1988. "We had a son working out there [at the Shell refinery]. We were hysterical for a little while," he recalled. Digirolamo blames human error for the explosion. "I would have to say it was a mistake. It had to be that someone didn't do what they were supposed to do." With 400 to 600 people working you are bound to have a "bad apple" he said philosophically.

Digirolamo also contested the claims of many Diamond residents that the air in their community is unfit to breathe and causes disease. If this is the case how did they explain the longevity of residents in Norco, he asked? Pointing at houses up and down his block, Digirolamo described many residents who are in their 70s, 80s, and 90s. "What I like about Norco . . . is the longevity we enjoy in this community," he said.

"Not that some of these chemicals couldn't affect you," Digirolamo conceded, but he did not see evidence that people were getting sick from exposure to toxics from the plants. In fact he worked in one of the most highly toxic units that Shell ever ran—the vinyl chloride monomer (VCM) plant. "We had it up and running like a clock. I was all over that unit," he continued, "until Shell realized how bad that stuff was" and tore the unit down and sold it off. Some Norco residents were not happy about Shell decision to close the unit because they lost their jobs, he added, but Shell was looking at the long-term implications of having a unit on-site that produced a chemical that became a poster child for its adverse health effects. "If the air is so bad for your health here, how do these people in Diamond explain the fact that lots in Norco are selling for $35,000 and new houses are selling briskly?" he asked. "If the air is killing me why would I stick it out?" If Diamond residents are complaining that many of their children have asthma, why are residents of Norco not seeing any cases? How can that be when we both breathe the same air?"

Diamond residents have to be honest about why they want to move, Digirolamo insisted. "Is it because of the air or because they want to make a few bucks?" he asked. The clear implication was that Digirolamo thought those who were complaining about Shell wanted to make some money off their relocation. "In other words what they are telling us now is if you start bitching the chemical plant will have to pay you big bucks to get out."

Digirolamo said he is puzzled about the different views of whites and blacks hold about what it is like living next to Shell plants. "It is tough to explain why we don't feel, hear, or think the same things. It is impossible for me to explain it," he said. Perhaps it has something to do with attitudes about lying, he suggested. "We are both [he and his wife] good Christians. We both believe that lying . . . you can't be saved," he said. And to say that living next to Shell was harmful would require lying, he said. "And we are not going to lie." His decision not to lie about being harmed by Shell and making a profit from those lies has nothing to do with protecting Shell, he explained. "I'm being selfish because I do believe it is a sin and that you can be condemned for lying," he added. Similarly, being party to a false suit is stealing, another sin, he concluded. "I am not saying that the residents of Diamond are lying; I am just saying that we are telling the truth," he added.

While Digirolamo was careful not to call his neighbors in Diamond liars directly, he was willing to take on the "outside agitators" who have come into Norco and Diamond to stir up trouble. One of those he singled out was Anne Rolfes of the Louisiana Bucket Brigade, a close ally of Concerned Citizens of Norco who had been agitating for relocation. "You see, Anne's job is a job as long as there is a problem," said Digirolamo. After Rolfes had made a presentation at a community meeting about the dangers of living next to Shell, Digirolamo said he told her: "You said a lot of bad things were happening in Norco but where are your sources? Where did you get your statistics?" She never did provide those statistics, he claimed, so the next time he met her he asked if she had seen a study that showed that most of the residents, other than white males, in so-called Cancer Alley had lower than average cancer rates. "Anne, did you read that article?" he asked. "Yeah, I'm thinking of moving to Norco," he recalled her replying sarcastically. "And I said: 'Well, we don't want you.'" Then, realizing that he might have gone too far, he pulled back: "No . . . I didn't tell her that."

At one point some residents of Norco and New Sarpy (an adjacent community) became so fed up with outsiders stirring up trouble that they voted them out of some meetings, Digirolamo recalled. One resident said: "Look, I don't want to leave. I have been living here all my damn life. So get that [the idea he will relocate] out of your mind. This is where I was born and raised." He went on to say that the issue about living next to oil refineries and chemical plants was between the local residents and the industries and did not concern outsiders. He then made a motion that no outsiders should attend the meeting and the motion passed.

Outside "agitators" were not the only ones attacked for complaining about pollution from Shell. At one meeting, a local woman who was grumbling about living next to the plants was asked by another resident if she loved her family. When she affirmed that she did, she was asked why she didn't leave town. If she thought it was so dangerous living in Norco, why didn't she leave instead of waiting for some money? The idea that she might find it too costly to relocate to a safer area, where property values had not been depressed by proximity to industry, didn't seem to enter into the calculation of the questioner.

Ask Diamond resident why the white residents of Norco don't mind living next to Shell and they will all explain that white residents are getting money for living next to Shell so they don't complain. "They don't want to lay down on the tracks in front of the gravy train," one Diamond resident observed.

"Why are they [whites] happy living right there [near Shell facilities]? If they are going to breathe the [polluted] air, at least they are getting paid. But Shell is not doing anything for me. You go back there [on the white side of Norco] and you see [Shell] uniforms all over. . . . Some of them feel obligated [not to bad-mouth the company] because they work there [at Shell]. But they [Shell officials] haven't hired anybody from my community in the last roughly 20 years," said Dewayne Washington, a resident of Diamond.

Wilma Subra, a chemist who works with communities on toxics problems, also sees the white side of Norco as exhibiting all the signs of a company town. When Subra gave a presentation in Diamond about how the entire community fell in what industry delicately described as a "vulnerable zone" where residents might be harmed by a chemical accident, she found that residents on the white side of Norco did not want to hear a similar presentation, she said. "These people work or worked for Shell. Their pension and their insurance are all tied to Shell. . . Every time Shell holds a meeting these people come out and support them one hundred percent. . . . And so this is a really nice little town but everything depends on Shell. So are they going to speak out against Shell and risk losing their retirement?" Subra thinks not. "Shell has let them know what is acceptable and what is not. Shell rules their lives," she added, and since it is such a small community they see Shell managers on a regular basis. Furthermore, a number of the big petrochemical companies make workers sign an agreement that "they will not talk bad about the company they work for or any other industrial facility in the area," Subra claimed. "And they also had to sign a letter that said they didn't sign the first letter." Though Subra had no specific information to prove that Shell is engaged in this practice, she thought it probably did.

Shell's Curator

Clarisse Vitrano Webb, 83, chairperson of Shell's River Road Museum, grew up on the white side of town next to Shell's refinery and chemical plant. The child of a Shell employee, she was raised in Norco and an adjacent town, spending the first eight years of her life in staff housing at the Shell refinery. She later landed a job at Shell as a nurse. "Oil is in my blood," said Webb, who was born in 1920 in Hahnville, directly across the river from Norco, in the home of her maternal grandparents. Her mother was a local woman of French ancestry; her father was an Italian-American laborer who started at Shell as a waterboy in 1918 and worked his way up through the ranks, running Shell's canteen in the 1920s and eventually becoming the company's fire marshal.

In the early days accommodations at Shell were relatively primitive, but as the years passed the company's on-site amenities became more lavish, Webb said. "This was a country club right here," she recalled. "[There was] a theater, gymnasium, bowling ally, swimming pool, golf course, tennis courts, American Legion home, and Norco School. . . . I could go on and on and write a book about it."[3]

In 1928 Webb's family moved out of company housing to the adjacent town of Good Hope where they stayed until 1960. Her father found a job working for the Sheriff's Department and the Louisiana State Highway Patrol. He later signed on as a bodyguard for Governor Huey Long. Long, famous for being "one of the boys," often played poker and relaxed with his bodyguards and a coterie of hangers-on when he was not bashing the oil companies and other malefactors in Baton Rouge and Washington who made life miserable for the common man. "When Huey died," Webb recalled, "it was like a death in the family because of how close he was to the guys.'

Webb finished nursing school in 1943, but it was not until 1966 that she landed a highly sought-after position as a nurse at Shell. That her father had worked at Shell probably helped. As she explained it, while Shell was at first reluctant to hire family members, company officials came to realize that it was to their advantage. "It [Shell] was like a family affair because the mothers and the fathers and the sisters and the brothers controlled each other," she said. If one of them was not doing his job properly the other family members would get on his case, she added.

Webb worked as an occupational health nurse and had her offices on the back side of the plant. This was not a job for the squeamish. "I remember a severed femoral artery, which was horrible. I was shoe-sole-deep in blood. I thought 'Oh my God we are going to lose this man,' and it scared me to death," she recalled. In the end both the man's leg and his life were saved. Though Shell's medical expertise was not put to work for community directly, Shell's ambulance was, Webb explained. "That was another give-away" that Shell provided the community, she noted. In fact, when her appendix ruptured while she was in high school it was in the Shell ambulance that she was taken to the hospital.

"I had a good living here. I mean I don't have a mint but I am comfortable and I enjoy my job. And they [Shell officials] were always decent to me until today," she said. She has lived by the Shell plants all her life except during six years—three years during which she attended nursing school and another three-year stint when she followed her husband from post to post while he was in the service. After the war "we came right back home. We didn't have to. We had every other chance in the world," she said.

Webb credits Shell with being generous in providing assistance to both their employees and members of the community. Sometimes the company ponies up money for the community directly, as it recently did with a gift of $350,000. Other times the support is more indirect. The company sometimes "works in strange ways," Webb noted. For example, there is the case of the 29-year-old employee who was hired by Shell in the early days who moved in with his pregnant wife and two children. At the time, company policy held that an employee had to work for Shell for 45 days before he became vested with full benefits. Before that time had elapsed the man climbed up on top of one of Shell's giant tanks and died. Since his widow could claim no benefits from Shell, her family sent her away to "beauty school" so she could learn a trade. When she returned Shell set her up in a beauty shop in the community, Webb recalled, and she had both a livelihood and a community to support her.

There have been many other instances of corporate compassion—some large and some small, Webb continued. For instance, there was the hard time in 1958 when Webb's mother died and she could not attend the funeral because she was lying in bed after undergoing major surgery. Some of her relatives offered to stay with her during the funeral but Shell made that unnecessary by sending a nurse to tend her so that her relatives could attend the services. It is thoughtful gestures such as this that helped win Webb's loyalty and appreciation.

But all has not been unremitting sweetness and light in the relationship between local residents and the industrial giants moving into their neighborhood, Webb conceded. Over the years, she witnessed Shell and other oil companies muscle into adjacent residential communities. In 1916, four years before she was born, Shell purchased 366 acres of sugar cane fields for $21,000 between the old Trepagnier Plantation and the Good Hope Plantation and built first its tank farm and then a refinery on the land.[4] It was in the worker housing on this land that Webb lived as a child.

From 1930 to 1949 Webb lived in Good Hope, a town adjacent to Norco which was built on the site of the Good Hope Plantation. The town was purchased, torn down, and transformed into the Good Hope Refinery, later becoming the Orion refinery, which still operates today. The town of Good Hope was as old as Norco before the oil company ran all the people out, Webb observed. "They destroyed a beautiful little community," she continued. Everyone moved out except for Charlie Andrews who lived in one house and his son who lived in another. Andrews lived to the age of 94 and died just recently, Webb continued. His house was totally surrounded by the refinery. People moved because they didn't want to live next to a giant refinery, she said "Let's face it: Who wants to live with a 'cat cracker' [catalytic cracking unit] in their back yard?" Webb is currently organizing a reunion of former residents of Good Hope "to relive all the good memories," she said.

The Good Hope Refinery (now the Orion Refinery) was not alone in its expansion plans. Shell was also adding to its holdings on the east side of its plant by buying out the community of Wesco, a settlement of about 50 families located on their fenceline between Norco and Good Hope. Wesco was purchased because it was located on a dead-end street that was surrounded by refineries, Webb recalled. "The only way out was River Road; there was no way out in the back. After a major fire at Shell some of the residents, recognizing how dangerous their situation was, approached Shell and negotiated a buyout. This purchase largely wiped out the residential neighborhood that separated the Shell and Orion refineries leaving a seamless industrial complex. Webb was intimately familiar with the disruption that expanding oil companies caused. Her sister, who lived in Wesco, moved her house adjacent to Webb's property in Norco.

In addition to the industrial land grab, the local residential population was also under pressure from the state government, which, in 1936, bought up property in Montz, a town on the west side of Norco. This land was turned into the Bonnet Carre Spillway to reduce flood pressure on New Orleans. Here again residents, including a number of black families who were farming the land, had to be moved.

It is in this context that Shell purchased the Belltown property in 1953 for its Shell Chemical plant. It was one more expansion of industrial facilities in the River parishes in a long series of industrial incursions into formerly residential areas. The difference was that with Belltown Shell was moving an historic black community where some residents had roots going back to plantation days. The Belltown community and the area adjacent to it that became Diamond had a long history and several different names, town historian Webb recalled. In addition to Belltown it was also called Wattown, Jewtown (because it was owned by Jews), and Sellers, she reported.

For Belltown residents to complain about being forced off the land is a hopeless cause, she opined. "Do you know how many places were moved because of progress?" she asked. "They have moved mountains because of progress. Lord, that is a poor fight. How can you stop big business? You tell me. How can you stop big business?" The people in Belltown could not stop Shell from moving them because they did not own the land, Webb noted. That is just the way it is. But Webb objected to the more recent industrial practice of forcing people to move even when they do own the land. "I think that is awful that a person owns something and they are going to force them out. . . . And it has been done. That is unfair. I would go down fighting for that," she said.

Having lived through this history of industrial expansion Webb has learned to coexist with powerful neighbors and her family has done well by getting along with them. She and her father both worked for Shell and they were treated well, she said. And she does not have much sympathy for people who yell and holler about the problems of living next to petrochemical plants. "I am glad I am not picayune about watching every breath of smoke.. . . . The thing that gets me is . . . the itch, the dandruff or the ingrown toenails that were blamed on Shell. That is stupid. I can't but say that and mean it," she said. Statistics show that residents of Norco are healthier than average Americans and all the tests of the air have not managed to show that there is anything very wrong, she claimed. If there were a real health problem all the residents of Norco would experience it, she reasoned. There is no "iron curtain" between Diamond and Norco and residents of both neighborhoods breathe the same air, she added. "We don't mind [the air quality]. We are not hollering and whooping about it," she noted. All places have their dangers, she continued. "You can make a mountain out of a molehill or you can accept what is there," she said.

Webb accepts the dangers of living next to the plant. She could have made a fuss when her sister's 35-year-old son, who worked for Shell was killed in the refinery explosion in 1988. "My sister's oldest child. . . . I never did blame the company," she said. "I stayed with my sister and her husband for 16 days until that boy's remains were found and we could bury him." Webb herself confesses to having been "on edge" after the explosion. "I wouldn't be human if I didn't: it was a horrible sound."

Shell gets blamed for a lot of society's problems, such as racism and poverty, Webb continued. "We are blamed for a lot of things that other people have done. I am telling you that. Shell is blamed for what the world has done," she said. Segregation was not Shell's fault, Webb pointed out.

There were quite a few African-Americans hired by Shell over the years and they were never mistreated, she asserted. Webb knew one of them well, a man named Joseph Cotton, who worked for her father when he was manager of Shell's canteen. "He was my dad's right hand, so he was my other daddy. You'd go to Joe if you needed something," she recalled.

Norco is racially divided geographically, Webb insisted, because the African-American population wanted it that way: "They separated themselves. . . . They wanted their own locations. You had sections the blacks wanted to live in: they wanted to be in the colored section. . . . They wanted their own separate everything and that is what they got." Part of their decision to buy homes in Diamond instead of in Norco also might have had something to do with the fact that properties on the white side of the line were more expensive and they couldn't afford it, she observed.

Webb also finds it unfair that blacks should continue to blame whites for slavery when "their own people did [sold slaves]. . . . I'm sorry, they are selling their own people until today and they are going to bitch about us over here," she argued. "What happened to the poor Italian immigrants, the poor Irish immigrants? Don't tell me about that. My grandparents were Italian immigrants and I can tell you they were treated far worse than some of the slaves. When they came here they were hard laborers in the sugar cane fields working arm-in-arm with some of those that are complaining the loudest today. They are trying to make us responsible right now for what happened to their ancestors and I could tell you about my own ancestors . . . and what I could complain about."

Webb also sees it as unfair that the residents of Diamond are now getting more than fair market value for their homes under Shell's relocation initiatives. Residents of Good Hope or Wesco only got fair market value for their homes—assessments that had been reduced because of the proximity of industry—so why should residents of Diamond get a special deal, she asked? It seems as if all the yelling and hollering is paying off; the squeaky wheel is getting the grease, she noted, and that rubs her the wrong way. The idea that this kind of organizing and protest is both legal and ethical does not resonate with her.

"I want to just tell you that the more you hand out and the more you give the more they expect. I have seen that. They want something for nothing and I mean it. I have been here long enough to know. . . . They [Shell] have bent over backwards . . . with their Good Neighbor Initiative and Good

Neighbor Policy. . . . I know the things they have given them and I know the handouts they have handed out. . . . I don't know what they [Shell] can do other than give blood," Webb commented. "I say reverse discrimination is beginning to show," she added. Shell has also contributed large amounts of taxes towards funding local education and they have paid mentors to work with young people. "It [Shell's generosity] doesn't have an end. . . . They [residents of Diamond] are looking a gift horse in the mouth. I'm sorry. I'm calling a spade a spade. I can't help it."

Walking the Line

The Constable of Norco, Milton Cambre, is a tall, soft-spoken man of French ancestry who knows the line that divides the black community of Diamond from the white community of Norco better perhaps than any other resident. While he lives on the white side of town in a brick home on Marino Street, Cambre's rounds take him back and forth across the Gaspard line making house calls in both communities. An exotic blend of hard-hat and environmentalist, Cambre has demonstrated a willingness to call on industry to clean up its act from inside the refinery gates.

Born about 25 miles upriver from Norco in the town of Polina, where his parents ran a tiny post office, Cambre described his upbringing as follows: "We were certainly not wealthy. My daddy worked, my mama worked, and the trains delivered the mail." The family owned a small strip of land they worked in partnership with a local African-American man. They provided the land, seed, and fertilizer; he provided the labor, the knowledge about farming, and the mule. Then they split the harvest of vegetables. Every day this farmer/partner would go to the train station with a wheelbarrow and bring back the mail, Cambre remembered: "He was the best man: he would bring sugar cane for us [children] and peel us pecans."

After graduating from high school in 1953, Cambre went to work at a refinery for five years in Destrehan just down-river from Norco before he was drafted into the Army. While in the Service the oil company where he had worked closed down. When he got out of the Army he went to work for Shell Oil for two years before being laid off in an economic downturn. He subsequently found work at General American, a tank storage outfit, where he worked as timekeeper and on payroll. But with a growing family of four children, Cambre took a better-paying job as an industrial mechanic at the huge Dupont facility across the river from Norco.

It was while he was at Dupont that Cambre started to lobby for change in the way the company handled waste disposal. At the time, he reported, a number of the petrochemical companies along the river (including Shell) were practicing deep-well injection of their hazardous waste. Cambre saw this as a flawed method because of its potential to contaminate groundwater, so he lobbied for ending it. Nor was Cambre satisfied when the oil companies abandoned deep-well injection of their wastes in favor of packaging their waste in metal barrels and sinking them in the Gulf of Mexico where he did his fishing and shrimping. Finally, an incinerator to burn the wastes was built, a method that was better but not perfect, Cambre observed. "I stayed in my role as hourly employee but I voiced my opinions and I was thought highly of by plant managers," he said. "They never did retaliate on me."

In his dealings with Dupont and Shell, Cambre said he had never been confrontational but that had not stopped him from tackling tough problems. "I was concerned with the episodic releases, the flaring and so on but I guess I am not one who just goes and criticizes. I want to solve the problem," he said. Cambre argued that he can get more accomplished working with the managers of the plants surrounding Norco than he could if he went outside and approached the media. When pressed about how concerned he is about illness induced by air pollution from the adjacent plants he seems to back off: "I would never have subjected my kids to something I thought was dangerous," said Cambre, who has four grown children who live within a mile of the Shell plants. He pointed to a controversial health study, which found no disproportionate health problems in the region, as a sign that the area was not dangerous.

This is not to say that Cambre had not seen firsthand how dangerous these plants could be. While working at Dupont, he came close to losing his life in an industrial accident. "I heard a tremendous noise out at the unit where I was working. I went to the doorway and I saw this big old plume of material coming out. I said: 'Something is wrong.' And while I was watching it ignited. I could not move. People tell you what you should do but I say you can't know until you witness it. Things were falling around me and I am stuck watching. . . . Somebody was in the shop and said: 'Let's get the hell out of here' and then I moved," he said. On the way out he saw men walking out of the unit that exploded with all the clothes burned off of them. "So it is scary stuff but you know what you are dealing with and it is the price we pay for getting the quality of life we have," he said.

By quality of life, Cambre explained, he means the good-paying jobs and the excellent educational system that is funded by taxes from the big industries. You have to look at the big picture when assessing the dangers of living next to oil and chemical plants and the benefits they bring, he said. Towns in southern Louisiana and the river parishes between New Orleans and Baton Rouge are poor and without the big industries to support the tax base and pay for schools and provide jobs there would be little opportunity in the area, he explained. He is concerned that so much will be asked of industry that they will pack up and move to another country where costs are lower and environmental regulation slacker. Having lost jobs at plants that closed down or laid off workers this is not just a theoretical problem for him, he added.

Some residents and activists were asking the plants to do too much, he said. "It is not the role of industry to be the savior" in all things, Cambre asserted. It is not up to industry to solve all of the economic and social problems of residents living near it, he argued. If there is a problem with air pollution and adverse health effects then government agencies should intervene.

Residents of Diamond complained about living next to the plant, but a few blocks away people were moving in and building expensive houses, Cambre pointed out. Most residents of Diamond, he said, were no more exposed to pollution from the plant than other residents of Norco. "I don't feel at risk. . . . I think a lot of it [the problem in Diamond] is an economic issue," he concluded. While he did not think there was a health problem, Cambre felt that residents of Diamond had every right to organize and express their views. He was disappointed, however, when only a few residents of Diamond came to meetings about environmental conditions attended by representatives of the Environmental Protection Agency and the state Louisiana Department of Environmental Quality at the VFW Hall in Norco. Diamond residents did not organize and work through the system, he noted. "They are getting the media to solve their problems. To me, they need to get to the [negotiating] table to solve their problems. I guess that is where our views differ," he added.

As for how close one can live to these plants and still be safe, Cambre suggested that a few blocks can make all the difference. The people in Diamond who were killed by the gas leak and explosion in 1973 lived on the street just opposite the plant, he pointed out. Living where he does nine blocks from the Shell/Motiva refinery and six blocks from the Shell Chemical plant he feels safe, he added. "I think it would be a black eye on all industry if we can't operate the plant in a safe enough manner where anyone can't live within a mile or two or five of the plant," he said.

For his work protesting the dumping of toxic materials in the Mississippi and his wetlands conservation efforts, Cambre was named a "point of light" by president George H. W. Bush. Now 67 and retired from his job in the petrochemical industry, Cambre has been able to devote much of his time to his volunteer work improving the quality of the cypress swamp, tupelo, and brackish-water wetlands behind the Shell plant and to help prevent further coastal erosion. He frequently takes reporters, filmmakers, and environmentalists for boat rides through the tangled and highly polluted bayous behind the Shell plants.

Some environmentalists who have accompanied him on these backwater reconnaissance missions described Cambre as a different man when he was helping to chart the depth of the industrial sludge dumped by Shell than he was in his formal role as a representative on community/industry panels. Clearly, Cambre left it to others to play the "bad cop" with industry, preserving for himself a more genial relationship with corporate managers as the friendly, local, blue-collar naturalist lobbying industry for incremental improvements. The fact that he had to stand for election as Norco's constable might also have been a factor in the diplomatic manner in which he dealt with the problems posed by industrial pollution.

Walking the tightrope between company-town constable and devoted naturalist, however, did not stop Cambre from numerous activist ventures including the scrounging of concrete from the foundations of homes that had been bulldozed in Diamond to use as riprap to protect the coastal shoreline. He also took school kids out along the bayou to build trails and nature parks, educating them and others about the rich natural diversity of Louisiana's wetlands. Clearly concerned about the impact that industrial dumping and emissions have had on the bayous and wetlands, Cambre nevertheless insisted that conditions were gradually improving. In the 1970s moss was rapidly disappearing from the wetlands because it could not tolerate the high level of pollution coming from the plants, he explained. But now that emissions have been cut the moss is reviving, he reported.

Middleman

Breakfasting at a popular restaurant tucked on a back street in New Orleans, Robert Thomas is frequently recognized and greeted by patrons. They knew him from appearances on television where he was often interviewed as a scientist who could translate complex environmental issues for the lay public. A tall man with tortoise-shell glasses, a neatly trimmed white beard, and the ruddy complexion of the outdoor biologist and naturalist, Thomas had a habit of inserting himself in some of the most contentious environmental issues in a state that was widely known for catering to highly toxic industries and its lackadaisical enforcement of environmental regulations.

Previously a founding director of the Louisiana Nature Center and then vice president for environmental policy at the Audubon Institute, Thomas is now director for the Center for Environmental Communications at Loyola University, where he teaches journalism students the fine points of covering an environmental beat. The fact that he is now firmly ensconced in academia, however, has not tempted Thomas to leave the hurly-burly of the public arena. Instead, he engages in what he called "intervention work" in which he positions himself as a mediator between industrialists and environmental activists and fenceline community grassroots leaders.

For the past decade, Thomas, 56, has made it a practice to sit down with industrialists and open a dialogue with them about environmental issues. "I go out and in some way get between the environmental community and industry," he said. He first started visiting Norco in the late 1970s because he was leading canoe trips on Bayou Trepagnier, a river that had as its headwater a pipe, 30 inches in diameter, which came out of the Shell Chemical plant and Motiva Refinery. The Bayou was heavily polluted and it was made worse when Shell diverted the water feeding it into the Mississippi in a state-ordered effort to dilute the company's effluent.

In subsequent years, Thomas participated in the Common Sense Initiative sponsored by the Environmental Protection Agency, in which representatives of both the local community and industry came together regularly to see if they could resolve some of the issues that were causing tension along their common fenceline. But his most effective work, he said, was done informally over endless cups of coffee with a variety of different Shell officials.

Thomas wanted to help company officials take some responsibility for the quality of life of people living along their fenceline. "Diamond is a very depressed area with all kinds of sociological problems that the company has ignored over the years," he said. "When you are poor, uneducated, and unemployable you have no options. . . . We are not talking about a normal situation. . . . We are talking about a situation where, for whatever societal reasons, people are living in an oppressed situation and someone has to step forward [to help them]." The state government had proved time and again that it was incapable of helping, so it was obvious that Shell was the entity with the resources to help solve the problem, he observed. The company, however, became adept over the years at deflecting demands made on them by the community, Thomas continued. For example, when the community wanted improved evacuation routes in the event of an accident at Shell or Motiva, company officials pointed out that they paid hefty taxes and that local government agents should deal with the problem. Furthermore, most Shell officials were so focused on making a profit and ensuring that their plant met environmental regulations that they did not think a lot about the quality of life of residents living near their plant, he added.

Environmental activists tend to approach industry head-on and confront officials at Shell with an ultimatum: "Unless you do this we will do that," Thomas pointed out. This often made corporate officials feel cornered and rendered it harder for them to change their behavior, he noted. Instead, Thomas took a more indirect approach. He pointed out that Shell was incredibly generous when it came to making large corporate donations to good works in New Orleans. But what had Shell done for the people of Norco, he asked?

After Shell officials talked a little bit about the baseball field, swings, and basketball hoops they had erected in Diamond, they were forced to recognize that the help they were providing to the local community, upon which they had the heaviest impact, was small compared with their generosity in the city. From there they moved on to a discussion about social justice, Thomas said. "You have to raise the issue with them [Shell officials] in a positive way so they can think: 'Well, this is my responsibility,'" he said. Thomas said he also made progress convincing Shell officials to take responsibility for the people living along their fenceline in Diamond by telling them that "it was in their best business interest to resolve the problems because they are not going to get smaller."

Gradually one could detect a painful evolution in the thinking of a core groups at Shell who were coming to grips with the issue, Thomas recalled.

Willing to concede that they had some impact on local residents, Shell officials were, nevertheless, concerned that once they agreed to relocate some residents that others would want the same deal. Shell officials wondered where it would stop. They were also concerned that once they gave in to one of the demands of the activist groups that they would just be pressured for more concessions, he said.

What he learned mediating between the entrenched positions of environmental activists and corporate officials was that each side had its own set of prejudices. As a result he had to convince the corporate officials that most environmentalists were sincere in their efforts to create conditions that would serve future generations well and that only a few were charlatans and crazies. On the other side of the conflict, Thomas tried to explain to environmentalists that just because industrialists were in business for a profit did not mean that they did not want to do the right thing by the community.

Thomas said that he had little patience for industrialists who do not care about the impact of their operations on the people along their fenceline; but he also found it hard to stomach the tactics of environmentalists who only criticized industry and could never acknowledge the good that they did. In Norco there was very little solid communication going on between the community and environmental activists on the one hand and the corporate officials on the other hand, he reported. The former tended to communicate by protest marches, lawsuits and media coverage, while the latter stayed behind their corporate walls and issued press releases. Thomas was particularly struck by the fact that some environmentalists were frank about their unwillingness to engage with corporate officials. "I don't want to get to know you because I might like you," one of them told an official at Shell. That was a real conversation stopper, he observed. Further, environmentalists refused to acknowledge Shell's generous Good Neighbor Initiative. "To me that is absolutely as bad as companies that won't help people. . . . It is absolutely incredible that they do that," he said.

Some environmental activists involved in the struggle in Diamond are less than enthusiastic about the role that Thomas played in the controversy. He is described by some as a "master of greenwash" and by others as "bought and paid for by Shell." Thomas is no go-between, they said—he never talked with the leadership of Concerned Citizens of Norco or with the environmental justice activists who were the allies of the Diamond residents. What this critique failed to take into account, however, was that Thomas might have interjected an environmentalist's perspective into the discussions he had with Shell officials without playing a formal role as a mediator.

What did seem clear from interviews with both Thomas and his critics was that he saw much of the conflict between Shell and Diamond residents as a communication problem between parties with radically different perspectives. When Thomas gave lectures about the intervention work he did in Norco trying to mediate between the interests of residents and industrialists he showed a photograph of a 93-year-old resident of Diamond who was looking out her front window at the Shell Chemical plant across the street. The cultural chasm in Norco was such that people had opposite reactions to this photo. On one side were people who live on the white side of town in Norco who loved where they live. They look at the snapshot of the old woman and said: "Isn't it wonderful that she could live to the ripe old age of 93 right on the fenceline?" While disgruntled residents of Diamond, who lived for years with the pollution from Shell but had landed few of the jobs and enjoyed few benefits said: "Man, can you believe it. . . . Would you like to live for 93 years next to all that pollution? It is horrible."

Similarly, people on different sides of the race line in Norco/Diamond looked at flares at the refinery and chemical plant differently, Thomas noted. "As it said in our report, when a flare goes off all the white people in Norco say: 'Oh, look, the safety system is working.' And all the black people say 'Oh my God, we are all going to die.'" It was obvious that while "black people don't trust the company or feel comfortable [living next to the plants], white people do," he added. "And believe it or not we went to the first meeting and nobody could explain why," he recalled.

Both sides were speaking from their heart and, as a result, thought that those who disagree with them were lying, Thomas observed. Many of the people on the white side of town had a long history of working at the plant, they had an informal network of communication that kept them abreast of what was happening within the plants, and they trusted those who were managing them. Whereas residents of Diamond did not know anyone who worked at the plant, they had only experienced the ill effects of living next to it, and they had little information about what was happening inside the gates, nor did they trust those running the operation. This leads to the opposing views of Shell, Thomas concluded.

The irony was that there were good people on both sides, he added. There were Shell employees who went into the plants every day and worked hard to see that environmental regulations were met and that they safely produced product that made the company a profit. When they were later accused of "being heinous and of having nasty motives" they could not recognize themselves in the caricature that was painted of them. They were trying to be good citizens but were accused of being bad people, Thomas said. On the other side of the equation were people who were terrified of living next to the plants but were too poor to move away, he continued. Both could speak from the heart and yet fail to hear what the other was saying.

III

Tension along the Fenceline

9

Winds of Change

In 1997, Barry McCormick, a 38-year-old former employee at the Lyondell/Citgo refinery in Houston, was hired to work as an environmental engineer at the Motiva refinery in Norco, which pumped out 250,000 barrels of oil a day and employed some 700 workers. A man of small stature and high energy, McCormick was given an important job at Motiva. He was put in charge of monitoring a program designed to meet new federal regulations that called for using the maximum achievable control technologies (MACT) for checking fugitive emissions from the thousands of valves and pumps at oil refineries.[1] This was a major undertaking. Not only would the price tag for carrying out this review cost the company more than a million dollars to conduct, what McCormick found would also paint a detailed portrait of how much pollution the facility was emitting into the adjacent communities of Diamond and Norco.

For decades the residents of Diamond had complained that they were being poisoned by pollution from the Motiva and Shell plants. The stink from the refinery and chemical plant was nauseating, and they were literally choking on the chemicals coming out of the plants, they reported. Many of them had respiratory problems, and a disproportionate number of residents had oxygen machines in their homes to help them breathe. Despite these anecdotal reports of a public health problem, the Louisiana Department of Environmental Quality (LDEQ) did not believe that there was a serious environmental health hazard in Diamond and consistently refused to fine Shell and Motiva or argue with its reports stating that the companies had an exemplary environmental record. In 1998, for example, the Motiva refinery at Norco turned in reports to LDEQ indicating that they had detected only two leaks in the 471 components checked among the thousands of valve and pumps at the refinery. This exemplary record of environmental compliance, however, was called into question once the new monitoring program went into effect. What McCormick found was that there were, in fact, many more leaks in the valves and pumps at Motiva. As a result, Motiva's reports about how many leaks the plant experienced skyrocketed, providing Diamond residents with additional proof to support their claim that unacceptably high levels of pollutants were crossing the fence into their neighborhood.

Whereas in 1997 only one leak was reported in the 695 components checked, and in 1998 only two leaks were found in 471 components checked, McCormick's work revealed that in 1999 there were 191 leaks detected in the 4,303 components monitored. "Motiva's reports on leaks changed overnight from an exemplary record to one of excessive leaks," observes John Biers, the energy reporter for the *Times-Picayune,* who blew the lid off this story in a piece of remarkable investigative environmental journalism.[2]

As McCormick found more and more leaks, he became increasingly aggressive about pushing management to report and fix them. Later reports were to reveal that the 1.14 million pounds of fugitive emissions from the Shell and Motiva plants in Norco in 1997 were actually two times greater than the 570,000 pounds of emissions coming out of their stacks.[3]

McCormick's drive to clean up Motiva regardless of who it embarrassed caused him to be fired from his job on March 8, 1999, some 26 months after being hired. According to Biers, McCormick's boss told him that, although he was one of the most ethical people he had ever met, he did not fit in at Motiva. McCormick claimed he was told he could stay on at Motiva until June 15 while he looked for another job if he remained silent about the company's environmental compliance record. Instead he went to the Louisiana Department of Environmental Quality and blew the whistle on his former employers, alleging that Motiva was emitting more gases than it was reporting to regulators and was doctoring its reports of fugitive emissions.

Jim Stone, an LDEQ inspector who had previously sided with Motiva in a number of regulatory controversies, was assigned to check McCormick's allegations. Stone subsequently verified many of McCormick's charges. On June 2, 1999, LDEQ sent Motiva a ten-page letter listing 26 problem areas in its fugitive emissions program. Motiva officials subsequently admitted that there were inconsistencies with the accounting system that the company used in monitoring the leaks, but they denied criminal wrongdoing.

As Stone became more critical of Motiva's leak-detection program, the company hinted that he was prejudiced against it. Stone was replaced by another inspector, Mike Alegro, who confirmed the most important of Stone's findings, Biers reported. McCormick subsequently sued Motiva for back wages and compensation for psychological counseling, loss of earning capacity, loss of enjoyment of life, embarrassment, and humiliation.

Barry McCormick's charges of wrongdoing at Motiva brought significantly greater regulatory scrutiny of the company and increased fines. From 1994 to 1998 there were 561 accidental releases from the Motiva refinery, which cost the company only $14,500 in fines. After McCormick went public with his allegations, fines against Motiva for leaks during the period from January to August 11, 1999 increased to $66,095.

The Common Sense Initiative

During the second Clinton administration, when Representative Newt Gingrich was advocating a rollback of environmental regulations in Congress, Vice-President Albert Gore Jr. took on the task of responding to the conservative push for a less intrusive, less expensive, more efficient way to regulate industry. Gore's approach was to establish what he called the Reinventing Government Initiative. Part of this effort examined industries sector by sector to see if environmental regulations could be better targeted. The idea was that air pollution regulations that might make sense for a printing company might not be appropriate for an oil refinery. The goal was to make regulation protect the environment while at the same time less expensive and cumbersome for businesses.

To make environmental regulations more efficient, the Reinventing Government Initiative organized the Common Sense Initiative, which was subdivided into a number of industrial sectors. On of these was the Petroleum Sector. Stakeholders involved in the petroleum sector—including government officials, refinery managers, environmentalists, and representatives of affected communities—were brought together to reassess the regulatory process to see if it could be improved. Among those invited to participate in this process from Louisiana were representatives of the oil industry and the bureaucrats who regulated their refineries. Also given seats at the table were Wilma Subra, the local chemist who acted as a technical consultant for fenceline residents; Denny Larson, who specialized in organizing communities located adjacent to petroleum refineries; and Beverly Wright of the Deep South Center for Environmental Justice, who had been knitting together a network of fenceline communities in the Louisiana river parishes.

A woman who does not suffer nonsense either quietly or diplomatically, Wright found the meetings of the Common Sense Initiative excruciating and did not trust the process, which she found heavily weighted in favor of industry. She worried that her name and the name of the Deep South Center would be used to legitimize a process in which she had little confidence. Instead of simply withdrawing from the process, Wright asked Margie Richard, then president of Concerned Citizens of Norco, to become the representative for communities in St. Charles Parish that were suffering the ill effects of pollution as a consequence of being the neighbors of the large refineries and chemical plants.

Richard wasted no time making her presence felt. "I represented myself and the common people who live near industry," she said. She asked what enforcement and compliance really meant when there were 420 episodic releases reported from Shell's Norco facilities in one year. "You have to stop having these things [regulations] written down and have no compliance," she asserted. Richard admonished the regulators for not doing their job. How could people of this level of intelligence with all these legal and scientific degrees work on these issues for all these years without requiring industries to comply with the regulations that were on the books, she asked? Someone in the regulatory system was not doing their job, she charged.

Further, Richard told members of Common Sense Initiative that while regulators were looking at chemicals individually and assessing their toxicity as a single chemical, "we, the people who are walking around [near these plants] and our children who are playing [next to these plants] are inhaling these chemicals collectively. . . . People are already damaged. To be truthful it is only the Grace of God that we have people living as long as they have lived who live near these facilities," she told them.

Richard was speaking from personal experience about what it meant to be exposed to industrial toxins. Not only did she live on Washington Street just across the fence from Shell Chemical, she had also "worked the turnaround." For those unfamiliar with industrial jargon, the turnaround described a period of time when a unit at the chemical plant or refinery was shut down for maintenance and repair. During these periods local residents were often hired on a temporary basis to clean out the facilities. When she was younger and a single mother Richard worked the turnaround and the collar of the sweater that she wore while she did the work turned green from exposure to some of the chemicals, she said. Curious about some of the chemicals she was working around, Richard went home and looked them up in a book. What she found was that some of the chemicals caused cancer, she said.

Denny Larson arrived for these Common Sense Initiative stakeholder meetings fresh from a tour of fenceline communities in the petrochemical corridor. On this trip he met with activists in Convent, in Baton Rouge, and in Texas City and passed through what he describes as "chemical ghost towns" where properties adjacent to large refineries and chemical plants were fast disappearing. There were numerous properties where you could still see the driveway and trees but where the house had been removed, he recalled.

One of the towns Larson visited was Norco, where he was introduced to Margie Richard. She took him on a walk down Washington Street along the fenceline with the Shell Chemical plant past the site where Helen Washington and Leroy Jones died in the pipeline explosion. Richard filled him on the local scene: "She was reeling off the names of residents who had died or were sick. This was the worst-case scenario. This was what it meant to live on the fenceline with a petrochemical plant and this woman, Margie Richard, had figured it out. She knew exactly what was happening and she knew exactly what she needed to do, which was to get the heck out of there," Larson said. In was with this background that Larson began to attend meetings of the Common Sense Initiative in 1995 and 1996. Right from the start representatives of refineries took a very aggressive stance. They asked if it would be possible to eliminate the "maximum achievable control technology" standards. Officials of the Environmental Protection Agency quickly nixed this suggestion. Next, industrial stakeholders tried to see if they could do away with their obligation to use hand-held air monitors when checking for leaks in their valves. Instead they proposed using a soap-and-water solution on the valves to see if there was a leak that would cause a bubble to form. EPA officials were aghast at this suggestion, Larson reported. This bald-faced effort to roll back pollution-control mechanisms backfired, Larson said, and the EPA sent out elite teams from the National Environmental Inspection Council to see how accurate industries' monitoring of their valves actually was. What they found was that refinery workers were holding the air monitors too far from the valves to collect proper readings. As a result they consistently reported lower levels of emissions from their valves than EPA enforcement inspectors found. A report was released which said that the underreported emissions from 17 refineries monitored was equivalent to the emissions one could anticipate from a quarter-million cars idling on the highway. In short, they were gaming the regulatory process, Larson said, and they were caught.

Refinery managers also complained that, when the various sectors covered by the Common Sense Initiative process were compared, petroleum plants were always rated as the worst environmental performers and targeted as the top priority for enforcement action. Here the demand by industry lobbyists that the regulatory process be better targeted came back to bite the refinery operators. They had asked for more targeted inspection and when comparisons were done about which companies were the worst offenders, refinery operators ended up at the center of a regulatory bull's-eye.

The facilitator of the process was clearly having a hard time persuading the various stakeholders to stop making outrageous charges against each other and get down to the business of negotiating marginal improvements that might be made to the process upon which they could all agree. Other sectors of CSI were making substantial progress while the refinery sector was stuck in an adversarial deadlock. To try to clear the logjam, the facilitator suggested at the start of one meeting that each stakeholder take a few minutes to tell other participants about their most recent vacation. The idea was that if the participants came to know each other better and see each other as real people they might develop enough trust to begin to seek compromise.

Stakeholders readily complied by describing their recent most vacation trip to see their granddaughters. Some told about exotic cruises and beach vacations. But when Diamond resident Margie Richard, the only stakeholder from a refinery-impacted community, was asked to tell about her last vacation, "she starts telling about people dying and getting sick in her neighborhood. She just lays it on the line . . . and throws in a couple of biblical references because she is a very religious person and that is the foundation of where she is coming from," Larson recalled. When Richard finished there was silence in the room. "She was a show-stopper. At every single meeting when she decided to say something it really shook up the decorum," Larson recalled. And while, on the one hand, this meant that some people did not take her seriously, because she was not following the narrative thread of the meeting, on the other hand a number of people were scared of her because they did not know what would come out of her mouth next.

"I spoke off the agenda," Richard conceded. "They were playing with people's lives, so when it got to me I said 'Lord, you have opened this door for me so I have to make a difference. I can't waste time; I may not be back.' . . . So I told them that where they lived they could go out and enjoy their backyards but where I lived when I go out I see a multi-million-dollar [chemical] company [next door]. . . . So I decided to turn the tide by talking about people coughing and I saw it was an opportune time for me to do it because all the big people were at the table. If I didn't come back at least they couldn't say that they hadn't heard the truth."

Despite the apparent impasse between the stakeholders, it was during one of the Common Sense Initiative meetings that chemist Wilma Subra first saw that Shell was willing "to open the door a little bit," she said. Subra was appearing on enough panels with one Shell official that the two of them came to know each other quite well. "In the beginning," the official from Shell's headquarters in Houston later said, "Wilma and I hated each other and didn't trust each other," but over time he came to see that they could work together. That official, Subra said, eventually became one of her "greatest supporters." At one point he turned to her and asked what Diamond residents really wanted. She told him that many of them wanted to be relocated. After thinking for a while, he asked "Well, what will it take?"

Yet at the Common Sense Initiative meetings Shell officials and Diamond residents remained hopelessly deadlocked on the big issues having to do with the health impact of industrial pollutants on the residents. Even agreement on small issues remained elusive. In a last-ditch attempt to find anything, however trivial, that all parties could agree upon, Subra and Richard asked Shell and Motiva officials to make a copy of their emissions release report available locally so that residents would not have to drive all the way to the state's environmental regulatory headquarters in Baton Rouge to see what chemicals were being released into the air they breathed. They suggested that a copy of the report be placed in a local public library. Shell officials said that sounded possible, but Larson noted that it never actually happened.

10
First Moves

As the grassroots campaign for relocation intensified and Concerned Citizens of Norco became more effective at airing grievances through the media, Shell officials began to feel the pressure. On November 29, 1999, they met face-to-face with Diamond residents on community turf for the first time. About a year later, after decades of ignoring resident demands for relocation, Shell officials offered to buy some 75 lots in Diamond belonging to the residents who lived closest to their facilities on Washington and Cathy Streets—about half the community. A similar offer was tendered to some 40 homeowners near the fenceline on the white side of Norco.

The rationalization for the change in the company's previous resistance to relocation was that Shell needed a larger buffer around its plants. "A long time ago, about thirty years ago, we recognized that it was not good to have people directly on the fenceline. We needed a buffer," said Shell spokesman David Brignac. The decision to create a buffer had nothing to do with either accidents or pollution from the plant, Brignac asserted.[1] "From the company's standpoint our vision was always that we want this space to provide a noise buffer and a visual buffer between us and the community. We think that is important from a nuisance standpoint."

Officially called the Norco Voluntary Fenceline Property Purchase Program, the plan included an offer from Shell to buy any property on the first two streets in Diamond and Norco along the fenceline. In Diamond that meant that Shell officials simply drew a line on the map that split the community in half: those properties on the front two streets Shell would attempt to buy out; those on the back two streets were of no commercial interest to the company. In practical terms what this meant was that 129 families in Diamond were left out of the program.[2]

While it was difficult for residents to understand why Shell would offer to buy half their community and leave the other half to breathe their fumes, there was a certain corporate logic to this offer. Shell was already in the process of purchasing the homes on the first two streets of Diamond closest to their fenceline whenever they came on the market in an effort to create a buffer zone around the Shell facilities. The Voluntary Property Purchase Program simply accelerated the purchase of properties in this area and alerted residents on the first two streets of Diamond and Norco that Shell stood ready to purchase their homes whenever they chose to sell.[3]

Diamond residents have another version of what was actually going on. Since the mid 1970s, Shell had been buying up lots in Diamond on the cheap as they became available. Shell purchased 13 wooden homes for an average of $20,908 and 7 brick homes for an average cost of $40,529, while empty lots went for an average of $9,560. Since 1977, according to a publication titled Shell Games, Shell had purchased 48 of the 269 lots in Diamond, at an average price of $26,933.[4] With few buyers willing to purchase a home in Diamond, Shell was able to pick up properties along the fenceline at bargain-basement prices. One home they did not succeed in buying was that of Deloris Brown, the daughter of a former Shell employee. They offered her only $20,000.

Monique Harden, former staff attorney at EarthJustice, suspected that Shell's decision to create a buffer zone around its plant might date from the 1973 explosion, although she conceded this theory remains impossible to prove. What is clear, however, is that Shell's quiet policy of buying out residents on the two streets closest to the property line for minimal amounts meant that residents who sold to Shell would have to have gone into debt to buy a home elsewhere, Harden asserted.

Shell officials rejected the charge that they were "landsharking" in Diamond and insisted that they were just purchasing properties at market prices. This explanation, however, ignored the fact that Shell could buy these properties cheaply because their facilities had dramatically lowered property values in the area. In effect the company had been able to buy the properties on their fenceline for minimal amounts by creating a nuisance that brought down property values, residents asserted. Determined to ignore past history and to focus on the new Fenceline Property Purchase Program, Brignac touted Shell's generous terms. Properties on the first two streets closest to their fenceline were assessed and raised by 30 percent. Concerned

Citizens of Norco negotiated with Shell over how properties would be assessed. Eventually a deal was worked out whereby assessors, instead of using comparable properties along the fenceline to determine the values of properties in Diamond, chose properties of a similar size in central (white) Norco. Furthermore, no property was to be graded as worse than average. The end result was that an uninhabited 1,200-square-foot structure in Diamond that was falling apart was assessed at $80,000, Brignac noted. In addition, owners were offered $5,000 in moving expenses. Residents could also choose to receive $5,000–$7,000 from Shell to hire someone to bulldoze and remove their home, and they could keep the balance after paying for the expense of the removal. The same offer was also made to residents of Good Hope and Norco Streets on the white side of town.

"We may not have gotten everything we wanted but I commend David Brignac because he opened the door and he began to talk and to listen," observed Margie Richard, former president of Concerned Citizens of Norco.

Asked why Shell offered to buy out only half of Diamond, Brignac responded "That is the $6 million question." The short answer is that Shell has no business interest in buying the back two streets because the purchase of the first two streets will provide a wide enough buffer for the company's purposes, he continued. Besides, just in terms of the costs of the program, while there are only about 60 homes remaining on the first two streets, there are approximately 160 homes on the back two streets, Brignac added. But it was more important that Shell be even-handed, he said. It would not be fair for Shell to buy four streets on the black side of town and only two streets on the white side of town.. And if Shell purchased properties on the four streets in Norco on the white side of town it would impinge on the central business district and destroy the economic backbone of the town, he argued. Buying out hundreds of residents would threaten the integrity of the town and generate a lot of anger and opposition from the residents who like living in Norco and do not want to see the town destroyed, he added. That was a pitfall Shell officials were determined to avoid.

Former Shell employee Sal Digirolamo supports Brignac's point. An ardent supporter of Shell, Digirolamo was nevertheless angry at the company for agreeing to pay to relocate some of the residents of the two streets nearest the fenceline in Diamond: "Shell made a mistake, I think, in buying the first house. Now it [the buyout] is never going to stop. . . . They are destroying a piece of Norco when they started buying out streets. And I did not like it at all. . . . I hate to see my community torn apart like that. . . . We will never have another Diamond in Norco."

Faced with a racially divided community, Shell found itself in a no-win situation where it had to make a decision that would alienate either one side or the other. If it were to give in to the demands of the residents of Diamond that they be relocated, the company would inevitably anger a large number of residents on the white side of town who did not want to see their town diminished. Shell wanted to do right by local residents, said Brignac: "We are committed to the long-term future of Norco and Diamond. . . . But it is not always clear to us how you proceed and maintain our relationship with the larger community."

Relative to other oil and chemical companies on the Gulf Coast, Shell was in the forefront of devoting money and staff time to finding a resolution to tensions with residents who live along their fenceline, said Brignac: "We want a good solution. We recognize that there is still a lot of tension. . . . We have been grappling with this for over a year now."

"I don't think there are bad intentions on any side," Brignac said. "There is a firm disagreement between some of the residents of Diamond and Shell, but I don't think it is because they are bad people or greedy people. When I look at Shell I think there is a genuine intention to want to do what is right for Norco and Diamond. . . . Norco as a community is tied to the success of Shell . . . and the success of Shell is tied to the success of the community. So we have a strong commitment to the community of Norco . . . the whole community."

Those who negotiated with David Brignac during this period admired him most for two traits. He was willing to listen to the residents of Diamond in a way that no representative of Shell ever had before. "Brignac did keep the door open. . . . Whether we agreed or disagreed he was not afraid. . . . He and his relocation team they listened to us and got the feedback. No longer was it one-sided: now it was listening and speaking," observed Margie Richard. "One of the things I appreciate about David," commented Dr. Robert Thomas (a journalism professor and naturalist who tried to play a mediating role between industrialists and environmental activists), "is that he doesn't sit there and sweet talk people to the point where they don't understand what he is saying."

When first asked about relocation, Brignac simply said "No, the company wouldn't do that. That is not negotiable." Though it eventually turned out that relocation was negotiable, Brignac was straight with people about what the company's position was at the time even if it meant that he had to sit there and take the heat for it.

"I can put myself in the shoes of someone living in Diamond. . . . If I am living on Diamond or East Streets and I am an African-American and I don't work for Shell nor do my relatives, I can begin too understand why I wouldn't like Shell," Brignac said. "Somehow we can't get beyond that. We want to say 'If you give us a chance we are going to really help you.'" Shell is sincere about wanting to address some of the inequities that have been in the area historically and the company is willing to spend serious money on these issues, he continued. "[T]he company is not blind. We know that there are socio-economic issues in Diamond. When you ride through Diamond it becomes immediately obvious that the homes are not as nice as in this [Diamond] part of Norco. But do you solve these problems by moving people? "I don't think so." Instead, Shell sponsored an educational assessment of Diamond and designed some programs to help both children and adults in the community, Brignac said. With input from the community and a variety of experts, Shell planned to spend $375,000 for an Adult Learning Center on Apple Street and an Even Start program for children.

To improve the quality of life of Diamond's residents, Shell was also considering a program offering loans of up to $10,000 so that residents could fix up their homes. These loans would be forgiven at the rate of $2,000 a year, so that if one stayed in the community for another 5 years one would owe the company nothing, Brignac said. "That is a way we could really demonstrate that we are serious: we want to help people, we want to improve their quality of life, and we are serious about being a good neighbor."

"There is a history here with Diamond where many [residents] are convinced that they can never be happy here. We don't believe that means that nobody can be happy here," Brignac continued, because so many people were moving into homes elsewhere in the community. In fact, new homes were being built in Norco that were closer to the plant than some of the homes in Diamond, he pointed out.

In addition to these incentives for residents to stay and fix up their homes, Shell and Motiva each contributed $500,000 for the purpose of starting a community trust fund. The goal of these contributions was to improve the quality of life in Norco, Brignac said. A committee of local residents would determine how the money would be spent. In 2001 some of the funds were used for jaws-of-life rescue equipment, home visits promoting literacy, outdoor lighting for the baseball field, and reviving the Christmas parade, Brignac noted. Shell intends to help establish job training, air monitoring, and help with a residential committee to develop a master plan for Norco, he continued. Shell also promised to improve the environmental performance of their facilities by decreasing their Toxic Release Inventory emissions by 30 percent over three years and their flaring by 50 percent.[5]

Representative Maxine Waters

One visitor to Diamond who was not impressed with Shell's decision to buyout only half of the community was Representative Maxine Waters. Waters was serving her sixth term in the U.S. House of Representatives and had chaired the Congressional Black Caucus. One of 13 children raised by a single mother in St. Louis, Waters began work at age 13 in factories and segregated restaurants before moving to Los Angeles and earning a Bachelor of Arts degree at California State University. With this background, she could easily relate to the experience of Diamond residents.

In a letter to Steven Miller, CEO of the Shell Oil Company,[6] Representative Waters said:

I am writing to reiterate what I think is in the best interests of the citizens of Norco and Concerned Citizens of Norco. Specifically, we are seeking the buyout of all four streets of the Diamond community, the community directly and severely impacted by toxins produced by Shell Oil Company. As you should be aware, Shell currently operates a toxic chemical plant just across a small one-lane road from the front doors of the all-African-American Diamond community. As a result of frequent chemical leaks and spills, as well as toxic chemicals that are spewed out into the air on a daily basis by Shell, those residents want to leave. They do not desire a "greenbelt" or other proposed refurbishments of their community.

Shell Oil Company's current plan to create a "greenbelt" and to address noise pollution is a clear example of Shell's insensitivity in ignoring the very real health threats that its chemical facility creates for African-American people throughout the Diamond community. Shell refuses to acknowledge that no development plan can change the fact that its chemical plant is a danger to all the residents in that community.

Shell's buyout plan of only two streets in the Diamond community disregards the life-and-death issues for the residents of that community. Residents routinely have to rush their children and grandchildren to hospital emergency rooms because they are suffering from asthma attacks, some of which require hospitalization. Both old and young people have to rely on oxygen tanks and prescription medicines to cope with Shell's toxic fumes. These people live on all four streets of the Diamond community, not just the two streets included in Shell's current buyout plan. In addition, Shell's chemical plant has devalued properties in the Diamond community. . . . I am disappointed by the tenor of your letter and strongly request that you reconsider its poor decision to limit the buyout to two of the four streets in the Diamond community.[7]

Divide and Conquer

Diamond residents were stunned by the Voluntary Property Purchase Program. For years Shell officials had told them that a relocation program was not on the negotiating table. Now suddenly the company had made a relocation offer, albeit to only half of the community.

Diamond residents had effectively forced Shell to come up with a relocation plan. But it really was only half a victory, and now Concerned Citizens of Norco confronted a whole new set of issues, the most important of which was that the Shell offer did not extend to the whole community. Equally aggravating to some residents, Shell had once again concocted a program for Diamond without their input.

For years, former Diamond resident Gaynel Johnson recalled, Shell officials had refused to attend meeting of Concerned Citizens of Norco in Diamond. The Shell officials who did come to Diamond would just target a couple of residents, talk with them, and conclude they had read the pulse of the community, Johnson continued. "That is what is messed up. You target two or three people in the community and talk with them. . . . You didn't knock on nobody's door and talk to them individually. . . . Did you go and ask each one of the people if they wanted to be relocated? No, because if you had they would have told you [that they wanted to be relocated]." Everyone has his or her own opinion, Johnson continued. "Gaynel talks for herself. I can't speak for my neighbor, my neighbor can't speak for her neighbor, in fact I can't even speak for my uncle.'

That Shell officials refused to meet with Concerned Citizens of Norco in Diamond was significant, Anne Rolfes observed. Until April 2001, all the meetings between Shell officials and Diamond residents had taken place in facilities owned by Shell. "Shell had always controlled the meetings by dictating the time and place," said Rolfes. "It was always convenient for [Shell officials], regardless of the needs of the working people of Diamond

... and ... it was always on their turf, which of course was intimidating. ...." Furthermore, Rolfes asserted, Shell made sure that these meetings were by invitation only, and excluded many of the Diamond residents who were most active in lobbying for relocation.

David Brignac admitted that Shell officials were worried about going into Diamond: "I don't exactly know why, but part of it is human nature: you don't want to go into a place where you know you are not going to get a good reception. ... It was like going into a place where you were not welcome and people were very distrusting. There was a fear on the part of Shell to go in, so in a lot of cases they didn't. That was not an easy wall to bring down."

In April 2001, Shell held its first meeting in Diamond. The meeting took place at night so that people with day jobs would be able to attend. Since the meeting hall was without electricity, extension cords were run from neighboring houses and makeshift lighting was set up.

Shell's first offer to move the two streets of Diamond residents closest to its plant's had been proffered in the autumn of 2000, so this meeting provided families of the back two streets of residents who had been excluded from the relocation program a chance to plead their case. One resident described a situation in which an elderly woman who lived in the excluded portion of Diamond would be left all alone while her children who lived on the front two streets would be moved. This would separate her from her children, who had shopped for her and had taken her to the hospital when necessary. Brignac suggested that perhaps an exception could be made to relocate this woman and her children. Once he uttered these words, Anne Rolfes noted, the "exceptions policy" was put into play. It was a very human moment, Rolfes added. Brignac was moved by the story and wanted to help. "The corporate shield was set aside for a moment," Rolfes observed.

Clearly the first meeting in Diamond with residents was difficult for David Brignac. "The first few meetings we had were tense," Brignac recalled. The meetings were very good but painful, he continued. "When people sit down and are serious about talking and are serious about trying to listen to one another, good things happen," he said.

"My [question]," said Margie Richard, "has always been 'Why didn't Shell get input from everybody earlier—way back—even before the

Voluntary Purchase Program?' They should have been communicating with the community all along to find out how people felt."

The most egregious part of Shell's offering to buy out half the population of Diamond was that it divided families who had lived next to each other and helped each other over the years, Diamond residents explained. "My twin brother, who lived directly behind me, sold to Shell," said Lois Parquet, 58, who has lived in Diamond all her life and has taught social studies at Destrehan High School for 30 years. Shell was taking "a segment of our family away from the nuisance" but was "going to let us stay here and continually be exposed to it," she observed.

Seeing that Shell was vulnerable to the accusation that it had callously excluded half of the Diamond community from the relocation program, Anne Rolfes and other environmental justice activists put out a publication, titled Shell Divides Families, that documented the relocation program's divisive effect on some Diamond families. They also posted heart-wrenching stories on the Internet. From a public relations perspective, this was not the message that Shell officials wanted to be circulated.

Faced with an offer to sell their homes to Shell and move to a cleaner, safer community, a number of the residents on the first two streets of Diamond jumped at the chance. Margie Richard and her ailing mother moved to a beautiful brick home in an integrated neighborhood in Destrehan, a 15-minute drive from Diamond.

Those who were left out of the deal were quick to note that Shell had managed to buy off many of the most vociferous activists by agreeing to move residents of the first two streets. As one resident said, Shell was glad to see Margie Richard leave town: "They just wanted to shut her up." Monique Harden echoes this suspicion: "I have been told by people in pretty connected positions with Shell that they understood that the reason to move the people on Cathy and Washington Streets was to get rid of the loudmouths and activists."

Shell was also able to effectively divide the town because of CCN's inability to recruit activists from the back two streets. Margie Richard, when going from door to door on Diamond Street and East Street trying to get people to come out and support the relocation struggle, had run into a kind of fatalism. The residents just did not believe Shell would ever relocate them, she reported. Their experience with Shell had been disappointing, and so they saw no point in fighting for relocation. "We want to go," residents of the back two streets told Richard, "but we know they are not going to include us." As a result, Richards noted, "turnout from the back two streets was very low during the whole struggle." It was only when residents of the first two streets won relocation and were made reasonable offers for their homes that those on the back two streets suddenly realized they also might have a chance. Richard regretted that the residents of the back streets did not organize earlier to demand relocation, but she felt compelled to take the deal for her family. Despite her decision to move, Richard emphasized that she never gave up the struggle to relocate all the residents of Diamond who wanted to leave.

Offering a buyout to only half the residents of Diamond divided a tight-knit historically black community that had roots going back to plantation days. It tore the social fabric that had enabled many low-income families to survive, and it split families and friends. Newly energized activists on the back two streets protested the dividing of their community. It was unfair and it didn't make sense, they argued. They were all subject to the same pollution and danger from explosion. Residents of the back two streets were just as prone to the ill effects of Shell's pollution as residents of the first two streets, and the 1988 explosion had damaged homes on the back two streets just as much as those on the front two streets. But Shell officials objected to this logic. They claimed that they were not offering to relocate people because of any pollution or danger of explosion from their plants. Brignac argued that Shell was meeting federal and state pollution regulations, that Shell's permit to operate had not been revoked, and that since the 1988 explosion Shell's safety record had been exemplary. The relocation program was simply the belated implementation of a 30-year-old Shell plan to expand the buffer zone around the facility, he reiterated.

"I think Shell's strategy is to divide and conquer, because they have taken families and split them apart," said Audrey Eugene, who lived in a handsome white-brick house on the wrong side of the relocation line.

Diamond residents have a remarkable capacity to cut to the heart of an issue, particularly when it affects them deeply. Margie Richard put it succinctly: "Because of the amount of pollution and the way it travels through the air you can't put a stop sign on pollution." Audrey Eugene agreed: "I am smelling the same thing as the people on those two streets [that are being relocated]. . . . Where is Shell's moral sense? Why are they doing this? The

Shell company is a multi-billion-dollar company and I'm quite sure that buying these few little properties is not going to break them. They can afford it." Janie Campbell had a similar opinion: "I can't understand how they think there is a shield between Cathy Street [where Shell is relocating people] and this street [where they are not]. Is there a . . . shield from the sky all the way down to the bottom? The same thing they get [i.e. pollution], we got it too. And if Shell said that they are not buying up homes here to protect people from their pollution I would ask them 'Do you want to swap homes for two days?' . . . I would let them live for two days in Norco and see what the pollution is. . . ." Campbell invoked the power of prayer to solve the community's dilemma: "I hope they will listen to us. I hope through the good Lord that they will listen to us and understand where we are coming from. . . . I just pray to God that God can open their heart and they can realize what we have been going through for years here and that it is just time for them to do something to help us. That is my prayer. . . . I know there is a God and I hope God is going to open their heart up. He is going to open it up . . . and they are going to do what is right."

A Tight-Knit Community

Residents of Diamond had strong ties to one another for a number of reasons, including shared bloodlines branching back to plantation days, the community's racial isolation, and the number of residents who went to school together.

Most residents of Diamond come from families that lived on this land generation after generation. This is typical of Louisiana, where people are statistically more likely to settle near where they grew up than are people in other states. In fact, sociologists describe communities such as Diamond as among the most stable populations in the history of North America.[8] Natives of Louisiana tend not to wander very far from their roots, and many of them settle close to their parents and friends. Those who try moving away report that they never found elsewhere the same kind of quality of life and closeness with neighbors that they experienced at home. This sense of community can be found in both black and white communities in Louisiana, but it is particularly intense in Diamond, where families and friends grew up together relatively isolated from the outside world. Diamond residents were hemmed in by industrial plants that refused to hire them and a white population that did not welcome them. There was not much room for the community to expand, so residents bonded within the community. Alumni of Mary Bethune High School continued to live in the neighborhood after graduation; a few even married classmates. As a result, it is not unusual to find grandmothers in Diamond who have known one another since childhood.

Devaliant Cole said he valued the sense of closeness he had with his neighbors: "I know everybody down the street in this area. I can walk down and talk to Stormy . . . or the brick house across the street is one of my best friend's grandmother's house. I always go over and check on her. I walk over there and say 'Mrs. Carter, how are you doing? Troy is talking about you.' And she says 'He always talk about me but he never call.' She gets a little peeved but I know he is calling her all the time." Then there is Cole's best friend from fourth grade, Eddie. Now a truck driver, Eddie is often at Cole's mother's house. Members of the community are so close that they have long disciplined one another's children or threatened to tell on them if they saw them misbehaving. "Troy's grandmother, when we were younger, she probably whipped me more than my mama did," said Cole. "Now you beat someone's kid and you will go to jail for 150 years. . . . I told one of the kids on the corner 'You can cut up all you want, but I am going to tell your daddy.' We have that closeness. Somebody told me that it takes a village to raise a child. That is true."

Cole is angry that Shell is bisecting the community by buying homes on the two front streets and skipping the back two streets. "It was a bad thing just to split up the neighborhood like that," Cole said. Shell would never have tried to split a white community, he continued. "If Shell went into another neighborhood, especially a white neighborhood, people wouldn't go for it."

Instead of splitting the community, Shell should have moved it whole, Cole argued. While the younger people will be able to adjust to life in a new location without the support of the Diamond network of relationships, the older generation, particularly those on fixed incomes, those living alone, and those who cannot read, will have a very hard time adjusting, he explained. "They need their neighbors for when they need a letter read. Here they can go to a neighbor [and say] 'Here, can you read this for me . . . ?'" Ernestine Roberts agrees: "With my lifeline being here it is kind of hard to pick up and go. . . . When you have been rooted in a place 50 years it is kind of hard to pick up and say 'OK, I'm gone.' . . . If I have to move out of here, it is going to take a mental and emotional toll on me. . . . I love my church, I love the people in my church because they are people from here. . . . I love my pastor, and it would be hard for me to leave my church." Shell is "taking families and breaking them up and sending them all over the place," Roberts continued. "When they [Shell] decided to uproot these people, I believe they should have found a place where they could put these people back as neighbors and family."

Some families are facing hard choices because Shell offers to move one member but not another. Such is the case with Delwyn Smith, 50, and her 74-year-old mother, who lives on one of the streets eligible for relocation. Smith's mother told Shell officials that she could not leave: "I will leave when you [relocate] my daughter. My daughter is all I have. She is my only child," she said. "I do all [my mother's] business," Smith explained. Wherever they move, they will have to live near each other, Smith continued. Smith's aunt, Luanda Charles, is in pretty much the same situation. It would be better, Smith suggested, if Shell "scoped out some property, developed it, and moved us all there." Smith was angry at Shell: "They dipped into the community which they shouldn't have ever done by buying up those two streets. Over there [on Cathy and Washington Street] it looks like a ghost town."

Dividing black families by purchasing only half the homes in Diamond has some unfortunate historical resonance dating back to slave days, when families were broken apart as slaves were sold to distant plantations. "Black folks have been separated [from their families] all their lives. . . . We want to stick together. I want to be around my family," said Brent Mashia, who moved to Diamond to live near his mother.

Also sensitive to the way in which the fabric of Diamond is unraveling is Lorita Jenkins, 62, a retired cafeteria worker who lives on the fourth street from the fenceline with the Shell Chemical plant. Jenkins faults Shell's two-street relocation plan for tearing the community apart: "I have members of my family who have moved from Washington and Cathy Streets [under the Shell relocation initiative]. I had friends who were in my wedding and we were in theirs [who moved]. . . . It is like we are scattering people all over: just like throwing dogs and cats out on the highway. It is like the town is just dead."

A tight-knit community has many benefits that are particularly critical to people who don't have a lot of cash. The network of relationships in

Diamond helps residents financially and in terms of the quality of their lives. The fact that residents can ask neighbors and friends to take care of their children after they returned from school permits many of them to take jobs out of town that keep them away from home until dinner time. Without this informal child-care arrangement many Diamond residents could not work. For example, Lois Gales, 52, took a job working for the Port of New Orleans. A graduate of Xavier College, Gales has four children and three grandchildren. A son and a granddaughter have asthma. In order to be able to work out of town, Gales had to arrange child care. While her children were growing up, a neighbor on Cathy Street, Mrs. Johnson, babysat all four.

"These people are related by blood, family, and marriage, and there is this really excellent network of people providing transportation for each other to the hospital, people taking care of children when their parents go off to work—all that is going on," observed Monique Harden, a former staff attorney at EarthJustice Legal Defense Fund.

Most residents I interviewed feel whipsawed by conflicting emotions about staying or leaving. On the one hand, they want to get out of Diamond to escape the pollution from the Shell plants; on the other hand, they want to stay because of the close ties they have with their neighbors. In view of the push and pull of these forces, most residents have decided that the environmental conditions are so distressing that despite their ties to the community they are ready to leave. Janie Campbell, for one, is torn about relocating: "This [picketing Shell] was not because we wanted to leave, because everybody loves their home where they have been for years, but when you can't stay you just can't. When you see water coming over the levee, you move." But neither Campbell nor most of her neighbors can leave unless they are bought out. "I couldn't go somewhere and pay rent," says Campbell. "I am not able to do that. I own this house and I've paid off this house. . . . I have two bedrooms, a kitchen, bathroom, and sitting room. I am happy and it is mine. I have everything I need . . . a washer/dryer. . . . And I keep it up. . . . I like a clean yard and a clean house. . . . Right now I live here by myself. All my children are gone. They all have their own place. I love my little home because I am used to it. It is not the house [that is the problem]. Everything is right where I can reach it. It is not that I want to move so I have a better house. No, no, no, no: that is not me. I just want to get out of here. . . . I am happy with my house. I am not happy where I am living. That is my problem."

The Racial Divide

For as long as anyone can remember, the African-American subdivision of Diamond has been separated from the larger white population of Norco by a long and narrow wooded strip of land that stretches from the levee to the railroad tracks. The property is known as the Gaspard Line, after the name of the owners.

"Let's be truthful," said Margie Richard. "You do have a split by race. From Apple Street on is predominantly white." There are about 3,000 whites in Norco and about 600 blacks in Diamond, she estimated. Gaynel Johnson made no bones about the racial divide: "Norco is a prejudice community. As you can see, the black are on this side and the white are on this side. It has been like this since I came out here." Others describe the racial dynamics in communities like Norco/Diamond as "stuck in a kind of 1940s time warp, with little overt racial animosity and little racial mixing."[9]

Whether one describes the race relations in Diamond/Norco as frozen in time or as ongoing geographic residential segregation, it is striking that people on the two sides of the color line have opposite views about why their community is split into two racially distinct sections. On the white side of the divide, some residents I interviewed claim that black people live together in Diamond because they want to. They also point out that there are a few black families that live on their side of the line while omitting the fact that there are no white families in Diamond. On the black side of the color line the view is different. People live in Diamond because this is where they were permitted to move when they were forced out of Belltown, residents explain. Those who came to Diamond more recently purchased homes here because the prices were low and they could afford to move in; those who made money often relocated elsewhere outside of Norco.

For generations the Gaspard property that divided the races was just a fact of life to people in Diamond, but some who moved into town found it strange that the community was so starkly divided, having come from places where the communities were more integrated. "I don't know why all the blacks live on one side of town and all the whites live on the other, but when I moved here that is the way it was. All of us were in one little [area] here, from the [railroad] track to the river, and we had these four little streets, and it was all black. They had the Gaspard Line in between us to divide us from the whites, you understand, and the whites were living over on the other side. Where I was living in La Place [before moving to Diamond] I had white people living near me . . . like a normal place. When I moved here I almost thought it was strange, you know . . . we were like all to ourselves and they were to themselves. We had our own black school right here where the swings are now," says Janie Campbell, who moved into Diamond in 1961.

The Gaspard Line is a part of the legacy of slavery and the Jim Crow era, observed Beverly Wright. For many years segregation was the law; subsequently it became a custom, Wright continued. "It will take a very long time for that to disappear," she predicted.

In the past some African-American residents of Diamond were reluctant to cross into the white side of Norco, where they felt unwelcome. Asked if he used to go into the white side of Norco when he was young, Brent Mashia dismissed the idea: "The police would pick you up. . . . You can't go over there. . . . You can't do nothing over there. They are a little racist. They don't believe in blacks going over there."

Though school integration has made important inroads into the old pattern of segregation and many blacks and whites now think little of crossing the color line, there are still aspects of the old-time prejudice that linger. Wendy Mashia, told two stories to illustrate the fact that the white side of town is still, in some ways, hostile to the presence of blacks.

The first story involved a call from a cousin of hers from Mississippi who is a long-haul truck driver like Wendy's husband Brent. Her cousin had just delivered a truckload of goods in the area, needed a place to spend the night, and asked if he could stay at Wendy and Brent's home. She said he was welcome to spend the night. After giving him what she thought were good directions about how to reach their house, she got a cell phone call from him. He was bobtailing (driving the truck without a trailer attached) and found himself lost on the wrong side of the tracks in the white part of Norco. "All of these white people are looking at me like I'm crazy," he reported. When he finally reached her house they both laughed about it, but then he said "Dang, they got all of you black folks here in a bowl." Previously Mashia had lived in a mixed-race community, but in Diamond the color line is clear. "I guess it is just one of those things," she said thoughtfully.

The second instance had happened just two years earlier, Mashia said. According to her daughter, the Norco school's cheerleading squad had been practicing outside when it started to rain. The teacher in charge of the squad inquired at the Sun Villa swimming club, a private club adjacent to the school, if they could temporarily use one of their roofed-in areas to finish their cheerleading practice. With her charges standing within earshot, the teacher was turned down. "No, only whites are allowed here," the teacher was allegedly told. "The little girls were devastated," Wendy Mashia recalled. "They had never experienced racism so thick like that. They were really in shock about that. . . . They knew from talk around the community that blacks weren't welcome but for someone to just tell you that to your face. . . . That was awful."

Not all residents of Diamond feel discriminated against in Norco. In fact there are many who went to school there and grew up in integrated classes who continue to have friendships with white schoolmates. They all noted, however, that after talking with their friends they all go home to geographically segregated neighborhoods. Jenny Taylor, 61, who has lived in Diamond all her life, does not see the problem as one of black and white: "The black people over here get along with the white people over there. That's not the problem at all." The real problem is that Shell "never did hire many blacks."

Another sign that some members of the white Norco community may retain some prejudicial reflexes from the old days is their willingness to generalize about how black residents of Diamond are just bellyaching about the problems of living next to Shell plants because they want to squeeze more money out of the corporation. This assertion is hotly contested in Diamond, where residents say they are hard-working Americans who have been wronged. Shell polluted their neighborhood, damaged their health, and reduced their property values. They just want what is fair. Shell has given them all the pollution and explosions but none of the benefits that those in Norco enjoy, they charge.

Diamond residents also have complaints about the way Shell has handled the racial division in their community. Local history is replete with instances where the African-American population of Diamond was treated shabbily by Shell officials, they continued. Their list of grievances ran as follows: To begin with, African-American residents of Belltown were pushed out of their homes and off their fields by Shell and given only token compensation. Then the few local blacks who were hired by Shell were given only menial jobs and not permitted to rise through the ranks as white employees could. Shell failed to desegregate its on-site recreational facilities. Shell continues to have a poor record of hiring out of the Diamond community. Finally, Shell split their community in half by offering to purchase only half the homes in Diamond. This is a tactic that Shell would not dare attempt in a white community, some residents argued.

Diamond residents also charged that Shell had been less than fair when compensating black residents for damage done to them by Shell facilities. First, Shell failed to provide adequate compensation for the families of the two Diamond residents killed in 1973, giving them only $500 and $3,000 respectively. Second, they alleged that Shell gave the white residents of Norco more than the black residents of Diamond after the explosion in 1988. There was also a long-standing policy of buying up properties on the first two streets of Diamond at bargain rates when residents moved out. It is only more recently, after Diamond residents organized and fought for higher prices, that those being relocated have gotten a fair price, they pointed out.

In fact, Shell being cheap with the black residents of Diamond is part of a long-term pattern, said Wendy Mashia. For example, when Shell laid a pipeline next to the home of Diamond residents they didn't pay them much either: "When Shell was laying pipe they gave those old folks little or nothing because those old folks don't know what is going on and half of them didn't know how to read or write . . . and they just came and swindled [them]." Now the people are saying that they don't want to tolerate it anymore, she explained. Shell offers people very little for their homes and then makes life impossible for them with its fumes, she continued. "It didn't just start happening the other day, and I guess the younger generation is just fed up with it," she said.

One long-festering complaint about Shell is that the company failed to dismantle segregation in its own facilities in a timely manner. When Shell had workers living in housing on company property, the plant had a variety of recreational facilities, including a swimming pool, a bowling alley, a gymnasium, and a movie theater. These facilities, however, were not available to the families of black employees. The closest young black men got to these facilities was being hired to set pins at the bowling alley. "My children used to go over there [to Shell] and stick them in holes for people bowling. They couldn't bowl themselves," said Josephine Bering, whose father worked for Shell during those days.

gie Richard (standing) and her mother, Mabel Eugene. Photograph courtesy of Lousiana
et Brigade.

esentative Maxine Waters (left) and Margie Richard (center) at a relocation victory
ration. Photograph courtesy of Lousiana Bucket Brigade.

A swing set along the fenceline with the Shell Chemical plant. Photograph courtesy Lousiana Bucket Brigade.

Young men playing basketball along the fenceline in Diamond. Photograph courtesy Lousiana Bucket Brigade.

rge Eugene (front, center) on his porch with members of his family. Photograph courtesy
ousiana Bucket Brigade.

Bessie Smith taking an air sample in her yard. Photograph courtesy of Lousiana Bu
Brigade.

Diamond residents and allies outside Shell's headquarters in New Orleans, deman
relocation. Photograph courtesy of Lousiana Bucket Brigade.

A young protester from Diamond. Photograph courtesy of Lousiana Bucket Brigade.

...nond residents protesting ...'s purchase of the Gaspard ... Photograph courtesy of ...siana Bucket Brigade.

...ond children protesting against Shell. Photograph courtesy of Lousiana Bucket Brigade.

Members of the Diamond Division of the Louisiana Bucket Brigade. Photograph courte[...]
Lousiana Bucket Brigade.

Margie Richard. Photograph by Steve Lerner.

Josephine Bering. Photograph
by Steve Lerner.

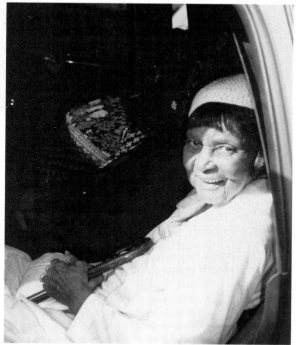

Jones riding in a limousine
g a celebration in her honor
amond. Photograph courtesy
usiana Bucket Brigade.

Iris Brown Carter. Photograph by Steve Lerner.

Gaynel Johnson. Photograph by S Lerner.

Larry Brown. Photograph by Steve Lerner.

Major Sampson, who grew up setting pins at Shell, thinks the company missed an opportunity to help integrate the town and reach across the racial divide. "With the bowling alley we could have bowled together," he said a bit wistfully. Instead he made a little money racking pins. Short of blacks bowling with whites during that period, Shell could at least have let their black employees bowl sometimes, he added.

"When Shell built its swimming pool, bowling alley, and all that," former Shell employee Janie Campbell recalled, "I never went there, and none of my kids did. My kids would swim in the spillway, and I used to beat them half to death because I was afraid they would get drowned. We never had a swimming pool, but Shell had a swimming pool and a bowling alley. . . . The only thing we ever had was the three little swings we have now and the basketball hoops. And before that we had nothing. . . . People feel bad about not being able to use the swimming pool, bowling alley or get jobs at Shell."

Shell has not tried to resolve the racial divide in Norco, commented former EarthJustice attorney Monique Harden, "and in some ways they were in the best position to do so because they control a lot in terms of the social fabric of the community." The way Shell handled hiring and the way the dealt with discrimination on the job site could have sent a very strong message to the rest of the community about what was acceptable. At least by the 1970s they could have made it clear that the nation had entered a new period of integration and opportunity. But Shell missed its chance, and instead segregation became more entrenched in Norco than in other communities in Louisiana, she continued. By the 1970s, Harden contended, "how the race issue was handled was tied to jobs."

When queried about reports that Shell's Norco facilities had been segregated in the past, spokesman David Brignac said "I don't know it firsthand, but I wouldn't doubt that it is true." Asked if Shell should admit that it made a mistake in segregating its facilities, Brignac replied as follows: "I have never seen the corporation come forward and say 'Yeah, we did some things that by today's standards were totally wrong and we admit it.'" Even researching the question is difficult, because most of the employees who worked at Shell at the time are now retired, Brignac continued. Reflecting on the question further, he said "Maybe we should go back and research our history and make some statements. . . . You have a lot of distrust and a lot of bad memories [about segregation] but I guess the hope is we can overcome some of this stuff." Shell is now committed to diversity, fairness, and treating people with dignity, Brignac continued. "So I think we are getting our act straight in terms of those things. But how do we overcome our past and not just our past, but the past of Louisiana and its history of segregation? To be blunt, you don't solve the kind of distrust and [racial] separation issues you have in Norco very quickly."

Brignac took issue, however, with those who describe the situation of Diamond residents along the fenceline with the Shell and Motiva facilities as a classic "environmental justice" case in which low-income African-Americans are living immediately adjacent to a highly polluting industry. That is not the case in Norco because 80 percent of the population is white, Brignac argued. While technically accurate, this answer failed to acknowledge, as Brignac did elsewhere, that Diamond and Norco were really two segregated communities separated by a deliberately maintained corridor of brush and trees. Thus, while Norco (including the subdivision of Diamond) was only 20 percent black, the community of Diamond was 100 percent black and was immediately adjacent to the Shell Chemical plant.

The Gaspard Line

Although Diamond residents have long seen the Gaspard Line (the wooded property that separates the black from the white communities in Norco) as evidence of a continuing pattern of racial discrimination, the issue did not become explosive until August 2001, when Shell purchased the property without warning residents of Diamond of its intentions.

The purchase of the Gaspard property outraged Diamond residents. As they saw it, after offering to buy out residents on the first two streets of Diamond to create a buffer, Shell officials said that they had no interest in purchasing any more land in their community. Then company officials went back on their word, skipped over two inhabited streets (where many of the residents were agitating to be relocated by Shell), and bought the Gaspard property. Some Diamond residents said this proved that Shell was duplicitous. "They [Shell officials] are not trustworthy. . . . They said they were going to do one thing and they did something altogether different. So they aren't thinking about us. They are just doing it for what is in it for them," fumed Carolyn Cole, a resident of Diamond for 30 years. Others saw Shell's action as disrespectful. "You [Shell] disregard me," said Ernestine Roberts, whose house Shell had declined to buy. "I ain't nobody. I'm nothing."

Gaynel Johnson also felt slighted. The purchase of the Gaspard property demonstrated that "grass and trees is more important to you [Shell] than I am," she said. The purchase also made residents feel further encircled by their powerful industrial neighbor. Shell has finally "boxed us in" or "penned us in," they complained.

"I have been here 50 years and sucked up all their fumes and now all of a sudden they want to buy the area behind me. That really confused me. It confused and angered me: a little bit of both. I couldn't understand how they all of a sudden got the property after saying they weren't buying anything else and all of a sudden they buy this strip of land. This was a buffer zone that looked like it separated the blacks from the whites in the first situation, and then they come back and buy it to keep us from moving anywhere. . . . It's too phony to me," observed Larry Brown.

Dewayne Washington, 40, who lived on East Street right along the Gaspard Line, was also dubious about Shell's plans. A broad-shouldered, outgoing man who works as a federal grain inspector, Washington said that a Shell spokesman told him that building a park along the Gaspard Line would help bring blacks and whites together. "I hear Shell say that they are going to try to unite everyone together when they bought the Gaspard Line [property] back there," he said, "but that is the buffer zone between whites and blacks. . . . Realistically I don't think cleaning up the bushes and putting up a park is integrating the neighborhood. . . . It is just [creating] a park that is separating black from white."

Trees on the Gaspard Line property were deliberately allowed to grow up in order to create a physical barrier between blacks and whites, claimed Devon Washington, a refinery worker. "You see that tree line on the Gaspard property? That has never been cut. If I let the trees and bushes on my property grow up ten feet like that I would have to cut it. So it is a deliberate barrier," he said. Washington doubts that Shell will cut the trees because if they did people on the adjacent streets on the white side of town would start selling their homes as the barrier between the races was eliminated.

The purchase of the Gaspard property was Shell's "greatest tactical error," observed Anne Rolfes, who was in Diamond when the decision was announced. The failure of Shell officials to walk the Diamond neighborhood and keep their finger on the pulse of public opinion caused kept them from fully appreciating what a hot-button issue the purchase of the property would be for residents, Rolfes said.

As an organizer, Rolfes jumped on this opportunity. She produced a big sign that read "Say No to Shell's Toxic Park. Why is Shell Buying Trees and Ignoring our Pleas? Relocation for all Diamond Now." The sign (in Shell's red and gold colors) was put up along the Gaspard Line. Then Rolfes and members of Concerned Citizens of Norco prepared a news release and invited the media to a protest. They brought folding chairs for some of the older members of the community (including Janie Campbell and Josephine Bering, who had begun their protest against Shell 30 years earlier).

At the press conference, residents who had previously felt the situation was hopeless and had become apathetic suddenly became angry and determined to force Shell to relocate the residents on the back two streets, Rolfes recalled. There was a dramatic turnaround in the way people felt about Shell, she continued. The purchase of the Gaspard property had a radicalizing effect on residents, she added.

Among those who began to speak up was Larry Brown, who began to ask publicly why Shell was buying the land and building walking paths instead of offering to buy him out. What good would a "toxic park" do him, he asked reporters? The park fails to address the fundamental problem Diamond residents confront, namely pollution from the Shell plants, he pointed out. "If the chemicals were killing me ten years ago and now they are going to build a park with flowers all around," he asked, "what is that supposed to do? Purify the air so I can breathe better?"

Shell officials admit that they did not handle the situation well and that they now recognize they should have explained their reasons for buying the property to the residents of Diamond before the purchase. Shell purchased the property for business reasons, said spokesman David Brignac. The company was worried that the owners might sell or lease the batture rights they had to the land (between the levee and the river) to a barge company. Having a number of barges tied up next to Shell's dock at Norco would make it difficult to safely maneuver the oil tankers coming in to Shell's refinery, so Shell made an offer on the property. Shell officials were told by the owners, however, that if they wanted the batture land by the river they would have to also purchase the rest of the strip of land, about 11½ acres in all, that had historically separated blacks from whites along the Norco/Diamond border. Shell agreed and purchased the property for $158,000.

Brignac denied that Shell had any plans to expand its facilities onto the property along the first two streets of Diamond or the Gaspard Line property. Shell had bought the latter property only to avoid having barges cluttering up its dock area and was willing to discuss with local residents and parish officials how to turn the Gaspard property into a linear park with walking trails and perhaps other facilities, Brignac said.

Clearly, Shell made a public relations blunder in not explaining to the community why it was buying the property. But part of the problem had to do with the history of this property. "Diamond residents tend to look at [the property] as having been left purposefully to keep this [racial] dividing line," Brignac observed. "And if you talk to white residents [in Norco] there is probably some truth to that . . . shamefully but true."

IV

Allies Support the Diamond Relocation Campaign

11

Supporters Converge

By 1995 all the ingredients were present for the Diamond community to become a "poster child" for environmental injustice. The struggle for relocation by Concerned Citizens of Norco had become a focal point for the environmental justice movement, and supporters converged on Diamond from across the United States. "A lot of us in national groups realized that this was . . . the flash point," said Denny Larson, coordinator of Refinery Reform Campaign, who came to Diamond from California. "The face of the environmental justice movement was Margie Richard's face and the faces of the residents of Diamond," he continued. "That was how to make this struggle real to other people."

There was also the recognition of the strength of Margie Richard's convictions about the need for relocation and the sense that she would keep pushing for this goal no matter how tough the struggle became, Larson recalled. Having a community leader with a core group of local activists willing to stay focused for the long haul was a big reason why Diamond residents had the potential to win an important victory against Shell, he added. But Richard and the other residents needed allies to help them make Diamond's plight known beyond the borders of St. Charles Parish and the state of Louisiana.

What is striking about the environmental justice activists who were drawn into the struggle in Diamond was how many of them had significant personal and work experience that would prove useful in the struggle for relocation. Some of them, like Larson, had a history of going up against large refineries or chemical plants on behalf of fenceline community residents. Others were long-term toxics activists before their involvement in Norco. They brought with them a wealth of experience about what corporate strategies could be expected from Shell and how to amplify the voices of local residents by using the media, the courts, and the regulatory machinery to expose the poisoning of the air and water in Diamond.

In this part of the book we will learn something about the lives and backgrounds of the people who came to support the local resident/activists fighting for relocation. We will also see in action members of a growing faction of the environmental and civil rights communities who are increasingly focusing on the impact of industrial chemicals on human health.

The activists who ended up working in Diamond came from widely varied backgrounds. They were black and white, rich and poor, hard-core environmental justice activists, environmental health advocates, philanthropists, preachers, and government officials. The diversity of this group of Americans who converged on Norco to help the residents of Diamond is an indication of the gathering strength of environmental justice movement in the United States. And it demonstrates that the issues that motivate environmental justice activists are beginning to resonate among a larger segment of the public.

Diamond was one battlefield for these activists. It is by no means the last. Many of these organizers see themselves as involved in a larger, long-term campaign to bring this nation's powerful industrial machinery under sufficient control so that it will cease to create Diamond-like conditions.

Workshops for Activists

At the Deep South Center for Environmental Justice, Beverly Wright runs what amounts to a school for activists who live on fencelines with toxic industries in the river parishes of Louisiana. Working out of Xavier University, Wright assembled a network of fenceline residents who had already shown interest in organizing their neighbors. Wright calls the Deep South Center a "community-versity." Its research, its workshops, and its community organizing are designed to be responsive to the needs of African-Americans in the chemical corridor and beyond, she said.

Academics do not have a good track record working with community residents, Wright contended. They tend to "parachute into" a community, work intensively for a brief period, and then disappear. This leaves the residents with unfulfilled expectations and without the resources to continue their struggles, she noted.

Instead of brief encounters, Wright worked to provide community residents with knowledge, allies, outside expertise, useful contacts and tools that would help them organize effectively. To this end, she held workshops for residents on a variety of environmental justice issues, and she created the Mississippi River Avatar Community Advisory Board so that community leaders from the chemical corridor could learn from and support each other.

Wright developed a procedure for involving fenceline community residents in the network. Any activist group that contacted and sought help from the Deep South Center was asked to write a letter requesting permission to become involved with the Center's workshops and board, Wright explained. The Center then wrote up a Memorandum of Understanding with the community group about what kind of help it could expect. This made everything clear from the outset and avoided unrealistic expectations, Wright continued. It also demonstrated that the community was buying into the process of its own free will and that it saw the potential benefits of being involved, she added.

The Deep South Center has been involved in a number of the environmental justice struggles in the region, including the battles in Convent, in St. Gabriel, and in the neighborhood around the Agriculture Street Landfill in New Orleans. "I am strongly convinced that the only way change comes is by empowering people on the ground so they can speak for themselves," Wright said. "If all you do is rush in like combat troops and fight one battle, then you leave the community with nothing. We have spent ten years building capacity within communities so they can fight their own battles with what technical assistance we can give them."

Often the people most affected by pollution from these industries have the least education, Wright pointed out. Some of the Deep South Center's workshops—which are conducted in churches and rented halls in affected communities—are basic "Pollution Prevention 101" classes, Wright said. Many residents are intimidated by and do not understand a lot of the jargon and abbreviations they hear when they go to hearings that concern the regulation of the industries in their communities. The Center's workshops teach them that LDEQ stands for the Louisiana Department of Environmental Quality, that EPA stands for the U.S. Environmental Protection Agency, and that ppb is an abbreviation for parts per billion. Residents are given a glossary of terms to keep and study. These workshops were useful to Margie Richard, then president of Concerned Citizens of Norco: "I had to read up on acronyms and study up on parts per billion but it happened and I gained knowledge," she said.

Other workshops familiarize fenceline residents with the Byzantine structure of the parish, state, and federal regulatory systems. This bureaucracy is diagrammed and explained to them when they attended a workshop titled "Who is Protecting You?" After the workshop there is a follow-up "face-to-face" session in which residents meet the state and federal regulators responsible for ensuring that the air they breathe and the water they drink are safe. These sessions help establish relationships between the residents and the regulators they telephone when accidents and releases occur at the plants adjacent to them. The workshops not only give residents a better idea about who to call when something goes wrong; they also give them a better chance of having their calls returned as a result of having had a dialogue with the relevant bureaucrat, Wright noted.

The Deep South Center's workshops are designed to meet the practical problems that residents face in their communities, Wright explained. For example, residents from the river parishes were invited to attend a workshop on how to monitor the air using the citizen air monitoring buckets brought in by Denny Larson, coordinator of the Petroleum Reform Campaign. A "Leadership Development Workshop" provided information about how to deal with corporate divide-and-conquer strategies and armed residents with information about communities with similar problems that had been successful in their struggles.

In the workshops held at the Destrehan Library (just down River Road from Diamond/Norco), one session was devoted to what environmental racism means and how it compares with other forms of racism. After hearing about the history of the national struggle for environmental justice, some Diamond residents began to realize that they were part of a larger movement. They could see that it was not just about their anger toward Shell for polluting their air. They came to understand that they were part of a larger campaign to fight corporate and governmental forms of racism, that it was important that their voices be heard as part of this movement, and that they were connected to other people who had resources that might help them, Denny Larson said. "The Deep South Center's work is sometimes underappreciated," Larson noted. Greenpeace and the Louisiana Bucket Brigade do a lot of media work and frequently get their names in the papers, but Dr. Wright is "linking people up and down the river through her Avatar Board so that all the community people can network directly among each other," he added.

Diamond residents Margie Richard and Gaynel Johnson both attended Deep South Center workshops and are among the graduates of this "community-versity." Wright recalled first meeting Richard in 1993 after a civil rights meeting that highlighted racial discrimination in the disproportionate siting of highly polluting facilities adjacent to African-American communities in the river parishes of Louisiana. Richard told Wright about the suffering of Diamond community and asked for help. Wright subsequently appointed Richard to take her place on the EPA's Common Sense Initiative. Richard found that this allowed her to meet and develop relationships with top executives at Shell and regulators at the EPA and LDEQ. "I think that was the beginning of Margie [Richard] really getting some attention for her community," Wright observed. Much of the work Wright did on the Diamond/Norco struggle involved helping Richard figure out a strategy for recovering from the legal defeat when Concerned Citizens of Norco lost its court case demanding relocation, dealing with Shell's divide-and-conquer tactics, and devising a successful media campaign. "We needed to shame Shell into doing the right thing because we were not going to get justice through the courts," said Wright. Shell wanted to maintain a "squeaky clean" reputation and did not like bad press, she observed. That was a point of leverage that could be exploited, she noted.

When it comes to looking for allies for community-based struggles, Wright's philosophy is to invite everyone in: "Our position has always been to bring in as many people as possible such as the National Council of Churches, the Black Church Council, the Black Caucus, celebrities, and Greenpeace." The idea is to get as many different groups pressing on Shell as possible. It takes a number of groups working together to bring about victory, she said. But chief among the necessary components for an environmental justice victory is a well-organized local group. Without that, nothing can really happen, Wright said. A strong community group, such as Concerned Citizens of Norco in Diamond, can usefully be put in contact with outside resources that can help them with their struggle.

Sometimes, however, grassroots community groups are so splintered by corporate divide-and-conquer strategies that the residents become angry and frightened. As rumors spread through the community about people selling their homes, the situation can become highly emotional, Wright observed. The way to heal a community that has been split apart in this fashion is to teach residents how to communicate better with each other so that the rumors can be put to rest and people can see what is really going on. This requires regular meetings and the ceaseless work of "walkers-and-talkers" who circulate through the community keeping people up to date.

There must also be motivators who lift the spirits of local residents who experience multiple defeats when going up against a multinational corporation such as Royal Dutch/Shell. Damu Smith from Greenpeace, for example, told residents not to give up, that people in a situation similar to theirs had won elsewhere, and that Diamond residents could win also, Wright recalled.

It is also important that local residents not only hear about other groups struggling with the same issues but also meet with them. By creating a network, these groups can support each other in very tangible ways, Wright pointed out. If, for example, one group is holding a demonstration or a press conference, members of the other groups can show up and give their support. This not only swells the ranks of the protest, it also widens the appeal to the media and demonstrates that there is a systemic problem that is worthy of news coverage. Weaving together this network of communities that have been heavily impacted by industry is at the heart of Wright's work.

Over time a coalition of nonprofit organizations formed to support the struggle for environmental justice in Diamond led by Concerned Citizens of Norco. Each group helped in its own way. The Deep South Center for Environmental Justice worked on educating Diamond residents in proven organizing techniques, the EarthJustice Legal Defense Fund provided legal expertise and organizing skills, the Refinery Reform Campaign introduced the air sampling buckets, the Louisiana Bucket Brigade did daily organizing work in the community, Greenpeace brought in politicians and celebrities, foundations provided critically needed funding, religious organizations added their moral authority to the struggle, the National Resource Defense Council did research, regional environmental groups such as the Louisiana Environmental Action Network organized press conferences, and organizations like CorporateWatch forged connections between the local struggle in Diamond and the international negotiations in the Netherlands. The struggle in Diamond was also given considerable assistance by a small group of anonymous whistle-blowing regulators within state and federal regulatory agencies who provided Diamond's nonprofit allies with inside information about regulatory deliberations, Wright reported.

In view of the sheer number of players involved, it is not surprising to learn that there was a considerable amount of infighting among the nonprofit organizations that attempted to support the struggle in Diamond. Even people pursuing the same goals can end up fighting because they distrust each other, because they are competing for limited funding, because of personality conflicts, or because they have very different (and occasionally mutually exclusive) ideas about the best tactics for achieving a desired outcome. Before the struggle in Norco, the infighting among nonprofit organizations involved in environmental justice battles in Louisiana was so intense that some foundations pulled out of the state.

The history of the environmental justice movement in Louisiana has not been one of seamless coalition building among good friends. Over the years Wright has sometimes felt that the Deep South Center was under assault. Some groups attacked the Center as racist because of its focus on African-American communities, she explained. Some white activists felt that the National Black Environmental Justice Network, which Wright helped found, sounded too racially exclusive. "Attempts were made by some of the other groups to separate Margie [Richard's] community from us," Wright charged, but the attempt failed. "Terrible things were said about us to [foundation] grant officers. But my approach has not been to respond to lies and instead to stay steady doing the work so that in the end people can see what you have done," said Wright. "There is friction but the positive side of this is that we managed to work it out. . . . I don't think that different groups can work together without having some conflict, to tell the truth." So activists working for nonprofit organizations always have to go back and reexamine their original intention to support the struggle of the residents on the front lines in the community, Wright concluded.

When a number of foundations became discouraged at the intense conflicts between environmental and environmental justice groups in Louisiana and reduced their funding, what they said was that they had been throwing a lot of money at community problems in the state and they were not getting much return for their investment, Wright recalled. "I told them they were doing it [the funding] wrong," she said. The problem was that foundations were giving money to groups that just "parachuted into" fenceline communities and then withdrew, she continued. They wasted a lot of money by failing to research the issue deeply enough before making their investments, she added. Now foundations are becoming involved again, she observed, and just in time; the support a number of the groups once received through the EPA has dried up.

Wright can be an intimidating presence, cutting with her words. Even the mild-mannered Shell spokesman David Brignac said "Dialoguing with Beverly Wright is particularly difficult: it is intensity one way and the intensity is insulting, which is not conducive to talking about issues." Hearing this description of herself, Wright laughs: "I have a lot of respect for [Brignac], whether he knows it or not. You can't show all your cards [in a negotiation.] I was the devil's advocate a lot. I was the 'bad cop' in the room. Someone has to be the bad cop, and I enjoy it anyway. It works for me."

Technical Assistance

The modest house on Old Jeanerette Road on the outskirts of New Iberia, Louisiana, looks an unlikely place for one of the nation's foremost experts on fenceline toxics to live. The Subra Company's offices are located in this small one-story structure across from a field of sugarcane 30 miles south of Lafayette in the marshy delta that fans out into the Gulf of Mexico. This is backroad Cajun country where every restaurant sells its own gumbo and boudin and the worn formica tables offer a variety of piquant sauces. It is also an area peppered with small towns that must deal with the airborne and waterborne pollutants the petrochemical industries throw off. Here there are waste pits where industrial effluents are dumped and "landfarms" where oil wastes are mechanically flung into the air to volatilize before the earth-clinging remnants are plowed back into the soil to degrade. Many of the residents of this economically depressed region do not have the resources to fight the big oil and chemical companies that frequently have their way with local officials.

Wilma Subra grew up amidst this tropical cocktail of industrial wastes. Now a 59-year-old chemist, Subra uses her expertise to help residents ferret out what chemicals they are being exposed to and how to protect themselves by skillfully navigating the regulatory process.

In Diamond, Subra played an important role in educating residents about what chemicals were being released, in what volumes, and what health symptoms they could anticipate from the array of toxics to which they were being exposed. She taught Diamond residents to keep diaries in which they listed what they smelled, how they felt, and what symptoms they experienced. Their journals would help document their exposures, she told them. Subra returned to Diamond periodically to conduct workshops in the churches during which she explained to residents what she had dug out of the company records about what chemicals they had released on which dates. She then helped residents match the company release data with their anecdotal diary entries about what health impacts they had experienced and recorded in their diaries. Before long, residents began to learn which smells came from which chemicals and what symptoms they caused.

Subra was a valuable ally for Diamond residents. She was a home-grown expert. They could communicate with her easily and have complex issues about chemicals, health, and the regulatory process translated into terms they could readily understand. She helped them see through some of the lies, half-truths, and omitted facts they were hearing (or not hearing) from industry. She was a chemist who could not be snowed by voluminous technical jargon, and she used her expertise in the service of fenceline residents. Best of all she, did not present the residents with a padded bill for services rendered. It is no wonder, then, that some of them referred to her as "Saint Wilma."

Subra's preparation to do this kind of citizen's toxicology started at a young age when she worked part-time in the factory of her inventor father. In seventh grade she started part-time work substituting at different jobs as employees at her father's factory took time off. Her father insisted that she and her five sisters learn all facets of the work, including details of the technical process and the accounting. This led to an early interest in science. When she enrolled at the University of Southwestern Louisiana she elected to take microbiology, chemistry, and computer sciences classes at the undergraduate and then graduate levels. Toward the end of graduate school she married and settled down in New Iberia, commuting to classes in Lafayette until a job opened up at the newly opened Gulf South Research Institute (GSRI), which performed analytic chemistry and animal studies at an old naval base in New Iberia. It was a perfect job for Subra, involving her in acute and chronic bioassays for all chemicals, animal studies, and fish toxicity studies.

GSRI did some of the quick-response work for the Environmental Protection Agency, including the early work at Love Canal, a community poisoned with industrial toxins. Subra and her colleagues would set up shop in small towns that were experiencing high levels of unexplained illnesses, she recalled. One project was at the Bluegrass Army Arsenal in an economically depressed part of Appalachia where trainloads of munitions from Vietnam were unloaded and stored. The munitions had been shipped on pallets that had been soaked in pentachlorophenol, a highly toxic concoction that kept the wood from rotting or being eaten by termites in the jungle. Unfortunately, once the munitions had been uncrated, much of the wood was scavenged by local residents and used for firewood or for paneling and bookshelves in their homes. As a result residents exposed to the wood fell sick. A GSRI team, which included Subra, was called in to do the detective work to find the source of the problem and determine the extent of the health impact.

After sampling the air, wood, blood, and urine for traces of pentachlorophenol the results were sent to the EPA and the Centers for Disease Control, Subra explained. But the people who were tested never learned what body burden of toxic chemicals they were living with. "I couldn't go back and say 'You know, you have the highest level of pentachlorophenol of anybody tested and you really need to do something about it,'" she said. "There was never anybody working on the side of the community," she added. "I had to go and deal with communities but never was able to give them the information. Even in Love Canal we couldn't deal with the homeowners. We would sample their air, their yards, their basements, but we couldn't deal with the homeowner. And these people had a right to know."

Unsatisfied with a system that kept residents in the dark about the extent of their chemical exposure, Subra left GSRI in 1991 after working there for 14 years and becoming the head of the Analytical Chemistry and Environmental Sciences section. During those years local residents who were experiencing problems with exposure to industrial toxins would come to GSRI about contamination problems in their neighborhood. Subra and her colleagues helped do some of the chemical detective work for them in the evenings and on weekends, but she continued to hope that one day she could help more directly. With this in mind, she set up the Subra Company, which takes calls from residents who have problems with toxics. "When someone has an environmental problem I get a call," she said simply. A lot of the work involves spill responses when a waste pit overflows into some-one's yard, she explained. Other calls come from citizens' groups (like the one in Diamond) that are sick of being poisoned by a neighboring petro-chemical plant, landfill, or incinerator. And some jobs involve helping res-idents oppose the construction of highly toxic facilities close to their homes, she continued.

Often residents exposed to toxic chemicals have very little money to pay for her work, Subra noted. To keep her business afloat, she takes paying jobs with local canneries and hot sauce manufacturers that need products tested for contaminants before they can be marketed. Subra's ability to do pro bono work was also given a boost when she was awarded a "genius award" by the MacArthur Foundation

One of the early calls Subra took was from a man in neighboring Vermillion Parish whose father and wife were dying of cancer. Subra started sampling water wells in the area and found evidence of concentrations of four heavy metals that were above the EPA drinking water standards. The heavy metals were associated with the oil-field wastes that were being dis-posed of in the area, she explained. "The health department called me in with their big muckety-mucks and said to me 'You need to quit telling the people not to drink the water . . . because you are creating a problem we don't have the resources to address.'" But Subra persisted. Eventually three of the pits were closed, and petitions led to their being listed as Superfund sites. This outcome only happened because citizens stayed involved and kept the pressure up and because Subra was able to help them gather and inter-pret the technical data and understand the regulatory process, she said.

Subra also worked on the *Morgan City v. Marine Shale Company* case. This high-profile case involved a man named Jack Kent who filed suit against open-pit and landfarm disposal of oil-field wastes and then started a company that would incinerate such wastes.[1] In his permit application Kent promised to burn only oil-field wastes and no hazardous wastes, Subra explained, but as soon as he started operations in 1985 he began inciner-ating hazardous wastes as a fuel and bulking agent. Subra joined local groups in protesting this illegal practice. Inspectors would constantly find violations, and suits would be won against the company in court, but Marine Shale was allowed to continue operations while the cases were on appeal. This went on for eleven years (1985–1996), Subra said, until a fed-eral court judge finally revoked the permit. "I worked with citizens to help them understand what was going on, what the emissions said, how to call in complaints, and how to develop data. . . . If you don't have someone to help citizens get information into the system you are lost," she noted.

In 1985 the residents of Diamond began to benefit from some of Subra's battle-tested techniques for taking on big polluters. It was in that year that she was asked to look into Shell's pollution of Bayou Trepagnier, a no-flow/low-flow stream that has its headwaters in Norco. Since the early 1920s, when Shell started operations there, it had been dumping wastes into the creek, which ironically had a "scenic river" designation because of its beauty and its popularity among locals as a place to fish.

Bayou Trepagnier "is one of the most gorgeous places in the world but when you put the paddle in all the industrial sludge comes welling to the top," Subra noted. "There is sludge out at Bayou Trepagnier that is as beautiful as molasses," she said. With help from resident naturalist Milton Cambre, Subra went out on the bayou. Navigating was difficult. They had to push their boat under fallen trees and step over them as they made their way downstream. In addition to taking samples for heavy metals, Subra also took depth samples that revealed the sludge was 6 feet deep in some areas. Gradually she mapped the sludge.

Once Subra had taken the samples and found high levels of heavy metals, Shell officials called and asked to take a deposition. "They bring out their super-whammy lawyers and all of that," said Subra, who explained that this process scares some people off. Then the Secretary of the Louisiana Department of Environmental Quality called her in to explain to her that his inspectors had been out there and found that there was no pollution. "He thought he was just going to shut me up and I was going to go away," she said. But Subra remained unimpressed and offered to teach LDEQ personnel how to take a proper sample. Eventually state inspectors went back out to sample again and found levels of contaminants even higher than she had.

After it had been established that there were high levels of heavy metals in the sludge in the bayou behind Shell's facility, the company responded that it had been discharging wastes into the creek since the 1920s but had never exceeded the amount specified by its discharge permit. In essence, Shell officials claimed that the buildup of pollutants was not Shell's fault because the amount discharged had never exceeded what was permitted, Subra observed. Shell also rerouted its discharge of wastes into the

Mississippi, whose waters ran much faster than those of the bayou and could dilute the wastes more efficiently.

Subra returned to Norco in 1988 when the huge explosion at Shell totally disrupted the pollution-control system. "The discharge [into Bayou Trepagnier] was of every color imaginable . . . spraying up into the air and coming down," she recalled. "Everything was out of compliance because the facility went boom."

Subra and others continued to press for a cleanup of the bayou, but for years nothing happened. Shell argued that it was better to leave the stuff in place. Then, in the mid 1990s, a huge storm that dumped 18 inches of rain caused the sludge to fluff up and overflow the banks, coating vegetation with toxic chemicals. "All the terrestrial animals were picking that up," Subra noted. "We are still arguing [with Shell] about what the remedy should be," she said. Local people still fish the bayou, and the effluent makes its way down to Lake Pontchartrain, where affluent campers are exposed to heavy metals when they catch and eat crabs, Subra added.

All this work in Bayou Trepagnier, especially after the explosion in 1988, introduced Subra to the conditions in which residents of Diamond were living. Then, a year later, the federal government began publishing Toxic Release Inventory (TRI) data which made public for the first time the volumes of toxic chemicals that specific facilities released into the environment. The TRI data permitted Subra to help Diamond residents match the symptoms they were chronicling in their diaries with the TRI release data from the Shell and Motiva plants. "I started doing composites of accidental releases and TRI data and looking at trends and making industry really nervous because I was putting it into a form the community could understand," Subra recalled.

After decades of debunking some of the misinformation or incomplete information put out by the petrochemical industry, Subra became adept at reading between the lines of the industry's reports. One well-known ruse is the paper shuffle, she explained. The way it works is that a company sells off one of its units that makes a particularly toxic chemical to a company that it partially owns and sometimes even helps run with its own employees. From then on the larger company can claim that it has nothing to do with the releases from the smaller, spun-off unit. Shell Chemical in Norco used this practice when it spun off a unit and called it Resolution Performance Products. The newly minted company, made up of Shell assets, took over the Shell unit that made epchlorhydrin, a chemical known to cause testicular dysfunction, Subra claimed. Shell also sold off an incinerator in Norco to which the company continued to send wastes to be burned, Subra added. By so doing Shell could claim to have considerably reduced its emissions, she observed. Knowledgeable about these paper transactions, Subra has had occasion to sit down with officials from Shell, Motiva, and the neighboring Orion refinery officials and show them how she is able to calculate the total emissions that residents are exposed to from their all their plants combined. Using data from the Local Emergency Planning Commission and other sources, Subra calculated that there were 248 days one year in which there had been leaks from their plants. "I sat in a meeting with Shell and Motiva and when I did this the manager of Motiva almost corroded," Subra said with some satisfaction. The fact these officials were nonplused by Subra's access to this information amazed her. "Guys," she said, "you all report this, and I have your reports." One graph that Subra assembled showing total emissions from their plants "blew them all away," she added. Apparently Shell and Motiva officials were not accustomed to anyone who could follow their paper trail in such detail and understand its implications.

It is essential to track chemicals releases from the footprints (geographic boundaries) of facilities, not by company name, Subra advised. If you look up the volume of releases from Shell facilities in Norco you will get one total for chemicals released; the answer will be quite different if you add up the releases from Shell, Motiva, Resolution Performance Products, and the other entities within the industrial complex next to which Norco and Diamond residents live, she explained.

While Shell officials were clearly not overjoyed when they heard that Subra was coming to town to give a presentation about the impact of their pollution on the health of Norco residents, there was grudging admiration for her work and her expertise. "Wilma brings the technical piece, which is good," said Shell spokesman David Brignac. "That helps bridge a gap for the community."

Taking on big industries, poking them in the eye with critical data, and providing damaging information about them to neighboring residents is dangerous work. Not only might there be retaliation, but local workers might become convinced that Subra's work as an industrial gadfly threatened their job security. Asked about whether she fears for her safety, Subra replies "I get threats."

Before moving into her current office, Subra worked out of two trailers on the other side of town. They were broken into so often that the local sheriff suggested that Subra was being harassed because of her work. Subra installed an alarm; it was tripped by burglars so often that responding to it became irritating. Then, while she was fighting an oil-field waste facility, her office was burgled and her computer and disks were stolen. Since then she has decided not to work in the office alone at night and has made it a practice to lock up backup disks of her work separately.

In addition to the physical danger Subra exposes herself to by going up against polluting industries, there is also the exposure to toxic chemicals that she endures when she visits the fenceline communities. Clearly, she is not exposed to as much as the people who live there but it affects her nevertheless, she said. In heavily polluted Grand Bois, the residents "stand there like it is normal, but I get sick every time I go there," she said. And the air in Diamond makes her sick when she visits, she added. The fact that many people who live in these communities can no longer smell the chemicals in the air does not mean that it is not affecting them. "You still get the health impacts," Subra argued, but because residents do not smell the chemicals they no longer associate the smell with the symptoms they experience. In fact, the inability to smell the chemicals is dangerous, Subra contended, "because you don't know when to run."

Are fenceline residents exposed to levels of toxic chemicals contracting chronic and degenerative diseases as a result of their exposures? Subra thinks they are: "Yes, absolutely, look at what they are being exposed to," she said. But she noted that the fenceline populations are often so small a sample that the number of people with a given disease is not seen as being statistically significant. This further complicates prosecuting a health-impact case against industry.

Intimate familiarity with the less-than-perfect regulatory process designed to protect the environmental health of the citizens of Louisiana may not have bred contempt, but at least it has engendered a jaundiced view in the way Subra sees the process working. At its core the problem is that there is a lack of political will to put in place meaningful protections, Subra said. It starts right at the top with the governor, she continued. Under the former Republican governor Charles E. (Buddy) Roener there were quite a few inspections and enforcement activities at industrial sites around the state, but during the administrations of the past two governors—Edwards and

Foster—the number of inspections dropped dramatically, she claimed. That could be because the 156 industrial facilities in Louisiana's chemical corridor constitute one of the biggest economic engines of the state's economy and generate 62,500 jobs and $1.4 billion in state tax revenues in 2002.[2]

Subra is not alone in charging that politicians and regulators in Louisiana are more concerned with attracting and keeping large industry in the state than they are with protecting their citizens from fallout from these industries. "Instead of protecting the citizens, the state [Louisiana] and its agencies are single-mindedly focused on protecting polluters like Shell Norco," said Carl Pope, executive director of the Sierra Club.[3]

Pope is joined in his criticism of the effectiveness of environmental regulation in Louisiana by high-level federal officials. The Environmental Protection Agency's own Inspector General recently blasted the agency's region VI office for having "failed to properly oversee Louisiana's enforcement of air, water, and hazardous waste regulatory programs," wrote *Times-Picayune* reporter Mark Schleifstein. The EPA's regional office, which has jurisdiction over Louisiana, "could not assure the public that Louisiana was protecting the environment," the report stated. The report went on to fault the agency's regional office for failure to ensure that the Louisiana Department of Environmental Quality did not collect bad data. "The region was unable to fully assure the public that Louisiana was operating programs in a way that effectively protects human health and the environment," the report added.

The EPA inspector general's audit of this regional office was instigated by a series of petitions asking the EPA to revoke LDEQ's oversight authority for a number of major regulatory areas including the Title V air permit program, which regulates the kind of pollutants emitted by industries such as Motiva and the Shell Chemical Company in Norco. The petitions were filed by the Louisiana Bucket Brigade, the Refinery Reform Campaign, the Tulane Environmental Law Clinic, the Louisiana Environmental Action Network (LEAN), and a number of other groups. The EPA report came on the heels of a state legislative audit that criticized LDEQ for failing to cite industries for environmental violations and collect appropriate fines.[4]

Between 1999 and 2002, the Louisiana Department of Environmental Quality levied fines in just 4 percent of cases in which they found evidence of environmental transgressions. That rate is right down at the bottom of states in EPA Region VI, along with Texas. Arkansas, in contrast, collected fines in 40 percent of all cases in which environmental regulations were broken, reported an article in the Baton Rouge *Advocate*. "If this were a report card we would be failing. We'd be last in the class," commented LEAN director Marylee Orr.[5]

Not only is LDEQ's regulatory process inadequate, environmental groups charge; there is also evidence that the cumulative volume of chemicals emitted by specific industrial facilities is not added up when making a determination as to whether or not the permit has been violated. Permits granted to industries specify what volume of chemicals they can release into the air, water, and land, Subra explained. These permitted levels of releases are based on health standards devised to ensure that residents outside the industrial fenceline will not be exposed to any concentration of chemicals that could cause them harm. That is the theory, Subra noted, but if you look at the compliance history of big refineries and petrochemical plants in Louisiana you find they are often out of compliance with their permit if you add up the volume of the chemicals they release through fugitive emissions, accidents, and permitted releases.

Talking with state inspectors it becomes clear that the system is deeply flawed, Subra observed. State regulatory inspectors go out to the big industrial complexes, do their inspections, find multiple violations, write up a report, hand a copy of the report to the industrial site manager, and then forward the report to regulatory headquarters in Baton Rouge, she explained. But the central office of the Louisiana Department of Environmental Quality does nothing, much of the time, Subra contended, because the governor has let them know that he does not want them to give industry a hard time. He wants to attract more industries to Louisiana not scare them off. In a few months it is time for the LDEQ field inspector to go back to the industrial site and do another inspection. The inspector arrives at the plant, does his inspection, and finds that the old violations have not been fixed and that there are new ones to report as well. Again he writes up a report and hands it to the site manager who laughs in the face of the inspector because he knows the whole regulatory dance is a charade, Subra said. In addition, before LDEQ inspectors appear at an industrial site, plant managers often get a warning call giving them time to fix up any problem that is really egregious, she added.

During the Clinton administration, those trying to force industries to reduce their releases at least had some federal Environmental Protection

Agency regulators on their side when the state LDEQ failed to do its job, Subra recalled. Some EPA inspectors would go undercover, check into a motel, rent a rowboat, and go out and catch industry red-handed dumping toxic chemicals in the water. But since President George W. Bush's administration took office even this kind of activity has subsided, she claimed. President Bush got a lot of his financial support from the oil and chemical industry, so he has told the EPA not too push too hard on enforcing regulations that are costly to the industry, Subra opined. "The EPA is still doing some enforcement . . . but it is like pushing a big rock up a big hill," she said. "The EPA is not the savior they were before . . . and without the EPA we have nowhere to turn."

Further evidence supporting this view of flawed regulatory enforcement nationwide emerged recently when an internal EPA audit found lax enforcement of Clean Water Act regulations during the period 1999–2001. The study looked at 6,600 major facilities and found that a 25 percent of them were in "significant noncompliance"—meaning that they were emitting a lot more toxic chemicals into the water than their permits permitted. Only 13 percent of the serious offenders faced formal regulatory action, the report noted. Further, 50 percent of all non-compliers were at least 100 percent over the limit for toxic emissions, 21 percent were 500 percent over, and 13 percent were 1,000 percent out of compliance, a recent article in the *Washington Post* reveals. "Fewer than half ended up paying fines— averaging between $4,996 to $6,455," the article added.[6] Big industries can afford to pay these fines and still continue to operate. Knowing this, Eric Schaeffer resigned as head of the EPA's Civil Enforcement Division. At the time of his resignation, Schaeffer indicated that he was leaving because of the agency's lax enforcement of the Clean Air Act.[7]

Despite these reports of industries routinely exceeding their emissions permits and being issued only minimal fines, it remains extremely difficult to prove that fenceline residents are being made ill as a result of exposure to toxic emissions. This is largely because of the way statistics are compiled, Subra explained. Attempting to do a longitudinal health survey of Diamond residents, for example, would run into a number of problems. First, many of the death certificates would indicate the immediate cause of death but not the long-term, chronic health problems that brought the deceased to the point of dying, she noted. Second, many Diamond residents had poor access to health care and as a result there is no medical history or paper trail that could be easily tracked that would demonstrate a pattern of sickness that led to their death. Third, there is the well-documented difficulty of proving that a specific chemical released from a specific industrial facility caused a specific disease. Finally, there is a dearth of air monitoring data from affected fenceline communities. Add all these factors together and it becomes clear just how difficult it is to prove that a given industrial facility is causing a certain level of disease in an adjoining residential community.

When she talks with residents of fenceline communities, Subra tells them that many officials who hold positions of responsibility "were not elected to protect you" but instead are "looking out for the people who gave money to their campaign." In short, she continued, "the political system is not looking out for their best interests." As residents come to understand this political dynamic some of them get angry and organize protests or run for office, Subra noted. They realize that the government is not protecting them so they have to protect themselves. The mayor of New Iberia, for example, first started out as a resident who advocated recycling but then became interested in broader environmental issues. School board members were radicalized when they learned that a new school was being built on contaminated soil, she continued. And there are now a couple of state representatives who ran for office after a neighboring landfill leaked into their backyard.

Some of the organizers, like Margie Richard in Diamond, with whom Subra worked closely, are growing older and slowing down, Subra observed. But younger organizers are springing up to take their place. It is this that gives Subra a sense of hope amidst the depressing failures of the state government to protect the people from industrial chemical releases. Asked if her work does not make her depressed, Subra responded "No, because when we get a win it is wonderful."

Lawyer in the Room

Beneath its hip, honky-tonk surface, New Orleans is all business when it comes to oil. Take the olive-green trolley down St. Charles Street under the bower of live oaks to Poydras Street and walk a few blocks to One Shell Square and you can stand on the sidewalk and gawk up at the huge megaliths that Big Oil has built for itself on the Gulf Coast. Shell Oil chose to erect a towering, white marble high-rise that anchors its Louisiana operations. A few blocks away the 34-story Texaco Center, sheathed in black marble, is further evidence that the wheels of business in Louisiana are lubricated with oil.

Conveniently located a few blocks away, in a four-story beige brick building with wrought-iron trim, were the offices of the EarthJustice Legal Defense Fund, one of the legal arms of the environmental movement.[8] Here Monique Harden had a base from which she traveled out to work with communities that experience the downside of living next to big oil refineries and petrochemical plants.

Every group of community activists that goes up against a large refinery or chemical company needs a lawyer, experienced in the field of toxics, who can help them stand up to multinational companies, such as Royal Dutch/Shell, which have armies of legal experts at their command. The tenor of a meeting with Shell officials changed dramatically once they realized there was a lawyer in the room, noted Beverly Wright. "Just having the legal mind in the room is important," she observed. The ability of lawyers to make arguments couched in legal terms, their expertise at following a paper trail, their knowledge about how best to intervene in the regulatory process, and their penchant for fighting like bulldogs all made their presence critical, she added. For all the above reasons, Concerned Citizens of Norco were fortunate to have in their corner Monique Harden, 35, formerly a staff attorney at EarthJustice Legal Defense Fund, who specializes in organizing fenceline communities.

The life path by which Harden became connected with the struggle in Norco suggests that she had prepared herself well to help the people who lived in the shadow of Shell's petrochemical plants. But there was also a more personal connection. Harden's family originally came from Kentwood, Louisiana. Her great-grandfather stepped on a nail while building the levees along the Mississippi adjacent to Diamond. Without access to antibiotics, he died from the wound. Decades later Harden returned to the scene of this family tragedy to help right some of the wrongs that had been done to the African-American population that lived there.

Born in San Francisco, Harden moved to New Orleans in 1978 at the age of 10. She subsequently attended St. John's College in Annapolis and then Law School at the University of Texas in Austin. Once finished with her schooling, she returned to "the fragrance of the sweet olive trees and jasmine that abounds in New Orleans" and purchased a home, which she shares with her sister. She found work with a local renewable energy organization called Alliance for Affordable Energy. She developed a utility ratepayers' bill of rights to help protect low-income families dealing with cutoffs and shutoffs of electrical services in the river parishes.

By 1997, Harden had gone to work for Greenpeace on a toxics campaign focused on vinyl production in Louisiana. She began to visit the river parishes and see the small and often dilapidated homes of African-American families located adjacent to towering industrial facilities next door. "I was absolutely shocked. I was embarrassed that I didn't know about these conditions," she said. She was particularly incensed to find that some of the industries retained the names of the plantations they were built upon. "This is unbelievably unjust what is going on here and I have to do something about it," she recalled thinking.

Harden's first organizing work in the river parishes was with a community group called the St. James Citizens for Jobs and the Environment in Convent, Louisiana. The group was fighting the development by Shintech of an industrial complex that had the potential to become the world's largest polyvinyl chloride (PVC) plant, with three incinerators and three processing units. From her previous work, Harden had decided that approaching community toxics problems with just legal tools was often ineffective and that it was important to "marry litigation with advocacy." The law could be a tool to support the demands of community groups, but it should go hand-in-hand with community organizing, she came to realize.

The residents of Convent were saying "enough is enough," Harden recalled. They already had 17 million pounds of air pollution being released in their area, and they were surrounded by at least a dozen large industries. As Harden looked into their case, she found that the CEO of the company, who wanted to build the PVC plant, had cut a deal with the governor of the state. He had pledged support for the project from all local officials who would have input on the decision about granting a permit. As a result, the decision had been made from the top down, and the environmental permitting for the project was really a pro forma exercise. The outcome was preordained, Harden claimed. All of this took place before the citizens of Convent, who would be affected by the project, had even heard about it. This was the basic template in Louisiana for how these plants got built, Harden contended.

To support the demand of the residents that the plant not be built, Harden and her Greenpeace colleagues drafted a petition challenging the permit and filed it with the Environmental Protection Agency's Administrative Division. The petition was based on environmental justice principles codified in the Executive Order 12898, issued by President Clinton in January 1994, which required all federal agencies to address the human health and environmental impact of their projects on low-income and minority communities. In addition to these legal interventions, Harden and her colleagues at Greenpeace and a network of other groups were also working to convince members of the Congressional Black Caucus to write letters to the EPA detailing what the construction of this project would mean to the residents of Convent. As time passed, the nonprofit coalition's efforts became increasingly organized and there were weekly telephone conferences and a newsletter circulated detailing developments in the case and strategies for future actions.

The challenge that Harden and other community organizers faced, first in Convent and later in Diamond, was how best to support the work of community leaders who had often been struggling for years with their corporate neighbors. Many of these grassroots activists felt unsuccessful, frustrated, and burnt out. They complained to Harden that they were not receiving any support from other residents who were convinced that they could not win. Residents told their activist leaders "We sued them and it didn't work, we protested and it didn't work, and I have work to do and children to raise."

Harden taught local activists how to encourage residents to contribute to the struggle at whatever level they felt was comfortable. That might mean lowering the threshold of involvement by asking someone to call just four or five people on a phone tree to urge them to attend a meeting. The idea was to set the bar low enough that everyone could participate even if at a minimal level, she continued. The other strategy was to set modest goals for activities in order to demonstrate to participants that their efforts could actually accomplish something. Mounting a visible protest encouraged others on the margins of the activist group to join in, Harden observed.

Harden also showed local activists how to counteract unrealistic industry claims about the benefits their facilities would bring to fenceline residents. In Convent, for example, Shintech promised that their new facility would bring jobs into the community. Local activists responded that there were a lot of plants within walking distance of the community that were not providing work for local people. The new facility would offer jobs that were poorly matched with the skills of the people who live in the area and most of the highly technical jobs would likely go to people outside the area. This made a lot of sense to residents who had been repeatedly turned down for employment at the surrounding plants.

The Convent campaign, which dragged on for years, was a battle of endurance. Finally a subtle negotiating process began in which EPA officials suggested that Harden withdraw the petition and cut a deal. But the community group decided to hang tough, and in October 1997 EPA Administrator Carol Browner blocked the Shintech permit on environmental justice grounds and found 50 errors in the air permit for the project that had been submitted by the Louisiana Department of Environmental Quality. This was the first time that the EPA ever denied a state-issued Clean Air Act permit and the fact that the ruling included environmental justice issues made it truly remarkable, Harden said. Working on this project taught Harden a lot about how the government works and showed her that a determined group of organized local citizens, supported by expertise from the nonprofit sector, could prevail in these cases.

One cool December evening in 1998, Harden drove to Diamond to attend a meeting of Concerned Citizens of Norco at the trailer of Margie Richard. When she arrived, she could see a white cloud of chemical pollutants coming out of the Shell Chemical plant and hugging the ground as it entered the residential section of the subdivision. As she opened the door of her car, the cloud of gas immediately began to seep in. Wading through the gas, she made her way to Richard's door and opened it. The gas followed her in. It was then that Harden made a commitment to help the residents of Diamond. "OK," she said, "I'm here to work with this community because this is godawful." It was unbelievable that this condition was permitted to be seen as acceptable, she added.

What Harden brought to the leadership of Concerned Citizens of Norco was some hard-won knowledge about what worked in terms of community organizing techniques in the river parishes. In concert with the Deep South Center for Environmental Justice, Harden, who was by then working at EarthJustice, began to help Richard and some of the other core community activists in Diamond solve some of their immediate problems.

First, Harden thought the CCN activists needed more information about how to organize a relocation struggle. She contacted the Center for Environmental Health and Justice. The Center's founder, Lois Gibbs, had experience that was relevant to Diamond. When large quantities of toxic chemicals were found bubbling up into the basements of homes in her community—Love Canal, in New York State—she had organized her neighbors in a successful relocation campaign. She subsequent founded the Center and published a manual titled Getting Organized and Getting Out. Copies of the manual were obtained, and a training session was organized in Diamond.

One of the most important concepts that the leadership of Concerned Citizens of Norco needed to absorb was how to keep their people united, Harden said. Many residents of Diamond had different ideas about what should happen: some wanted relocation but others wanted to stay. Some were homeowners while others were renters. What the Diamond activists needed to understand was that "no matter how important these differences were, they should not be allowed to stop a unified struggle," Harden argued. This required some fancy footwork. Instead of just putting out the demand for relocation, the wording had to be revised. The new slogan became "Diamond residents wanted the best possible conditions for the residents who want to stay; *and* for those who want to relocate they wanted a program that would do it in a fair way." Making this dual demand helped avoid division in the ranks and promoted a unified front. Another potentially divisive issue involved the different interests of renters and homeowners. Instead of just demanding a buyout for homeowners, there was also a demand made that renters be fairly compensated for moving expenses, as well as security and utility deposits. "The magic wand in all this was always stay united," Harden added. The solution was never to say "either/or" but rather to cluster demands so everyone was covered.

While Harden was getting to know the leadership of CCN, she was also traveling to a meeting of the National Environmental Justice Advisory Council (NEJAC).[9] While attending the meeting, Harden focused on the plight of residents living in the fenceline communities. One of these was Mossville, a fenceline town outside Lake Charles in southwest Louisiana. Mossville dates back to 1812 and is now adjacent to the largest complex of PVC facilities in the United States.

In December 1998, NEJAC stakeholders met in Louisiana to look into environmental justice concerns centered on the high concentration of refineries and petrochemical plants in the chemical corridor. Those attending the meeting were treated to a bus tour of the area. "We had four tour buses going down the Bonnet Carre Spillway, up River Road, down Washington Street [in Diamond] to Margie Richard's house," Harden recalled. As the buses passed through the Shell Chemical facility and the Motiva and Orion refineries, Margie Richard and other community leaders explained to the stakeholders what it was like living next to these plants. When such "toxics tours" are organized, Harden explained, the workers at the refineries and petrochemical plants are on their best behavior. While working for Greenpeace she had been told by one refinery worker "We love it when you guys do tours because we work double time and it is good pay cleaning up and making the facility presentable."

There was a certain irony in the fact that a gas leak occurred at Shell Chemical just days after the NEJAC bus tour passed through town while the stakeholders were still convened at a hotel in Baton Rouge. On the same streets where the NEJAC "toxic tour" buses had parked, residents of Diamond were waking up to find a gassy cloud coming in under their doors and causing their eyes to water and their throats to burn. It was an inopportune time for what plant managers refer to as an "upset."

But to tell this story properly first we need to meet Denny Larson, who played a pivotal role in capturing an air sample of this "upset" that provided Diamond residents with some of the first concrete evidence that could help prove they were being exposed to toxic chemicals leaking out of the Shell plant.

A New Tool Delivers Hard Evidence

Four years before the big bang of 1988 changed the landscape in Norco and sparked a grassroots movement in Diamond demanding relocation, a young man named Denny Larson moved to San Francisco and started working with fenceline refinery communities in the Bay Area. Larson would later disseminate a tool that would permits people who lived near highly toxic industrial facilities to prove that they were being exposed to chemicals emitted by their neighbors. That tool, the air-sampling "bucket," would later prove crucial in the Diamond residents' struggle for relocation.

Larson grew up in Helena, Montana, the son of the owner of an independent meat-packing company. After college, he worked as a freelance photographer in Austin and subsequently as a lithographer in a printing shop in Los Angeles. Some of the employees in the printing shop's plating room were exposed to a lot of solvents, and one of them developed a rare form of liver cancer. A short-lived attempt to organize a union and improve working conditions ended when all those involved were fired.

Larson next went to work for California governor Jerry Brown's ill-fated senatorial campaign, serving as a gofer. When Brown lost, Larson moved to San Francisco, where he took a job as a canvasser for Citizens for a Better Environment (CBE), an organization started after Earth Day 1972 by an encyclopedia salesman named Mark Anderson. Anderson became convinced that if he could sell second-rate encyclopedias by knocking on doors maybe he could convince residents to donate a dollar each to operate a recycling center or do other environmental work in Chicago. Thus environmental canvassing was born and idealistic young people have been knocking on doors ever since asking for contributions to green causes.

Not a lot of people are cut out for canvassing, Larson observed. The 95 percent rejection rate tends to wear on the faint of heart. It also takes a certain attitude to be willing to disturb countless people in their homes and demand their attention and some money for a good cause. Larson was made for it, he said. He started on August 30, 1984. "I liked going to people's doors because it was like shouting 'Wake up, America,'" he continued. "We were going to rankle people with money and get them to do something for people who didn't [have money] who lived where the toxic hazards were."

Larson started hearing horror stories about what it was like living next to the plants as he went door to door working as a canvasser in the East Bay out near the big oil refineries. As he collected citizens' complaints about toxics, he became educated about what it was like living on the fenceline. After hundreds of such conversations, he became convinced that there was a need for a network of refinery communities that connected community groups fighting pollution in the same way in which the Silicon Valley Toxics Coalition had created a network of groups around electronic plants.

Larson soon led a drive within CBE to launch its first corporate campaign against Chevron over their dumping of toxics into the Bay. By 1986 the newly organized National Toxics Campaign came west and joined with the venerable Citizen's Action League to form the West County Toxics Coalition, of which Larson was a founding member. It was then that Larson and others began to see the potential effectiveness of concentrating organizing efforts in fenceline communities where the residents who lived next to these plants were most affected by their pollution, he recalled. To this end, he started organizing among residents who lived next to the Chevron, Pacific, Shell, and Tosco refineries in Richmond, Rodeo, Martinez, and Crockett.

By 1992, CBE had a toolbox of strategies crafted to influence the behavior or the petroleum companies. One of these tools was the "Good Neighbor" agreements which established a formal protocol for refineries to deal with their residential neighbors. It soon became obvious that the best time to push for a Good Neighbor agreement was when a plant was applying for a permit, Larson explained. Blocking the permit could give residents leverage with the company and sometimes even get the Good Neighbor Agreement written into the permit itself.

Larson and other activists also became increasingly sophisticated about the availability of improved technologies, such as the leakless valves, that companies could install to reduce pollution. CBE had its own research and legal staff to look into these emerging technologies making it possible for

Larson and others to make public arguments calling for the upgrading of refinery equipment. "We became experts in solutions," Larson said. This all paid off and resulted in 300 tons a year less venting of volatile organic chemicals at one Shell plant, for example, he added.

This success did not go unnoticed. The C. S. Mott Foundation awarded CBE a $250,000 grant to write manuals and do training to help other fence-line communities around the country make similar gains and to build a national refinery network When Larson started doing this in 1994 and visited a community next to a Sun refinery (formerly a Chevron plant) outside Philadelphia, he learned that the residents had lost the fight to stop the building of a benzene plant there in 1982—a year after activists in Richmond had kept Chevron from building the same benzene plant in their community. The lesson was clear if depressing: the not-in-our-backyard campaign in Richmond had just pushed the problem into someone else's back yard in Philadelphia. Clearly a broader national strategy was called for that would organize a movement which would ensure that highly polluting facilities that poison the air would not be built in anybody's back yard, Larson said.

Traveling around the country training fenceline communities in how to intervene in the permit process of oil refineries and extract concessions that would reduce pollution, Larson began to patch together a National Oil Refinery Network designed to help coordinate the work of groups dealing with similar problems around the nation. It was while he was doing this work that he first met Wilma Subra, the chemists who helped fenceline communities in Louisiana; and Margie Richard, the grassroots activist from Diamond. Since Subra was in high demand from communities faced with toxic problems Larson asked her for a list of communities along the petrochemical corridor that runs from New Orleans to Texas. This list subsequently became the backbone of a network of communities that have since shared expertise and war stories—learning from each other and supporting each other.

Larson also came to know Beverly Wright, who had also been networking among communities in the river parishes outside New Orleans. CBE subsequently made mini-grants with the C. S. Mott money to the Deep South Center to run workshops that brought in a variety of outside experts to educate local residents about how their struggle with the Shell Chemical plant and the Motiva refinery fit in with the larger struggle for environmental justice.

Birth of the Bucket Brigade

The saga of how a cheap variety of air-monitoring equipment came into existence began with a chemical release by a large industry into a neighboring fenceline residential community.

This time it took place near the towns of Crockett and Rodeo, California not far from a Unocal refinery that boasted a 174-foot tower used to reprocess and cleanse hydrogen used in the refining process. In 1994 the tower sprung a leak from corrosion near the top and catacarb, a chemical that is dangerous and capable of causing blindness among other ill effects, began to escape. "Imagine the tower is a giant aerosol can under 1,700 pounds per square inch (psi) pressure and it starts to leak," said Denny Larson, coordinator of the Refinery Reform Campaign. When the leak started workers looked up what they should do in their process safety manuals and found that they were instructed to shut the tower down immediately. It later was revealed that a similar tower in a plant in Illinois took off like a rocket and landed in a farmer's field 7 miles away killing a number of workers in the process.

Unocal workers were called into a management meeting where they were told not to shut down the unit, Larson claimed. The fact that they would lose a large pay-for-performance bonus if they pulled the plug no doubt played a role in that decision, he continued. Instead of shutting down the tower they were told to "limp it along" and keep an eye on it. They were also assured that catacarb was no more dangerous than detergent, Larson said. One of the workers, a man named Don Brown, objected to this characterization of catacarb as harmless. He reported that he had looked it up on the Occupational Safety and Health's (OSHA) Material Safety Data Sheet, which indicated that the chemical could cause blindness and serious health effects. His objection was overruled, however, and the tower was kept in production.

Over the next 16 days the hole in the tower grew larger and began to spray so much catacarb that it covered the neighboring town of Crockett in a brown goo that residents had to scrape it off their windshields. Since it was September the catacarb also covered the vegetables in the gardens of residents and infiltrated their homes permeating their carpets and curtains. People began to get sick and then became furious, Larson recalled. Eventually, the leak got so bad that it began to eat the paint off the tanks in an adjacent oil tank farm and the owners called up Unocal and insisted that they shut the offending unit down. But by then the damage had been done. "People were waking up to realize that while they couldn't see the plant it was poisoning them," Larson said.

At that point Larson began to organize local residents to block Unocal's permit application and demand a Good Neighbor agreement. During the same period a tort attorney named Ed Masry and his research assistant, Erin Brockovitch, came to town to collect clients for a suit against Unocal. This was the same toxic tort team that later successfully won a massive claim against PG&E, a struggle later made into a feature film titled *Erin Brockovitch*, starring Julia Roberts.

As if the leak of catacarb from the tower was not bad enough, a new leak of hydrogen sulfide from an old compressor sent 80 kids to the hospital, Larson recalled. Subsequently it was discovered that Unocal had plans to sell the plant and that explained why they were not investing in maintenance or new equipment, he said. They were just running the plant into the ground and squeezing every penny of profit they could out of it, he charged. "Then we realized what was happening: that they were going to kill people if they weren't stopped," Larson asserted.

In June 1995, Masry and Brockovitch were in their office in Crockett when Unocal sprung another leak of sulfur. It made both of them sick and injured Brockovich's eye. Now they were not just representing people who had been hurt by the plant: they had been hit themselves. Masry called up the Air District and other agencies and asked what substance had escaped so that he could inform their doctors so they could be given proper treatment. He was told that company air monitors indicated no problem. It was then that Masry blew his top, Larson said. Now it was personal. There and then he decided to equip his clients with air-sampling equipment and surround the plant with forty air monitors so they could gather their own data on what the plant was releasing. But where would he get the equipment?

An environmental engineering firm told him could purchase Suma Canisters at cost $1,000 each that would take air samples but this was too expensive even for a wealthy tort attorney. Masry asked Don Brown and an environmental engineer to come up with a cheaper model. After some tinkering they devised an air sampling bucket that cost $300 to produce. With the data they gathered, Masry and Brockovitch won their cases against Unocal in 1997, collecting $80 million for some 6,000 residents. Larson asked them to donate the thirty air sampling buckets and the design specifications for building them so that he could write up a manual and begin teaching other fenceline residents how to use this new technology.

Larson subsequently reduced the cost of building a citizen air-sampling device even further. He replaced the stainless steel canister with a five-gallon plastic paint bucket that can be purchased for $5 at a hardware store and equipped it with a Tedlar bag that could hold the air sample. (Tedlar is a plastic that does not give off or react with other chemicals so it will not contaminate the sample.) He also bought a cheap pump for the air monitor from Radio Shack and switched the stainless steel fittings for brass. When the remodeled air sampling "bucket" was completed it could be built for $175–$200—a fraction of the cost of the fancier model. This made it affordable for groups of residents who were serious about proving that they were being poisoned by a neighboring facility, Larson pointed out.

It was Larson's hope that this new tool might prove to be "the missing link" for a lot of groups that currently had to depend on data supplied by the offending companies, which tended to put their air-monitoring equipment too far out of town, upwind from the plant, or calibrated only to detect chemicals at very high levels. The company air monitors were akin to speed radar guns that would not find a problem with drivers going 1,000 miles per hour, Larson contended. Furthermore, a lot of industry's air monitors were set to detect the wrong chemicals and were not targeted on volatile organic chemicals (VOCs) such as toluene and benzene—chemicals typically found in the vicinity of a refinery. This was the case in St. Charles Parish, where three ambient air-monitoring sites were located in Destrehan, Hahnville, and Luling but none in Norco. Further, none of the three monitoring sites tracked toxic pollutants produced by chemical plants and instead were limited to detecting total suspended particulates, lead, ozone, and particulate matter.[1]

While Larson was pioneering the use of these buckets, he convinced an EPA official from Region IX in California to do side-by-side tests that compared samples taken by the conventional Suma Canister and the cheaper citizen's air-monitoring bucket. The EPA test showed that when properly used the buckets took accurate air samples that could be sent to a lab and analyzed by gas chromatograph mass spectrometry to find out what chemicals were in the air.

Larson's idea was to set up what he called "Bucket Brigades" in fenceline communities. He hoped to use the bucket as an organizing tool to get fenceline community groups off the ground. He did not just want to come in with the bucket himself, take a few samples, and then leave the community without equipment when he left. Instead, he insisted that a community raise the money to build the buckets and get training in how to use them. Only in this fashion would they be empowered to protect themselves. The bucket could help put citizens in control of the data, he argued.

For a number of years no community took Larson up on this offer. He had set the bar deliberately high and no one wanted to jump over it. Then, finally, the community of Mossville, Louisiana (surrounded by a polyvinyl chloride plant, a refinery and a vinyl chloride monomer plant) was awarded a Greenpeace grant to build and learn how to use the citizen's air-monitoring bucket. About 100 grassroots activists came to the training session, including Margie Richard and Gaynel Johnson from the Diamond subdivision of Norco. Participants assembled their own buckets and learned to use them.

"On February 28, 1999, an air sample on Mossville captured vinyl chloride and benzene in excess of air criteria," noted a report by two MIT researchers.[2] An accidental release of vinyl chloride by one of these plants occurred on the same day the sample was taken. The sample showed traces of EDC and ethyl benzene, chemicals associated with the production process of the nearby plants, Larson reported.

A number of groups bonded around the making of their buckets, Larson recalled. After they build their buckets "there is a tremendous pride of ownership. They have built their own slingshot. It is their slingshot and they are going to slay Goliath," he said. They stencil the name of their group on their buckets and differentiate roles in their bucket brigade. Some residents serve as samplers and keep the buckets in their homes ready to use. Others are "sniffers" who call those with the bucket if they smell intense chemical odors. Still others are assigned as coordinators who check to make sure that samples are properly taken, that the valve is turned off after use, that it is properly stored, and that the paperwork is done creating a chain of custody for their evidence. They are also assigned to ensure that a narrative is written when the sample is taken describing the odor, the physical reaction of residents to the chemical exposure, a rough estimate of wind direction, and the time and date the sample is taken

Maura Wood, a member of Louisiana's Delta Chapter of the Sierra Club arranged to have the organization provide funding for residents of Norco to learn how to build and use air sampling buckets and paid for the analysis of a couple of air samples. The bucket was ready for action. It had been used effectively in northern California but questions remained as to whether or not it would catch on under different cultural conditions in the South of the United States and in other parts of the world.

MEK Leak

On the cold, cloudy morning of December 8, 1998, a 5,000-gallon reactor tank at Shell Chemical's resin unit became overpressurized and started leaking just across the street from Diamond residents.[3] The vessel contained methyl ethyl ketone, a substance listed as a hazardous air pollutant by the U.S. Environmental Protection Agency.[4] As a result of the leak, a fine, cloudy-white mist descended on the residents of Diamond causing burning eyes, throat irritation, and nausea. Some residents reported a smell like burnt garlic; others felt the skin tighten on their faces.[5] "Hazel Davis, unsuspecting, walked through the fumes and the strong smell stung her eyes and nose. Other neighbors were caught in the cloud or saw it leak into their homes through cracks and under doors."[6]

A level two alert (one is the lowest and four is the highest level of danger) was announced that morning. As part of the emergency preparedness routine a telephone alert system was activated and an announcement of the leak was made over radio stations.

Shell workers fanned out through the communities of Diamond and Norco warning local residents that there was an incident in progress at the plant and passed out a flyer that read: "Notice to Our Neighbors. . . . Shell Norco wishes to apologize for this morning's incident. . . . At approximately 8:00 A.M. this morning an overpressure of a small vessel occurred at the resin unit. There were no chemical releases to the community. An investigation into the causes of the tank overpressure is underway."[7] Residents were advised to "shelter in place" by closing their doors and windows and turning off their air conditioning and heating systems. Norco school administrators decided that the fourth- to sixth-grade students who were already at the school should "shelter-in-place" but they diverted school buses carrying kindergarten through third-grade children to a high school in Destrehan a few miles down River Road.

Diamond resident Wendy Mashia first heard that there was a problem in Norco from a co-worker at the Macy's department store where she works as a sales clerk. "I left work half scared to death," recalled Mashia who has three children in school in Norco ages 6, 10, and 13. When she arrived home she found two of her children had been evacuated to the high school.

Other residents took matters into their own hands. "I was on the highway coming [to Diamond] from Bible college when there was an announcement [on the radio] that they had evacuated Norco, recalled Margie Richard, former president of Concerned Citizens of Norco. "I panicked because my mom was home. People came up the street and their eyes were burning and nose running and everything. So I told my mom to get in the car that we were getting out of here," Richard said.

Just after 10 A.M., officials from the Louisiana Department of Environmental Quality arrived at the site and were told by Shell officials that there had been no releases into the community. State regulatory officials decided not to do any air monitoring. At 11:28 A.M. Shell officials sounded the "all clear" signal and it seemed that the crisis had passed. At 12:18 P.M., 400 pounds of hydrochloric acid were released when a railroad tank car was overloaded.

The first sign to Gaynel Johnson that there was some kind of a leak at Shell came when an attorney in New Orleans called her and asked what was going on in Norco. She told him she had heard nothing new. Then a neighbor called asking the same thing. Taking the telephone with her Johnson walked outside. "I was looking toward the back of Shell and I saw this white stuff is walking clean across that-away," she recalled.

Many Diamond residents assumed that the second release was a continuation of the previous incident. This led them to conclude that the "all clear" signal had been sounded too soon. It also resulted in considerable skepticism among residents as to whether or not Shell was giving them accurate information: on the one hand they were told that the leak had been fixed; on the other hand they could clearly see evidence that some kind of problem was still occurring.

It later emerged that there were two separate incidents on the same day and that while Shell felt obliged to report the first incident, they did not report the second release because it was under 400 pounds—below the legal reporting limit for that chemical. Shell did a good job in the morning of alerting residents about the first leak but failed in the afternoon to keep residents up to date about a problem they could clearly see, said Robert Thomas, a professor of environmental journalism. "They should have immediately told the people that there was a [second] release," he added.

The timing of the MEK leak could not have been less fortuitous from Shell's perspective. The 24 executive council members of the National Environmental Justice Advisory Council (NEJAC), who had recently toured Norco, were still meeting in Baton Rouge at the time. Denny Larson, coordinator of the Refinery Reform Campaign, who was attending the meeting, called Margie Richard in Diamond to see if she planned to travel to Baton Rouge to give a presentation the following day.

Richard was very upset when she received Larson's call. She told him she was not sure if she could come because there had been a big release and people were sick in Diamond. Some of them were going to emergency rooms to be treated. Hearing this Larson and a colleague grabbed one of his air-monitoring 'buckets' and a video camera and headed for Diamond. On the way out the door he met one of the EPA officials and told him about the release. "There has been a toxic release. We're going [to Norco] to take an air sample: what are you going to do," he asked? It later became apparent that the EPA had no one at the time in Louisiana equipped to take a sample, Larson claimed.

By the time Larson arrived in Diamond it was dusk—about 8 hours after the release. Margie Richard was so glad to see him that she wept for joy. With a colleague, Larson walked up and down Washington Street until they found a spot where the smell of MEK was still strong and took a sample. They both recognized the smell from earlier exposure to the chemical, he said. He then rushed the sample via Federal Express to Performance Analytical Laboratory (now Columbia Laboratories) in Simi Valley, California—one of the few certified labs willing to run an analysis of bucket brigade samples. (Other labs did not want to antagonize the industries they service, he said.) Larson explained the circumstances of the sample and pleaded with workers to analyze it and return the results within 24 hours. But the next day, when Larson received the data, he was puzzled because there was no sign of the MEK.

At first he thought that the delay in taking the sample—a period of at least 8 hours after the release—had allowed the chemical to dissipate to the point where it was undetectable. It was a big let down. There was, however, one chemical listed in the sample analysis he did not recognize called 2-butanone. When he finally found a reference book and looked it up it turned out that it was another name for MEK. "I ran around the hotel screaming: 'We got 'em. We got 'em,'" Larson recalled. This was the smoking gun. The fact that he had found traces of MEK in the sample combined with the symptoms experienced by Diamond residents, which were associated with MEK, proved to him that the residents had been exposed.

Shell officials told residents immediately after the release that no dangerous chemicals had escaped into their community but here was proof that they had been. Larson wrote up a report about the air sample findings and Margie Richard read it out at the NEJAC speak-out session for fenceline residents the next day. Richard also brought with her a mother and her two children from Diamond who had been so badly affected by the release that they went to the hospital. "This was a watershed event," Larson observed.

While he had been in Norco the day before taking the sample, Larson had also videotaped a large flare coming out of Dow Chemical unit across the river from Norco. He showed this to EPA officials at the NEJAC conference and they were surprised having been told by Dow officials that there was no flare. They requested a copy of the videotape. The combination of the MEK sample at Norco and the videotape of the Dow flare convinced EPA officials that they were being lied to by industry. As a result, when Margie Richard and a group of Diamond allies approached EPA officials at the conference and demanded to know what they were going to do about the exposure of residents in their community to dangerous chemicals, Sam Coleman, director of Enforcement for EPA's region VI said: "It is on the top shelf. . . . I have questions about why these things happened and I think they are legitimate questions." The situation in Norco was a "historic and serious problem," he added.[8]

The air sample Larson took in Diamond found 12 parts per *billion* of MEK—far less than the Louisiana state's legal limit of 3.98 parts per *million*. As a result, Shell officials could say that they had not broken the law with this release. But the sample was taken 8 hours after the release and the likelihood is strong that if the sample had been taken at the height of the release it would have been considerably higher. Further, Shell claimed that it had taken air samples that morning and had not detected a problem. Larson contended that Shell's monitoring equipment was not set low enough to detect the chemical making it possible for them to report to residents that there were no harmful chemicals in the air. "They lied by omission," Larson asserted. His air sample proved that there was MEK in the air and that residents had been exposed. The bucket had proven its worth in Norco.

"Denny brought the bucket to Diamond. . . . When the MEK leaked he came down and did some testing. And that gave me relief and I said 'Thank you God' because facts work," said Margie Richard. People had begun to dismiss Concerned Citizens of Norco as just a bunch of malcontents who were "making a bunch of noise," she continued. But after the bucket air sample "we could deal in facts," she said.

Catching that bad sample "really put a fire under Shell," commented Beverly Wright. There was no doubt that this "very nasty stuff" that had been detected in the air was coming from Shell, she continued. "So the Bucket Brigade proved to be a very powerful tool," said Wright who admits to having been initially skeptical of Larson. But in the end Wright realized that the bucket sample not only provided evidence of a chemical exposure in Diamond, it also gave residents in the community a feeling that they could take some control over what was happening to them, she added. Shell was eventually fined $27,000 for the December 8, 1998 releases.

"Residents were so angry because they thought they had been lied to," Wright recalled, "but I told them 'What do you expect from a polluting facility? They are not going to tell you what they are doing and confess.'"

In addition to not being able to explain why there was MEK in the air sample, Shell never offered a satisfactory explanation of what happened to the overpressurized MEK. How did Shell resolve the problem? How did they reduce the pressure, Larson asked? Where did it go? There was never any evidence that they vented it to a containment vessel and the only other logical explanation is that they released it into the air next to Diamond residents, he added.

This is a routine practice in the industry, Larson said. "It is outrageous to have flammable, explosive, and deadly chemicals in spheres and process units all the time and the routine method for dealing with an emergency is to vent it directly to the air where you know it is going to blow off site into the neighborhood; or to flare it [burn the chemical at the top of a stack], which often times has been shown—particularly with Motiva and Shell— that the flare can't handle it and the combustion rate is poor. You don't get 98 percent combustion. You get all kinds of nasty chemicals in huge amounts coming off the flare into the neighborhood," he added.

Other bucket samples detected chemicals in the air in Diamond on other days. A resident-captured air sample taken on June 19, 1998 confirmed the long-standing contention of Diamond residents that "there are no good air days in Norco." Analysis of the sample detected nine harmful chemicals in the air on a "normal day" when there had been no reported accident.[9]

Subsequent bucket samples taken in 1999 found a "noxious mix of chemicals" reports Anne Rolfes of the Louisiana Bucket Brigade. Samples included carbonyl sulfide and carbon disulfide at levels above Texas state standards. (Louisiana does not have standards for these chemicals, she explained.) In addition the samples included trace amounts of benzene, toluene, styrene, and methyl ethyl ketone, she added. A later sample taken on June 5, 2001 recorded dangerous levels of carbon disulfide, a chemical that attacks the cardiovascular system, Rolfes added.[10] Based on the citizen air-monitoring results collected in Diamond, Wilma Subra calculated that "residents of Norco were being exposed to 100 to 1,000 times higher concentrations of toxics than people living in rural Louisiana."[11]

The Louisiana Bucket Brigade has been exceptionally important in Norco and in other communities in Louisiana," observed former EarthJustice attorney Monique Harden. It permitted residents to gather some tangible proof of what is in their air and to prove that adjacent companies have been less than candid with them. The air sampling bucket gives residents some control over the collection of data and they can believe the results because they captured the sample themselves, she continued. Before the air-sampling buckets arrived in Diamond, some residents had given up calling the state authorities; they knew nothing would come of it. But the arrival of the buckets in town motivated more residents to participate in the relocation struggle, she noted. It also made governmental regulatory agencies and companies like Shell more accountable, she added.

Who Heard What When?

The single-day, double-barreled accident at Shell Chemical and the way it was handled caused long-simmering anger among Diamond residents to boil over. Residents said that once again they had been lied to by Shell officials only this time they had evidence of the lies. Responding to the sense of outrage in the community, Margie Richard, then president of Concerned Citizens of Norco, called for a public meeting to analyze what had gone wrong and devise a warning system for Diamond residents that would work better in the future.

Richard called for a face-to-face meeting to be held in January, 1999 with Shell officials, representatives from the Louisiana Department of Environmental Quality, parish representatives, and U.S. Environmental Protection regulators. She also invited representatives of Greenpeace, the Sierra Club, the Deep South Center for Environmental Justice, and EarthJustice Legal Defense Fund. Also in attendance were members of the Norco Civic Club and other residents from Norco and Diamond.

Shell officials initially lobbied to hold the meeting at their facility and they wanted to know who would be attending it, recalled former EarthJustice attorney Monique Harden. But Harden and others advised Richard that Concerned Citizens of Norco should keep the meeting under their control and feel fully entitled to set it up the way they wanted it. There was also the problem of not having the $50 to rent a meeting hall, but Harden told Richard that the allies of Concerned Citizens of Norco would come up with the money.

The January 14 meeting was to prove one of the most contentious ever held in Norco. "Obviously the white folks were very pumped up and pro-Shell at the meeting; and the black folks were very indignant about how they had been treated not only on December 8 but about their whole history with Shell," observed Denny Larson, coordinator of the Refinery Reform Campaign. This was a critical juncture for the struggle for relocation in Diamond. The residents' anger at Shell was white hot. Large numbers of them had been affected by the gas release and had been worried about their children. There was a groundswell of antagonism toward Shell among residents and a widely held sense that now was the time to demand relocation.

On the other hand, calmer heads were calling for using this incident constructively. For the first time the issue of air pollution in Norco and Diamond had become a top priority at the Environmental Protection Agency. EPA officials insisted that they could not do anything about relocation—that was a local zoning issue. The EPA could only relocate residents adjacent to Superfund sites under certain conditions. But they were willing do intensive air monitoring in Norco with a mobile air sampling truck that could take multiple samples upwind and downwind of the plant. Wilma Subra, who had been working for years to patch together data proving that Shell was releasing toxic chemicals into Diamond, saw this as a critical breakthrough. With the promised new EPA air-monitoring equipment residents would finally be able to collect the hard data to prove that Shell was out of compliance with their permit and endangering the health of local residents, she said. This could prove critical in making the argument for relocation, Subra added.[12]

There were others, however, who did not want to wait for months to collect more data. They made the following argument: first, they already knew that Shell was polluting the air because there was ample evidence from Shell's own statistics that they were releasing hazardous chemicals into the community; second, now was the time to demand relocation while the people were angry; third, inviting the EPA in to Norco to do air monitoring would just give Shell an excuse to put off any decision about relocation; and fourth, the message should be that the EPA had not done its job until everyone in Diamond who wanted to be relocated had been moved.

The meeting at the American Legion hall in Norco had been arranged so that there were a bunch of tables in the back of the room where people could place food. At the front of the room there were a cluster of chairs—or hot seats—where representatives of Shell, Concerned Citizens of Norco, and the EPA could sit and answer questions about the release on December 8. When some of the white residents of Norco filed into the room (some dressed in Shell jumper suits worn on the work site) they mistakenly assumed that the tables in the back were where the action was going to be and sat there. As residents of Diamond entered the room they all sat near the hot seats at the front of the room. Already the dividing lines had been drawn.

Margie Richard opened the meeting by presenting information about the MEK leak on December 8 and followed up with a discussion of the frequency of accidents at the Shell and Motiva facilities. Other Diamond residents vented their frustration about the confusion that arose out of the school's decision to keep some of the students in the school buildings during the crisis while diverting younger children to a neighboring high school. A few Diamond parents described how confused and frightened they and their children had been. At that point one of the white parents from Norco said that her children actually enjoyed being sequestered with the "big kids" and that it was an adventure for them. A black parent replied that while it might have been fun for other children it was terrifying for hers.

The discussion then addressed the question of why an "all clear" signal had been sounded an hour before Diamond residents saw the cloud of hydrochloric gas released. To respond to this Randy Armstrong, director of the environmental section at Shell Chemical, explained that a "misunderstanding" had occurred. Shell did not report the second release because it was under 400 pounds and that amount did not have to be reported, he said. "He laid it out and when he was finished the lady [from Diamond] who had been concerned about her children got up to the microphone and said: 'Why didn't we know this two months ago? I have spent two months so upset,'" recalled Robert Thomas, director of the Center for Environmental Communications at Loyola University. This exchange illustrated how profound was the communication gulf between Shell and the residents of Diamond and here was a chance to work it out, suggested Thomas. But it was not to be.

Instead the discussion became even more heated when the question arose about who knew about the MEK leak and when were they informed about it, recalled Monique Harden. "The people in the room were asked: Who didn't receive a [warning] call? All these brown arms go up in the air. [Then the question was asked:] Who did receive a call? And the white people all raise there hands. So we have a problem here," she observed. Immediately, the white residents from Norco started getting very angry and said: "You are trying to make this a race issue," she continued. But Diamond residents replied that there was a problem with who in town had been alerted.

It was at this juncture, that Damu Smith, an organizer from Greenpeace, who had long been involved in the struggle for relocation in Norco, said: "I am not going to allege racism but there is something very strange going on here," Robert Thomas recalled. He went on to point out that more white people appeared to have gotten warning calls than black people and suggested that this indicated that there was a serious problem. "Smith drove a racial wedge into the discussions," Roberts charged, and the meeting descended into a shouting match with the representative from Greenpeace and a woman from the EPA screaming at each other. A contingent of white residents from Norco then stormed out in disgust, he recalled. An opportunity was lost to bring the two communities closer. "It had come very close to coming together," Thomas lamented.

Denny Larson had a different interpretation: "Damu hit the nail on the head." The meeting was unprecedented because there were members of both the black and white community present, he continued. "From the very first time you go to Norco you cross what I call The Great Divide—the thicket between the black and white communities that has a ditch running through it. This makes the point rather starkly that racism is alive and an issue in Norco. St. Charles Parish has a history of Klan activity that goes way back." Racism determines who works at the refineries and who lives where, he continued. Whites and blacks in Norco tend to be polite to each other in public and greet each other at the grocery store but when any real issue comes up—such as the handling of the MEK leak—the community is racially polarized, he added.

What was particularly revealing was how members of each race perceived that members of the other race had submitted to pressure from their peer group. Black participants observed that when asked if they had been notified about the chemical release most whites put up their hands and the few who had not been telephoned looked around and saw how their neighbors were voting and decided to put up their hands. Similarly, a number of white participants reported that when blacks were asked if they had received a warning call some of them who had received calls started to raise their arms but, seeing everyone else of their race with their hands clenched in their laps, decided not to. Of course, both observations could be correct. Clearly no one wanted to indicate anything other than what the majority of their race was signaling.

Even the composition of the people who came to the meetings was called into question. From the Diamond side of the fence, Gaynel Johnson observed that white residents who attended the meeting were not truly representative and included a disproportionate number of Shell employees, retirees, and caterers instead of the parents of children who had to deal with the confusion at the school. "So you see what Shell did? They targeted people," she claimed.

What puzzled Richard about the position taken by the white residents of Norco was not so much that they reported that living next to the plant was no problem from their perspective but rather that they wanted to insist that the experience of Diamond residents was the same. "You have your problems in Norco . . . that is natural . . . but why do members of the Civic Club want to tell us in Diamond that we don't have problems?" she asked.

One of the most telling signs of how powerfully Shell controls the white side of Norco occurred when participants in the meeting were polled as to who wanted cleaner air to breathe, noted Monique Harden. All the blacks voted for clean air and clean water while all the whites kept their hands down. "That is pretty scary that whites can't even vote for clean air and clean water," Harden observed. But Larson is not surprised: to the whites calling for clean air and clean water are code phrases for shutting down the plant, he explained.

Some of the white residents from Norco who attended the meeting complained that there were "outside agitators" present who were determined to make the issue a black against white problem. One member of Norco's Civic Club got up and denounced Greenpeace's Damu Smith as nothing but a troublemaker. "He sinks ships," Richard remembered the speaker warning. Robert Thomas also felt that some of the outside environmental activists were unhelpful. Some of them were putting their own agendas ahead of serving the real needs of the residents, he observed.

The charge that outside agitators were causing the problems in Norco was patently ridiculous, Denny Larson argued—residents of Diamond had been lobbying for relocation since at least 1988 and some since 1973. This was a homegrown movement by residents who wanted to be relocated, he added. The "outside groups" only helped local residents amplify their voice by bringing in the media and other resources to help them be heard, he said.

After the race issue came up, the meeting degenerated into people yelling at each other. Someone said that Damu Smith should leave the meeting or the police would be called. Richard quickly nixed this idea pointing out that the meeting had been called by Concerned Citizens of Norco and that Smith was an invited guest. EPA representatives were also miffed because they felt that their offer to monitor the air had been snubbed by local residents. As a result they decided to back off. A number of white participants walked out on the meeting once voices were raised.

While the meeting was tense and at times even ugly it did serve the purpose of bringing a long festering wound into the sunlight. "We aired all of differences and indifferences. It was so chaotic until there was yelling and screaming. . . . That is when the real communication started," observed Margie Richard, by now an accomplished master of finding hope in even the most depressing circumstances. "That was another door opening and out of the chaos there was a change in the way the people in the Old Diamond Plantation were treated by Shell," she added.

13

Helping Hands

The environmentalist organization Greenpeace came to Norco in the person of Damu Smith, 52, a veteran civil rights and environmental justice organizer. Like others who made their way to Margie Richard's trailer on Washington Street, just across from the Shell Chemical plant, Smith had worked on a number of social justice campaigns before coming to Norco. In addition to this organizing experience, he brought with him Greenpeace's considerable resources, its bulldog reputation for sticking with campaigns for years, and its penchant for using headline-grabbing tactics.

Born in St. Louis, Smith grew up in the Carr Square Village housing projects, where he lived until he was 17. "I grew up in a working-class/lower-income family. My father was a fireman and an air pollution inspector and my mother was a licensed practical nurse. So I was born of working-class parents. My mother and father went through a lot of difficulties at times in their own relationship and sometimes it resulted in us going on welfare. My father was in prison for about five years. I mention this because much of what I am today has been shaped by the fact that I grew up in not wretchedly poor surroundings but we struggled. I know what it is to go to school without heat at home and study by candlelight and not have enough money to get adequate clothes. So I have great sensitivity to the plight of poor people. I grew up under those circumstances. I grew up under food stamps and welfare and government handout cheese and milk and meat and all that. I experienced all of that as a child," Smith recalled. He also grew up in the 1960s, during the height of the civil rights and black power movements. At age 10 he watched television news reports of Martin Luther King Jr. leading voting rights marches in Selma. As a junior in high school, he attended Sophia House, a Jesuit-run after-school program for "disadvantaged black male youth." It was designed to help prepare young black males for college, he said.

In 1969 and 1970, Smith was reading Malcolm X, H. Rap Brown, and Eldridge Cleaver and having long conversations with his friends about the politics of the civil rights movement and the war in Vietnam. The Jesuits took Smith and his colleagues on a field trip to Black Solidarity Days rallies in Cairo, Illinois, where they heard Ralph Abernathy, Julian Bond, Nina Simone, and Jesse Jackson. They toured neighborhoods where the houses were pocked with bullet holes caused by gunfire from white supremacists. "Seeing those bullet holes . . . that changed my life. I decided then that I was always going to be a freedom fighter in the movement for liberation and justice and I have been doing that ever since," Smith said.

In October 1970, as a freshman and the president of the Organization of Afro-American Students at St. John's University in Collegeville, Minnesota, Smith led a takeover of the school's administrative offices in a protest over absence of a black studies program. "I led the takeover of the administration building and the president's office for a couple of hours," Smith recalled, "and the police came in and arrested us and we went to jail for a couple of days. A photo of me looking out the window of the president's office was flashed on the front page of most newspapers in Minnesota." His celebrity put Smith in touch with other black activists, and he began to study the lives of heroic black figures both living and dead. "This helped shape my political views," he said.

In 1973, Smith moved to Washington to be at the heart of the action. He attended Antioch College's Center for the Study of Basic Human Problems. In 1991, while organizing against the Gulf War, the director of Greenpeace heard Smith speak at rallies. He was offered a berth in Greenpeace's minority fellows program, which recruited people of color who had organizing experience. After a year in the program he was hired by Greenpeace. He worked for the organization for the next 10 years. He served on the planning committee for the First People of Color Environmental Justice Summit, where he rubbed shoulders with what he describes as "the giants of the environmental justice movement," including Benjamin Moore, Pat Bryant, Dana Alston, Bob Bullard, and Beverly Wright. "I learned everything listening to them because this was my introduction to the Environmental Justice Movement. . . . I was at their feet learning," he recalled.

Smith was asked to travel around the country and invite grassroots leaders in communities of color to come to the Summit. "In the process I got to know a lot of people and I traveled extensively all over the country meeting all these people. So that was a real blessing and experience for me. It was like going to school: I was getting paid to go to school."

In addition to working with the Toxics Campaign at Greenpeace, Smith was seconded to serve as a full-time staff position for the Southern Organizing Committee for Economic and Social Justice and became its first coordinator for the environmental justice. He was also designated the director of the Southern Community Labor Conference for Environmental and Economic Justice and coordinated the largest environmental justice conference ever held, bringing together 2,500 activists from all 14 states in the South as well as people from elsewhere in the country to New Orleans. This outreach effort required that Smith travel to 40 towns and cities in nine states in six months in 1991–92.

"I went to all these communities impacted by environmental racism where I saw the contaminated conditions that people were living in. The strategy of the Southern Organizing Committee was to not only get these people to come to a conference but to help them with their struggles for environmental justice. So we would bring in support to their communities at the same time we were mobilizing them for the conference," Smith said. He convened five statewide meetings in Mississippi, North Carolina, Georgia, Alabama, and Louisiana. In the process he built up a network of grassroots environmental activists and was subsequently named the southern regional coordinator for Greenpeace when the organization's Toxics Campaign targeted PVC production in Louisiana.

Having traveled all over the South as an environmental justice organizer and visited several hundred communities on the fenceline with toxic industries, Smith observed that conditions in heavily minority fenceline communities in Louisiana were among the worst he had seen. In fact, along with those in Texas, particularly Brownsville Texas, conditions in Louisiana were the worst.

"What struck me about the South today was just how bad things were. That is the only way I can put it. **BAAAAD!** all caps, bold, exclamation point. And by bad I don't mean good. Here were all of these low-income black people in rural and semi-rural communities surrounded by all these toxic industries. It was incredible to see the vastness of it, the scope of it, especially in Louisiana. There were acres upon acres of polluting industries surrounding these people in the communities. People were in such close proximity to these facilities and the fact that these noxious fumes were coming out and the wrenching stench of this toxic soup swirling around people's homes and the playgrounds and schools just hit me like a sledge hammer. This was such a devastating set of conditions for people to be living under. It was shocking," he asserted. This was ground zero for environmental injustice, he added.

Smith first came to Norco in 1991 around the time of the Southern Community Labor Conference. But the first time he really had a chance to meet and talk with members of the community was in 1995–96. "By then I was knowledgeable enough to have a pretty informed conversation with them about what was going on and to offer suggestions. At Greenpeace Smith assignment was primarily focused on the PVC industry. Unsatisfied with targeting one class of chemicals exclusive, he argued that winning victories in Louisiana on PVC required winning victories in other heavily polluted minority communities such as Norco.

At a meeting with Margie Richard and other members of Concerned Citizens of Norco, Smith was told about the lawsuit that the community had lost against Shell. Instead of pursuing a legal strategy, Smith argued for a different approach. "The only way we are going to be able to win against Shell is ultimately to shame them into moving everybody because legally there is no basis for a lawsuit any more. Morally there might be but legally there was no basis," he explained. Smith also told them that Greenpeace was prepared to help bring their plight national and international publicity.

Here was an opportunity to win an environmental justice victory in Norco because the issue could be framed as "black people and toxics," Smith continued. "You can't get much closer to the fence. They were right there: toxics looking them in the face and they were black. I knew that the positive invocation of race would help do the job in these situations. We had to tell the truth about what was going on. We had to tell the world that the reason why these communities were being dumped on and the way they were being dumped on was because they were black," he said. "I knew we could embarrass them [Shell] to death with the combination of race and toxics. I knew we would be able to use that to our advantage. And I don't mean it in a crass way because this was the truth of what was happening. I knew that if we exploited that reality that ultimately we could win," he added.

Smith conceded that there were also whites living near the Shell plants but argued that the black population was closer to the source of pollution. "The people who were on the street right across from Shell [Chemical], all of them, were black. . . . That was the in-your-face part. And the houses immediately behind them were all black. The white people were in the same vicinity and were being poisoned. The problem was that they were so co-opted by their racism . . . that they couldn't even see that they were being polluted or were unwilling to admit it publicly," he said.

Smith began bringing prestigious people to Norco for "toxic tours" including African-American church leaders. "People started making the pilgrimage to Norco. This was getting a lot of attention and Shell did not like it. They were getting a bad name and they started getting letters and phone calls from people," Smith said. In April 2001 Greenpeace sponsored a celebrity toxic tour that included actor Mike Farrell, writer Alice Walker, Representative Maxine Waters, and the Chicago poet Haki Madabuti. Among those who made appearances, wrote letters, or gave money for the struggle in Diamond were Stevie Wonder, the Neville Brothers, Danny Glover, and Bonnie Raitt. In addition to Maxine Waters, other politicians who weighed in included John Conyers, John Lewis, and Paul Wellstone.

The struggle in Norco was significant, Smith said, because "here was a community so badly poisoned, so enormously affected, a community in so much pain, a community that had suffered so much. The Diamond community was the poster child for environmental racism. It was such a blatant travesty of justice. And we had to win that one. We had to help set a precedent for relocation in that type of situation: relocation by a fenceline community." Shell's resistance to a settlement in Diamond can be partially explained by the fact that the company was concerned about the precedent it would set if they agreed to relocate residents on the fenceline, Smith explained. "You do one and all the others are going to be calling for the same thing so they resisted to the end. This was David versus Goliath. Residents were standing up against these huge industries that have so much power and so much money. . . . They have lawyers and public relations people, they have engineers and scientists and there you are . . . little David . . . so it is easy to feel alone. But the people drew strength not only from themselves but also from us for being there with them supporting them.'

The role played by Greenpeace was crucial because Greenpeace is big enough and has enough money that it can commit to a struggle for a long period of time, said Beverly Wright. Often, fenceline industries are able to simply outlast the energies and resources of local community activists but once Greenpeace takes on a battle there is a new equation and enough resources to see the struggle through, she added.

In addition to its celebrity toxic tours, Greenpeace was also able to publicize the plight of the residents in Norco by bringing the Greenpeace ship up the Mississippi River and mooring it next to Shell's facilities in Norco. "Greenpeace scared the hell out of Shell," said Wright. "They brought down these kids who scale incinerator chimneys and put up banners and Shell just didn't know what they were going to do. Just knowing that Greenpeace could send one of its big boats up the river and park it next to the Shell plants and bring in all the media made Shell very nervous and gave the local residents more bargaining leverage than they would have had if Greenpeace were not involved.

The Greenpeace ship moored next to Shell's facilities in Norco in 1999 and 2000 and became a focal point for press events. "We came on the shore and did a little snooping around and then we brought in the Greenpeace bus, the Toxic Patrol. Those were the fun days. What we did was to put Shell on notice that we were there and we were going to watch. We were able to bring the media in tow so you had all this bad publicity churning out for Shell. It was just building and building," Smith said.

Greenpeace was such a lightning rod and so feared by industry that Smith deliberately kept his distance during the residents' negotiations with Shell. The subtext to industry was that if the negotiations did not go well Greenpeace would be back, he said. Greenpeace's role was to do the heavy hitting, Smith added. "We were just slamming Shell for all the bad things they were doing," Smith recalled. "We were just staying on their case and pressuring them . . . putting all kinds of pressure on them. And they became very hostile. They [Shell officials] would see me and they wanted me arrested. . . . It was very hostile. . . . They ran me off their premises a couple of times. . . . They hated me, but they respected me."

Keeping It Hot

In late January 2002, the offices of the Louisiana Bucket Brigade were located one flight up behind a door with a missing windowpane on Daneel Street in the university district in uptown New Orleans.[1] On a Tuesday evening, pizza night, the small suite of rooms was jammed with canvassers who were just back from making their rounds soliciting contributions and memberships. This hard work—walking door-to-door in the rain—was aimed at raising money so the Bucket Brigade could continue to help organize residents in fenceline communities in the river parishes.

The canvassers sat around a card table on folding chairs sorting crumpled dollars, wet change, and checks as they toted up the evenings take, munching on pizza, their coats and scarves still on. Keeping careful watch over their accounting was the head of a huge puppet that had been carried in a protest against Shell along the fenceline in Norco/Diamond. Also leaning against the wall was a canvassers' map of New Orleans with color-coded pins indicating where contributions came from. On the walls hung blown-up photos of Diamond residents looking out their windows at the refinery next door; and a schematic map with snapshots of all the houses in the community indicating which were occupied and which were vacant or had been bought by Shell.

This urban outpost was one of the war rooms of the many allied groups that were supporting the Diamond community's struggle against Shell. Clustered in a corner, amid supplies for making protest signs, were a couple of specially designed and equipped white plastic buckets (from whence the brigade takes its name) used by residents to capture air samples and subsequently sent to labs for analysis.

Overseeing all this activity was Anne Rolfes, 32, an energetic woman who is constantly on the move and can often be seen wandering from one room to another in her offices engaged in animated conversation with an invisible confederate as she talks on her cell phone. Rolfes, who had grown up in Lafayette, Louisiana (which she describes as the urban heart of Cajun music), was a relatively recent recruit to the environmental justice struggle in Louisiana, having begun her work in Norco in August 1999. During her three year stint organizing in Diamond, however, she brought to the movement a fierce energy and genuine commitment to work for the relocation of residents for "as long as it takes."

Of all the "outside" environmental justice activists who helped the residents of Diamond with their relocation struggle, Rolfes was on location organizing in the community more than anyone else. During a one year period from April 2001 until April 2002 her calendar shows that she made a total of 161 visits or about three visits a week. Not all of those visits were entirely devoted to organizing and many days Rolfes would stop by and sit on the back porch of Diamond resident Clara Smith or Ruth Jones, go to a baseball game with Iris Carter, attend a Bible study class with residents, or play chess. This everyday social contact permitted her to come to know residents well and gain their trust and respect. That trust and affection was summed up once by Margie Richard, former president of Concerned Citizens of Norco, who described Rolfes, a blue-eyed blonde, as "my vanilla sister." "I really learned about the community," Rolfes said, "and consequently how best to fight alongside them."

Rolfes came to Diamond by a roundabout route, although looking back her personal journey had a certain logic to it. She grew up in Lafayette which, at the time, was geographically segregated with blacks living in one part of town and the whites in another. Her mother taught a special education class at Vermillion Elementary School which was attended by African-American students. At the age of 10 Rolfes remembers her mother pointing out a store on the African-American side of town that looked old and rundown. She noticed that the store had none of the new signs, modern cash registers, or automatic doors she was familiar with on the white side of town. "With that one gesture my mother pointed out a world of difference" between a poor, African-American neighborhood and an affluent white one, she recalled. Rolfes credits that evening as the one on which she learned the telltale signs of an unequal society.

After graduating from college at the University of Colorado at Boulder in political science, Rolfes joined the Peace Corps. At the time she was reading John Steinbeck's dust bowl story, *The Grapes of Wrath*, and was inspired to try her hand at working the land in a community that could use her help. In its wisdom, the Peace Corps assigned her a job as a "forester" working out of a farming family in a remote village in Togo, West Africa. Rolfes lived there for three years and gained a deep understanding and appreciation for what the lives were like of people who were dependent for their survival on the crops they grew. She also learned about the hardships suffered by the Ogoni people in the neighboring Niger delta who were being pushed off their lands as Royal Dutch/Shell and the Nigerian government collaborated on exploiting the region's oil supplies.

Back in the United States, after her stint with the Peace Corps, Rolfes gravitated to Berkeley where she landed a job with Project Underground, a group working to expose the depredations Niger delta farmers were experiencing at the hands of Royal Dutch/Shell operations and the brutal troops fielded by President Sani Abacha. Her recent experience in Africa gave Rolfes a leg up in winning an assignment to return to the continent where she researched a report about what was happening in the Niger delta based on the accounts of refugees who had fled into Benin.[2] Stationing herself in Queme, Rolfes interviewed Nigerian refugees and learned first-hand about how they were being displaced from their fertile farmland as pipelines and well-heads were constructed; and how the land and water they depended upon for their livelihood were being polluted with the by-products of oil drilling.

This was dangerous work. Shortly before his death in June 1998, just before Rolfes reached Benin, President Abacha of Nigeria was sending agents across the border into the refugee camps were she was working and kidnapping people. While she was scared at first, Rolfes soon discovered that she could move among the refugees unmolested and found support for her work from local church groups. Rolfes recorded harrowing stories about the cruelty of Abacha's soldiers and police who were dispatched to make sure the oil companies experienced no problems from the local farmers. She also learned about the complicity of the oil companies in the police action against the local farmers. "Shell bought weapons for the local police," she charged. Since then, she said she has "a special place in my heart for Shell."[3]

One photo in particular served to radicalize Rolfes. It captured an elderly Ogoni woman, clearly from a Niger delta farming family, being shot by Nigerian troops as they secured an area where a pipeline was to be built. "If anyone ever did that to the family I lived with [in Togo] I would have to go and bear arms. I could just never stand by and watch that happen. . . . I would see these pictures of these old women defending their fields or getting shot. . . . I felt like I knew these people. Farming is not a hobby for them. If they don't farm that is it for them," she recalled thinking. "Who was speaking up for that old lady," Rolfes asked herself?

Her personal answer to the question emerged when she returned home to Louisiana. "There is no question that witnessing Shell's atrocities in Nigeria was, initially, the energizing force behind my work in Norco. Before coming to Norco I spent four years working with the people of the Niger delta, documenting Shell's decimation of their homeland and the murders, rapes, and tortures that took place with Shell's tacit support. When I arrived home in Louisiana to start working on pollution issues the first problem I heard about—Norco—had Shell's fingerprints all over it. I was supercharged and energized from the get-go because of my experience in Nigeria. . . . Since Shell had done such damage in Nigeria I wanted to take them on in Louisiana and make them pay for the harm they had done people all over the world," she said.

It dawned on Rolfes that the same companies were "doing bad things in Nigeria and in Louisiana: we should link this up." So she decided to try to create a "delta to delta" project that would permit those who had suffered at the hands of the petrochemical industry in Nigeria to share their stories with residents in Louisiana who lived along the fenceline with the same multinational oil companies.

But first Rolfes, who was sleeping on a sofa at her brother's house in New Orleans, had to find a paying job. As fortune would have it, Denny Larson came to New Orleans. Larson was a veteran toxics activist from California who had started out collecting air samples in a residential community in Richmond, California adjacent to a giant refinery. He was in New Orleans holding a workshop to train local activists in the best technique for taking air samples as a way to prove that industry was contaminating residential neighborhoods. Rolfes took the training and apprenticed herself to Larson with whom she continued to collaborate. She did some work for Larson and for the Sierra Club and then founded the Louisiana Bucket Brigade to create a local center for the fenceline organizing work. Since then she has been working full steam to help the residents of Diamond win their struggle for relocation.

Rolfes first visited Norco in 1999 with Denny Larson. She had passed through the town earlier in her life and had been struck by what appeared to be dark and spooky industrial works. But on her first real visit to the community she ended up at the home of Percy Hollins, son-in-law of the venerable Janie Campbell. Hollins later came to be one of the residents who most consistently took air samples whenever he smelled something funky wafting across the fence from Shell. Rolfes said she kept returning to Diamond because the residents were so receptive to her coming to help and because they were so determined to get something accomplished. "Diamond is a real treasure . . . because it has such deep roots," observed Rolfes, who visited the community frequently, occasionally cruising the streets in her red 1965 Mercury Monterey convertible.

It was after Larson captured the "smoking gun" air sample of MEK and after the big meeting about the accidental release on December 8, 1998, that Rolfes started visiting Norco. Shell officials made a huge mistake during that accident because they told residents there was no problem while residents clearly knew better, she said. Photos of children on school buses with handkerchiefs over their noses and mouths made it clear that something out of the ordinary was going on, she said. And then the MEK sample nailed the problem. "They [Shell] got caught and that was crucial. It was the first time anyone had any evidence," she added. Now the leadership of Concerned Citizens of Norco could say that Shell was "putting MEK out on us and not telling us." Worse they were denying it. This confirmed all the suspicions that residents harbored that Shell was less than candid with them and that they had been subjected to elevated levels of toxic chemicals coming from Shell for years.

Rolfes helped to write and publish a report titled *Shell Norco Toxic Neighbor*. As those involved in the production of the publication talked about how best to use it, they decided to peg its release to an EPA-sponsored meeting that was to be held at the Holiday Inn in downtown New Orleans on November 5, 1999. Among those expected to attend the meeting were top-level executives from Shell. Fenceline toxics activists saw this meeting as an irresistible target for a protest and at first the idea was to do a sidewalk picket of Shell outside the hotel. But then Denny Larson suggested they try to get a room inside and Rolfes volunteered to look into the possibility.

When she approached the events manager at the Holiday Inn the next day, Rolfes said, she "lucked out." Yes, the manager said, they did have room for another environmental group. The EPA was only taking up only half of a very large conference room that could be separated by a sliding divider wall. Without revealing her groups agenda, Rolfes booked the other half of the conference room and the network of environmental groups began to make their plans. The day of the EPA conference anti-Shell activists held a press conference at noon during the conference lunch break "slamming Shell for being a toxic neighbor," Rolfes said. All the local television stations covered the press conference, the Toxic Neighbor report was released, and there was a story on the front page of the next day's *Times-Picayune*. Shell officials were not amused: "Shell people were huddling; they ran into this room and they were talking and fuming," Rolfes recalled with a certain mischievous delight. "That was huge."

Looking back on the many protests and events she helped stage, Rolfes said that what the Louisiana Bucket Brigade did best was to keep things percolating and never let a month pass without staging some kind of event or activity out in Diamond. There was one moment in particular, in March

2000, when Rolfes felt that the Louisiana Bucket Brigade helped residents avoid being divided by Shell tactics. Company officials were saying different things to different residents. As a result, residents began to argue among themselves about who heard what when and why so-and-so had been left out of certain conversations. "So there was this distrust and that wasn't good," Rolfes noted. To help residents over this rough patch, Rolfes suggested that they make a list of all the best promises they had heard from Shell and then pick the promises they liked the best and agitate for Shell to actually implement them. One of the promises that residents said they had heard that they liked was that Shell would purchase Diamond properties for their commercial value instead of the lower residential value. So residents turned that verbal promise into a demand, Rolfes recalled.

On October 2, 2000, Rolfes and her colleagues published Shell Games, a report that criticized Shell for purchasing properties in Diamond at depressed prices. Denny Larson had urged Rolfes to visit the county courthouse and find out who owned the properties in Diamond and how much they had been purchased for. The first one Rolfes looked up belonged to Helen Washington who had died in the pipeline explosion in 1973. It was lot 22 square 14 in Diamond and Shell had purchased it for $3,000 from the family of Washington after her death. As Rolfes continued to search through the property records she found more lots in Diamond that had been purchased by Shell at bargain prices. In fact, the average price being paid by Shell for homes in Diamond at the time was $26,000, Rolfes said. Diamond resident Margie Richard was outraged at the small sums that Shell had offered to her neighbors for their homes. "How could they give people $10,000 when they knew what was going on?" she asked.

Just before the release of the report, on September 17, 2000, Shell decided to make their first formal offer to buyout the first two streets of Diamond. It was a victory for the residents who had been agitating for years for relocation but it was also "a cruel blow" because half of the Diamond community was excluded from the offer, observed Rolfes. Furthermore, the prices Shell was offering would require residents to go into debt in order to relocate, she continued. But when the Shell Games report came out describing how Shell had been buying up homes on the cheap, Shell sent around a flyer improving their offer by promising to give qualifying homeowners a minimum of $50,000. "You never know what is casual" in these struggles, Rolfes said, but she did find it probably more than a coincidence that two days after the release of their report Shell upped their offer to a minimum of $50,000 per house. It smelled of damage control.

Shell put their spin on the buyout program for the first two streets in Diamond and then the Shell Games report "was the gut punch to follow it," Denny Larson said with considerable relish. Immediately after the publication of the report, Concerned Citizens of Norco and their nonprofit allies held a press conference in Diamond on the fenceline with Shell Chemical and released the report. On the back cover was a photo of the home of the manager of the Motiva refinery. "We put his house on the back cover of this report without naming him or giving his address," Larson said. It was a photo of a wealthy home owned by a Motiva manager who lived far from the fumes in Diamond and Norco. "We were sending a message directly to him—that we knew would be forwarded to Houston and London—that these guys are playing hardball, they are making it personal, and they've got my address," said Larson. It was not appreciated, he observed.

Rolfes credits Denny Larson with coming up with a number of other effective ideas about how to publicize the suffering of people who live along the fenceline with industry. One of his schemes involved challenging Shell officials to a public debate about the problems residents were experiencing in Diamond. The local debate was to take place at the same time as the presidential-election debates between Al Gore and George W. Bush. Larson's idea was to challenge Shell to a debate and have a big American flag and a podium as the backdrop for the newspaper and television cameras.

The challenge for the debate, set for November 1st, 2000, at 7 P.M., was made public in an advertisement placed in the *St. Charles Herald Guide*, a small parish newspaper widely read in Diamond and Norco. "Open letter to Shell and the Norco Community," the ad read. "Time to come out of your shell for a good old-fashioned debate on the issues: relocation of the Diamond community. Concerned Citizens of Norco challenge Shell officials to a debate on the issue of the community's new relocation program and the Norco fenceline property purchase program." Shell's decision to decline the invitation was carried in the parish newspaper the next week under the headline: "Shell Ducks Debate." A Shell official was quoted as saying that "A debate by its very nature is divisive." Rather than leave it there, Diamond residents decided to hold the debate in absentia. This also was covered by the press: "Imagine if there was a debate and the other side didn't show up," a follow-up article read.

This was just one of many protests in Diamond and all of the various nonprofit organizations that worked with the Diamond residents contributed to the community's victory over Shell, Rolfes observed. "Our unique part is that we are there consistently, very present in the community and in the campaign. . . . We were there all the time, we kept it alive, we didn't let it lie for a few months and then come back. . . . We kept it hot," Rolfes said.

Keeping it hot involved placing stories about Diamond in the media. Rolfes became adept at this and in one year was instrumental in initiating 61 stories about the Shell/Diamond controversy in newspapers and magazines as well as broadcasts on radio and television. Rolfes took a pugnacious delight in seeing these stories aired: "When I would see a TV story or a print story I got real joy and envisioned it as a left hook to Shell's chin. I loved nothing better than following it up with a right," she said.

Even officials at Shell began to take note of the effectiveness of the Louisiana Bucket Brigade. While events such as the one-sided debate were distressing for the company, Shell spokesman David Brignac could not help but admire Rolfes's skill at bringing in the media and her credibility with the community. "Anne is in the community all the time. She knows people, she knows their situation, so she has credibility with the community that I think most of the environmentalists don't have. This gives her credibility with us. When we have someone who really knows the community, knows what is going on, knows the situations, we are willing to talk because this can help. . . . Anne does what she does well. She knows how to work the media and of course that can be painful to us at times. But in terms of getting us to work with the community she has been real helpful," Brignac added.

Rolfes was also working to get various student groups involved in publicizing the plight of the fenceline community in Norco and Tulane students demonstrated on campus. Antioch students came to Diamond and worked with some of the kids in the community to make huge puppets and signs saying "Don't Divide Diamond." Rolfes took advantage of any group passing through New Orleans that could be hooked into the Diamond struggle. "My thought was: never have anyone in town and not use them to support the local campaign," she said.

One of those she linked up with the Norco/Diamond struggle was a loose coalition of environmental groups focused on industrial chemical pollution known as Coming Clean. They were invited to a big demonstration at Shell

Plaza in New Orleans in June 2001. Among those in attendance were Lois Gibbs, who organized one of the early fenceline struggles for relocation at Love Canal; and Ted Schettler of the Greater Boston Physicians for Social Responsibility, who outlined the health impacts of living close to toxic industries. "It was a great demonstration. We tried to deliver a letter and they [Shell officials] wouldn't let us in. It was all very dramatic," Rolfes remembered. A number of Diamond residents showed up, some 700 leaflets were passed out, and there was good media coverage. Members of the Coming Clean Coalition were also invited out to Norco for a picnic during a day when there was a big release of toxics from the Shell plant, she said. The company said it was not serious, that it was just a power outage, but chemist Wilma Subra later found out that it was part of a 16-day release of some 452 tons of chemicals that blanketed the surrounding area. The true extent of the release was not known for six months because it took that long to dig it out of the records, Rolfes said.

That same spring, a group of investors put pressure on Shell to clean up its act with its neighbors. Trillium Assets, a socially responsible investment fund, which owned Shell stock, used its newsletter to urge Shell to improve its corporate behavior in Diamond and shareholders began to bring up the subject directly with the company. Public education about exposure to toxics was also an integral part of the protest strategy. Early in 2002, Peter Oris came to town and gave a talk titled "Communities, Chemicals, and Common Sense." There were also several delegations of philanthropists who came through Diamond including program officers from the Ford and Rockefeller Foundations. The Environmental Grantmakers Association did a toxic tour of Norco during a meeting they held in New Orleans. Rolfes saw her role as helping to coordinate these out-of-town activists as they passed through Norco, maintaining the pressure on Shell, and keeping it hot.

While much of the organizing in Diamond involved conflict and hard work, some events were designed to bring the community together to have fun. For example, in the spring of 2001 Rolfes had a little bit of money in her budget that she wanted to use to allow the residents of Diamond to celebrate their struggle against Shell. This was part of the "Celebrate and Agitate" strategy that was pursued to keep people in the local community positive about the struggle, noted Denny Larson. With this in mind Rolfes approached Concerned Citizens of Norco and asked them how they wanted to use the money. After some deliberations they decided to honor the older residents of Diamond as a way of educating the younger generation about the foundation of their community.

"The greatest [organizing] ideas come from the people themselves. They are the ones who live in the community and know the right thing to do," Rolfes observed. In their wisdom, the leadership of Concerned Citizens of Norco decided to rent a limousine and take the elder residents for a luxurious ride around the community. The idea was to honor the older generation for its work in the struggle against Shell. As a focal point for the celebration they decided to commemorate the life of Ruth Jones, the mother of Leroy Jones who died in the Shell pipeline fire.

As an organizing tactic this choice was brilliant, explained Rolfes, because as soon as the limo started cruising up and down the narrow Diamond roads (where the possibility of driving into an open storm water ditch requires a driver's full attention) all the residents poured out of their homes to see what was happening. The elder women of Diamond had such a good time that none of them wanted to stop making the rounds of the community.

A year later, when Ruth Jones died, a photo of her emerging from the limousine in her best hat and dress was used on the announcement of her funeral. Margie Richard, then president of Concerned Citizens of Norco, also enjoyed limo day. She made a crown for her mother to wear for her limo ride and still has a photo of her mother coming out of the limo with a big smile on her face. "It just picked up [the spirits] of all the elderly people," Richard said. As the afternoon wore on, Richard asked Ruth Jones if she was tired. As Richard recalls it, Jones replied "Humph, tired? I could sit in here all night." Then Richard asked Miss Thelma the same question, and she replied "Could we go around the block one more time?"

Help from West Harlem

Further help for the relocation campaign in Diamond arrived from West Harlem in the robust and animated form of Vernice Miller-Travis, 45, a veteran community organizer and environmental justice advocate who worked for the Ford Foundation as a program officer.

Miller-Travis had a suitcase full of life experience that was relevant to the struggle in Diamond. Born in Harlem Hospital in 1959, where her mother and father both worked, she grew up during the heyday of the Black

Power and Civil Right movements. Her father was a labor organizer and a follower of Adam Clayton Powell Jr., the radical African-American congressman who was pastor of the Abyssinian Baptist Church of Harlem. On some days Rev. Powell would stop and talk to her and the other children playing on 138th Street on his daily walk to church from Lennox Avenue.

"I knew all my life that I would be engaged in some way in the struggle for civil rights and in particular the struggle for equality of African-Americans," Miller-Travis said. After attending public schools in New York City through the eighth grade, she won a scholarship to attend the elite Fieldston School in the Riverdale section of the Bronx. Miller-Travis then attended Barnard College through her junior year, after which she withdrew for financial reasons. It took her two more years to graduate because of the time she devoted to working as an administrative assistant. She subsequently graduated from Columbia University in 1982 with a BA in political science. Law school would have been her next step, but she did not have the money.

After college, Rev. Benjamin Chavis, then Deputy Director of the United Church of Christ's Commission for Racial Justice, offered her a research assistant position working with Charles Lee, the Commission's Research Director, who described to her their Special Project on Toxic Injustice. "I had no idea what Toxic Injustice was at the time but that job would change my life," she said.

Her work with Lee would lead to the publication of the landmark report *Toxic Wastes and Race in the United States*, on which she served as the principal research assistant. The report documented the disproportionate siting of hazardous waste facilities in low-income communities of color and created one of the first collections of hard data on which the environmental justice movement was founded. Miller-Travis soon found an opportunity to organize local residents against the kind of "locally unwanted land use" that the report highlighted. In 1988 she joined with Peggy Shepard and other residents in forming West Harlem Environmental Action, a group that opposed the construction of the $169 million North River Sewage Treatment Plant, which was to be half a mile long and six stories tall. Despite their efforts to stop it, the plant was eventually built.

Miller-Travis subsequently worked at the Natural Resources Defense Council and helped write the brownfields legislation—passed during the Clinton administration—that dealt with the cleanup of contaminated properties. While at NRDC she organized the Partnership for Sustainable

Brownfields Development, which leveraged brownfields restoration funds for the revitalization of low-income communities of color.

Her introduction to Diamond came in 1991 when she went to New Orleans as part of the advisory board of the First People of Color Environmental Leadership Summit. On that trip she traveled by bus to Diamond and other river parish towns in the chemical corridor. She was particularly struck by her visit to Sunrise, Louisiana, a town so heavily contaminated by adjacent industrial facilities that the entire population had to be moved. "These people had been put in harms way to such a degree that the only resolution was to physically relocate them," she said. "All that was left of the town was the street grid: there were no structures, no houses, no building . . . nothing. . . . It was like you were standing on somebody's grave in the cemetery and you feel a shudder go through you. . . . It was a really eerie feeling."

How does it come about that communities like Diamond and Sunrise have to be destroyed to save the residents, Miller-Travis asked? The circumstances that people in Diamond had to live under makes no sense, she continued. "You go down there and you see the facility, you see the [toxic] outputs of the facility, you see where the people are, and common sense will tell you there is a problem here. This doesn't require geo-sensing, it doesn't require hydrothermal examination. . . . It doesn't require any of that. Just look at the place and you can see it is no damn good. This is not good land-use planning. People cannot sustain themselves living next to a major petrochemical facility." When you look at the huge Shell refinery and chemical plant and the tiny little community of Norco/Diamond you know it does not make sense, she said. "These people are in a fight for their lives: this is not simply a rhetorical discourse about environmentalists versus industrialists," she added.

Miller-Travis went to graduate school and studied urban planning because she wanted to understand how decisions such as the one to locate the Shell refinery in Diamond and the North River Sewage Treatment Plant in West Harlem came to be made; and how communities of color could intervene in the decision-making process and protect themselves from similarly pernicious land-use decisions in the future. What she learned, she said, is that frequently the decision about where to locate highly polluting industrial facilities overlaps with where people of color live.

Decisions about where industrial development is placed are made by local zoning boards, often without input from residents in the area where industrial development is targeted. Federal agencies, such as the Environmental Protection Agency, which should logically play a role in protecting residents from living too close to highly polluting industries, are powerless to do anything about this because the right to make these zoning decisions is jealously guarded as a local prerogative protected by states' rights.

Bonehead decisions are also being made at the state level in Louisiana about the siting of industrial plants inappropriately close to residential areas, Miller-Travis continued. Little thought is given to the potential of these facilities to contaminate important ecological resources in the area, she asserted. "I can tell you that there is not a more organized constituency of ignorant people in one place than the people who work for the state of Louisiana at the decision-making level," she charged. Industries are permitted to operate unfettered and poison the air, soil, and water. Then whole communities have to be relocated, a situation that could have been avoided if state regulatory officials had been doing their job, she claimed.

In addition to the human suffering that this intense pollution causes, there is also damage being done to the entire ecosystem, Miller-Travis noted. The crayfish, the shellfish, and the bayous are being poisoned, and that contaminates the food supply. The natural wonders that make Louisiana attractive to tourists are being destroyed because state officials have yet to grasp that to protect human health and to attract tourists requires protecting the ecological health of the region, she added

Even the economics of relaxed regulation of industries in the chemical corridor does not make sense, Miller-Travis argued. The state is "giving all kinds of tax abatements to these chemical manufacturers and petrochemical industries to come down and do business in Louisiana so it is not like the state is making truckloads of money," she continued. In fact, these industrial facilities often cost the state more than they generate in tax revenue if you factor in cleanup and liability costs the state faces from future suits, she observed.

The Sierra Club

If most of the ten largest, traditional, largely white environmental organizations have paid more attention to environmental problems facing grizzly bears, whales, and redwoods than they have to the plight of low-income minority residents living on fencelines with polluting industries, it is not true of all members of this group. Greenpeace and the Sierra Club stand out as exceptions to this rule for their attention to environmental justice issues.

At the Sierra Club, external criticism and internal self-examination began to move the organization toward engagement with fenceline communities. "The Club was slow to recognize that minorities and the poor didn't want pollution and degradation any more than anyone else," wrote Mike McCloskey, former executive director and chairman of the Sierra Club. But eventually the organization did come around to seeing that environmental justice issues are deeply connected to the organization's mission. "The quest for environmental justice is based on the principle that environmental protection must serve everyone, not just the privileged," continued McCloskey, who began his work with the Sierra Club at the age of 27 as a Pacific Northwest Field Representative. The Sierra Club has stood for comprehensive solutions, not ones that shift ecological burdens into pollution havens and "sacrifice zones," he added.[4]

To put this growing awareness into action, in 1991 the Sierra Club established the Gulf Coast Environmental Justice Organizing Project, bringing together about 100 communities on the fenceline with toxic industries. Sierra Club activists played a supporting role in a number of these communities, helping local leaders publicize their cause in the media and gain access to government and business officials. Among the groups they worked with were Jesus People Against Pollution (Columbia, Mississippi) and Citizens Against Toxic Exposure (Pensacola, Florida). "I've worked with an African-American community that was built on top of an old municipal landfill that is now a Superfund site," commented Barbara Vincent, chair of the Gulf Coast project and of the Delta Chapter of the Sierra Club. "Louisiana is full of such cases. You can't live here and not feel outraged by what some people have to live with."

Efforts like these helped the Sierra Club recognize that the nascent environmental justice movement could help significantly expand the base of American citizens fighting pollution. It also helped answer the charge of some critics that the Sierra Club had previously failed to "incorporate the viewpoint of communities most victimized" by pollution, stated a report published by the Sierra Club Foundation.

The national scope and activist-led structure of the Sierra Club makes it ideally suited "to form partnerships with grassroots community groups . . . and to bridge the gap between local environmental justice grassroots groups and the rest of the environmental community," the report continued. This outreach initiative has the potential to enable the two camps—traditional environmentalists and grassroots environmental justice activists—to "overcome long-standing mistrust and forge a unified agenda," the report concluded.[5]

The Sierra Club's dip into the environmental justice pool began tentatively with the organization's hiring of John McCown as its first National Environmental Justice Coordinator. He remained the organization's lone ranger on the issue until 2000, when environmental justice organizers were hired to work out of Sierra Club offices in Washington, Memphis, Detroit, and Los Angeles. New sites in Central Appalachia and in the Southwest were opened in 2001. And members of the Sierra Club Environmental Justice Committee are also working in North Carolina, Maryland, Illinois, and Louisiana. To cover the inevitable legal issues that arise in environmental justice struggles, the Sierra Club hired attorney Denise Hoffner-Brodsky to work full-time on EJ issues. The environmental justice initiative within the Sierra Club is like a "movement within a movement," said Hoffner-Brodsky. "Its activists are dedicated to fighting for a clean and healthy environment for people of color and others whose communities are disproportionately targeted by polluting industries."[6]

In addition, through its Environmental Public Education Program, the Sierra Club funded grassroots environmental justice activities to the tune of $50,000 in 2001 and $75,000 in 2002. "This is about the Sierra Club making a commitment to the people as well as the natural environment," writes Kirstin Repogle, chair of the organization's national Environmental Justice Committee.[7]

From the outset of its commitment to environmental justice issues in 1993, the Sierra Club began to sponsor "toxic tours" of low-income communities that suffered from disproportionate exposure to toxic chemicals. Some members of the organization's board began to question why it was involved in nitty-gritty industrial battles. Though the Sierra Club has a track record for fighting pollution, the organization's historic focus remained primarily targeted on getting members to trek into wild places so that there will be a committed constituency primed to fight to save the remaining wilderness.

Nevertheless, there is a certain logic to an extension of the Sierra Club's work sponsoring treks into the high Sierras to leading toxic tours of blighted neighborhoods in the Louisiana chemical corridor, argued Sierra Club president Robbie Cox. Long ago, David Brower, the organization's first executive director, set its strategy by saying "Show people the places we care about. Then they will fight to protect them." Toxic tours are just "a natural evolution of our mission to 'protect and restore the quality of the natural and human environment,'" Cox continued. Using toxic tours as a vehicle, the Sierra Club began to "forge a partnership with communities fighting exposure to dangerous substances" and reach out to a segment of society that had long been neglected by mainstream environmental groups, he added.

Cox recalled an early toxic tour in 1993 when he traveled to an abandoned chemical plant in southern Mississippi with a young local activist named Charlotte Keys. Both Cox and a reporter who accompanied them were moved by the stories they heard when they visited with local families who lived adjacent to the Reichold Chemical plant, where there had been a big explosion. When asked by the reporter what evidence there was of ill effects caused by pollution from the chemical plant, Keyes explained that "the evidence is in my body." It was then that the reporter began asking more questions about the chemical company and what had happened there. Thus, from the outset, it was clear that toxic tours could shine a public spotlight on the previously ignored plight of fenceline residents.[8]

Today the Sierra Club has environmental justice work underway in Detroit, where Rhonda Anderson is leading tours of abandoned industrial sites in low-income African-American communities; in Los Angeles, where Jessy Cardenas is working to organize protests against the extension of an airport that would degrade environmental quality in a predominantly African-American and Latino neighborhood; in Washington, where Julie Eisenhardt is working with two neighborhoods pitted against each other over the location of a trash-transfer facility; in Memphis, where Rita Harris is working with residents in a low-income community on the north side of the city who oppose the re-permitting of a hazardous waste incinerator; and in Arizona, where Andy Bessler is involved with a community of Native Americans whose water supplies are being degraded by a coal processing plant. In Diamond/Norco, Maura Wood provided fenceline residents with funding and tools for their relocation struggle.[9] Each of these Sierra Club organizers is informed by the organization's "guiding principles" to support and train grassroots activists and link them to resources, "fight alongside residents in their struggle to end pollution of their communities," share information and strategies, but not try to tell them what to do.

Sierra Club activist Darryl Malek-Wiley has long been involved in exposing the plight of residents in the Louisiana's chemical corridor. In November 1988, shortly after the huge blast that leveled homes in Norco, Malek-Wiley helped organize the Great Louisiana Toxics March, in which thousands of people walked segments of the 80-mile "Cancer Alley" to protest the exposure of local residents to high levels of harmful chemicals.[10]

Since 1993, the Sierra Club has sponsored guided toxic tours of the chemical corridor three to four times a year. Malek-Wiley, who has conducted many of the tours, reports that he takes anywhere from a handful of people up to 47 in a big tour bus. The tours are often narrated by residents from the affected communities and stops are made in their homes so that those who take the tours get a close-up view of what conditions are like.

The Sierra Club is by no means the only organization running toxic tours through the chemical corridor and Norco. Members of the National Environmental Justice Advisory Council (NEJAC) came through Diamond when they were holding a conference in Baton Rouge. Similarly, members of the National Council of Churches of Christ toured communities in the chemical corridor in 1998. Some of the ministers who went on the tour were particularly struck by the "haunting sight of children playing in the shadow of the Shell complex" in Diamond, a Sierra Club publication reported.[11] The next year, in 1999, the Sierra Club's National Board of Directors toured communities in the chemical corridor during a day trip from their meeting in New Orleans.

Sierra Club activists also joined the coalition of nonprofit organizations that worked with Concerned Citizens of Norco in their fight for relocation. Maura Wood, a long-term Sierra Club activist from Baton Rouge, arrived in town and negotiated a grant from the Sierra Club that enabled some residents of Diamond to form a "bucket brigade" in their neighborhood to sample air quality. The grant allowed local residents to learn how to build and operate a simple air-monitoring device and paid for laboratory testing of the air samples captured in Diamond.

Wood also managed to place a video camera on the roof of a trailer, located on the fenceline with the Shell plants, that was owned by Margie Richard, then president of Concerned Citizens of Norco. The video camera provided a live feed to the Sierra Club website showing the Norco Complex flaring chemical wastes. The "flarecam" provided viewers an opportunity to check the Sierra Club website and see what was being released into the air over Norco. Those who did tune in were informed that "a yellow-smoky flame indicates bad engineering and a poorly run plant."[12] Viewers were also told that, by law, flares were permitted to last only 15 minutes. The Diamond Bucket Brigade and the flarecam provided new tools for local residents to show people outside their community what they were experiencing and to increase the pressure on state regulatory officials to monitor the situation in Diamond more closely.

In a 1999 initiative aimed at advancing the argument that environmental racism is a human rights violation, the Sierra Club provided a grant that enabled a few residents of Diamond and the Agricultural Street Landfill fenceline community to travel to Geneva to participate in the U.S. Environmental Justice Delegation to the United Nations Human Rights Commission.

The Louisiana Environmental Action Network

Marylee Orr did not plan to be an environmental activist. The problem of environmental contamination came to her in a very personal way. One of Orr's children was born with Hyland Membrane Disease—a respiratory illness exacerbated by pollution from chemical industries and incinerators near Baton Rouge. As a result, Orr's environmental activism came out of a primal urge to protect her child. "That brought out the tiger in me," she said.

A single mother running a small art gallery in Baton Rouge, Orr decided to fight to make the air in her community safe for her son to breathe. She joined with other neighbors in founding Mothers Against Air Pollution, a group that patterned itself after Mothers Against Drunk Driving. Their first target was the huge Rollins incinerator, located on the outskirts of Baton Rouge near the community of Alsen.

"My world was pretty small at the time," said Orr. Alsen was a completely new experience. It was a 98 percent African-American community on the north side of the city where the air was so foul that it made you gag, she said. "It was a real education for me. When I went out there I couldn't believe it. . . . It was frightening," she added. Alsen residents sometimes had to put wet towels over their heads when the pollution was strong she recalled. "I had no idea that conditions like this existed and that people were being poisoned like this right here in the United States," she continued. Some Alsen residents were getting nosebleeds that were so bad they had to be taken to the hospital, she reported. Others were suffering from respiratory illness, asthma, rashes, and skin discoloration. "Marylee," she recalled thinking, "you are stupid that you didn't know this was happening."

In preparation for a public hearing about the Rollins incinerator, Orr and other members of MAAP began knocking on doors in Alsen and elsewhere in Baton Rouge. In six days they collected 2,400 signatures of people concerned about pollution from the incinerator and about the quality of the air in their community. "People were so wonderful to me and accepting of my presence," Orr said of her first foray into political organizing. Introducing herself as a Mother Against Air Pollution she found that other mothers, aunts, and grandmothers in Alsen could relate to her easily when they heard her story and her concerns. "I think they understood that I was really there to help," she said.

The campaign against Rollins effectively prevented the incinerator from burning polychlorinated biphenyls (PCBs) and eventually led to its shutdown, she said. It was a demonstration of People Power, Orr observed. From then on, when residents would complain about how little the government was doing to protect their air quality, Orr told them of what she called a well-kept secret: "We are the government."

Orr and another woman were appointed to a municipal committee that dealt with health and environmental issues. "She was the token black lady and I was the token white lady," she recalled. At first other members kept dismissing the stories of illness that Orr and her colleague brought to the committee as only anecdotal and without scientific merit. "They called me Miss Hennypenny and Chicken Little," implying that she thought the sky was falling, she said. But Orr remained undeterred. "Now we have the scientific studies to back up what we knew then with our gut," she said—that industrial air contaminants were making people sick.

In 1986, Orr and her colleagues invited Lois Gibbs—the woman who had mounted the successful Love Canal relocation campaign—to give a talk to people from similarly contaminated communities in Louisiana. Some 75 activists from a number of parishes came together at the meeting and decided to establish the Louisiana Environmental Action Network (LEAN), a statewide coalition of groups focused on environmental and toxics issues. In the beginning "we had no office, no staff no phone, and no fax," Orr recalled. Meetings were held at her house because she had the youngest child. Finally, in 1987, a grant came through that permitted them to open an office and hire a full-time director. But the office burned to the ground and the director quit. Since then, Orr has directed LEAN, which has grown into a coalition of over 100 membership organizations. What the organization at first lacked in terms of financial resources it made up in diversity. Member groups include fishermen, unions, faith-based groups, environmental groups, and an organization fighting an incinerator. There were also civil rights activists from Geismar, one of the most polluted communities in the United States—"a real hell-hole," Orr claimed. LEAN's board of directors is very diverse, Orr said. There are a lot of African-American women in the organization, gays, and environmentalists. "Our diversity is our strength . . . and it scares the hell out of some people," she added with satisfaction.

Like many other grassroots toxics activists in Louisiana, Orr is deeply religious—in her words, "prayed up and ready for action." She also feels that she has a deeply personal stake in reducing exposure to toxics: "We here in Louisiana are the canaries in the mine. . . . We are the disposable people. . . . We are the price society pays for its conveniences." Not only has her son with respiratory problems been affected by airborne toxics; she is also convinced that her other son, who has learning disabilities, contracted his problems through the umbilical cord when she was drinking contaminated "river water" during her pregnancy. "We are number one in developmental toxins," Orr claimed. The correlation between exposure to these developmental toxins and the epidemic of learning disorders will be confirmed at some future date, she predicted. "We laugh a lot among ourselves but our road is paved with personal tragedies."

LEAN became involved with Diamond through its technical consultant, Wilma Subra, who helps a number of local communities translate complex scientific issues into lay terms. "We wanted to get the chemical plants to be better neighbors (and we still do) but in Diamond, in my estimation, relocation was the only option," she said. Orr is careful not to go into communities and try to tell people what they should do. The residents are the one who have to live with the problem, and so they are in the best position to decide whether they need to leave or not, she explained.

In Diamond, as elsewhere around Louisiana, fenceline residents had to go up against industry officials who "wanted to give as little as possible for as long as possible," Orr observed. "Those are their [corporate] instructions and they are darn good at it. We have to force these companies to do the right thing." But Orr also believes that reaching an agreement between company officials and residents in fenceline community can be a win/win formula. "I tell company officials that it [reaching an agreement with local residents] is good for them too," she said.

Over the years, LEAN brought the resources of its statewide network to bear on a number of battles over communities contaminated by industrial toxins. With its large membership and high media visibility, LEAN helped communities like Diamond by holding press conferences and turning out members to swell the ranks at local demonstrations. The diversity of its membership also underscored the fact that a large segment of society in Louisiana was concerned about the impact of industrial chemical releases on human health.

Before the campaign in Diamond, environmental and environmental justice groups in Louisiana had cut their teeth on the effort to keep Shintech from building the world's largest PVC plant in Convent. There were also a number of relocation campaigns before the one in Diamond (for example, those at Morrisville, Placid, and Revilletown), Orr pointed out. All these experiences helped the environmental movement in Louisiana mature and educate the public about the health hazards faced by fenceline residents, she added. By the time the campaign took place in Diamond, the coalition of support groups that came together to help Concerned Citizens of Norco was "an All Star Team . . . a dream Team," Orr said.

V

Endgame

14

The International Arena

Margie Richard, president of Concerned Citizens of Norco, was convinced that the struggle for relocation had to "go beyond Norco." She realized that there was just not enough power in Diamond to turn around a huge multinational corporation. At first her outreach efforts involved contacting other grassroots fenceline groups in the chemical corridor in Louisiana and environmental justice groups in New Orleans and elsewhere around the United States. But eventually Richard began traveling abroad to spread the word about the conditions of life along the fenceline in Diamond. The strategy behind these trips was that a multinational corporation such as Shell cared a good deal about how it was perceived in the international arena and thus was susceptible to pressure on the international stage.

Richard's first trip abroad took her to Geneva in April 1999 to attend a meeting of the United Nations Commission on Human Rights. She was part of a delegation of fenceline activists that included Elodia Blanco of the Concerned Citizens of Agricultural Street Landfill in New Orleans, Haki Vincent of the Concerned Citizens of Mossville in Lake Charles, Louisiana, Beverly Wright of the Deep South Center for Environmental Justice, Monique Harden of EarthJustice Legal Defense Fund, and others.

Members of the delegation wore buttons that read "U.S. Environmental Racism Must Stop" and passed out information packets about their struggle, recalled Harden. They were promoting the idea that environmental injustices suffered by people of color in the United States were human rights violations. The message was surprisingly well received by delegates from a wide range of countries, she added, and the 500 leaflets she brought from Norco were quickly snapped up.

Richard's testimony at the UN conference on April 7 paints a quick but vivid portrait of what Diamond residents experienced on the sliver of land between the Motiva refinery and the Shell Chemical plant:

My name is Margie Richard, I am the president of Concerned Citizens of Norco. My hometown is located in the southeastern section of Louisiana along the Mississippi River. In 1926 the Royal Dutch Shell Company purchased 460 acres of the town of Sellers and began building its oil refinery. When Shell purchased the town of Sellers, which is now Norco, they displaced African-American families from one section to another.

We are now surrounded by 27 petrochemical plants and oil refineries (and counting), refineries from which Norco received its name: Norco is an acronym for New Orleans Refinery Company. Our town is approximately one mile in radius and home to 5,000 residents. There are four streets near the plants occupied by African-Americans: Washington, Cathy, Diamond, and East. My house is located on Washington Street and is only 3 meters away from the 15-acre Shell Chemical plant expanded in 1955. Norco is situated between Shell Oil Refinery on the east and Shell Chemical plant on the west. The entire town is only half the size of the oil refineries.

Nearly everyone in the community suffers health problems caused by industrial pollution. The air is contaminated with bad odors from carcinogens, and benzene, toluene, sulfuric acid, ammonia, and xylene. . . . Runoff and dumping of toxic substances also pollute land and water.

My sister died at the age of 43 from an allergic disease called sarcoidosis, a disease which affects 1 in 1,000 people in the United States, yet in Norco there are at least 5 known cases in fewer than 500 people of color. My youngest daughter and her son suffer from severe asthma; my mother has breathing problems and must use a breathing machine daily. Many of the residents suffer from sore muscles, cardiovascular diseases, liver, blood, and kidney toxicant. Many die prematurely from poor health caused by pollution from toxic chemicals.

We know that Shell and the U.S. government are responsible for the environmental racism in our community and in other communities in the U.S. and many communities throughout the world. There must be an end to industry pollution and environmental racism. . . .

We are not treated as citizens with equal rights according to the U.S. law and international human rights law, especially the Convention on the Elimination of All Forms of Racial Discrimination, which our government ratified as the law of the land in 1994.[1]

In 2001 Richard was given another chance to put pressure on Shell to relocate Diamond residents by exposing their untenable situation to another international audience. For years, activists had been making the connection between the contamination suffered by Nigerian delta farmers at the hands of Shell and the harmful environmental conditions created by Shell for residents of Norco. Margie Richard was one of those who had traveled to

Nigeria to make personal contact with Nigerian activists and consolidate a "delta to delta" alliance.

Then Amit Srivastava at CorpWatch, a nonprofit organization that monitors corporate behavior, began making the connection between the international problem posed by global warming and the localized plight of fenceline communities suffering the effects of pollution from neighboring refineries and petrochemical plants. After visiting Diamond, in November 2000—in a tour arranged by the Louisiana Bucket Brigade and Denny Larson—Srivastava provided funds so that Margie Richard could attend the climate treaty negotiations (COPVI) being held in The Hague in the Netherlands, corporate home of the Royal Dutch/Shell Group.

Denny Larson, coordinator of the Refinery Reform Campaign, came and knocked on Richard's trailer door and told her that her long-term wish to be able to go and speak directly with the owners of Royal Dutch/Shell had been granted. "I jumped in the kitchen of my trailer and said 'Hallelujah,'" Richard said. This opportunity appeared like a gift from above for Richard, who had always thought that if she could just meet the leaders of Shell in person in the Netherlands and explain to them what life was like in Diamond she could convince them to relocate Diamond's residents. Suddenly that dream was not as far-fetched as it first appeared: Richard and a number of colleagues including Larson had tickets to the Netherlands, and preparations for the trip were underway.

Richard brought with her a documentary film crew, a bag of polluted air from Norco, and a jar of polluted water from Nigeria. "The great thing about Margie is that she always recognized that these struggles are connected. . . . So she went there [to the Netherlands] to publicly question Shell about the situation in Norco," observed Anne Rolfes.

On the flight to the Netherlands, Richard was excited: "This was like a dream come true for a child. I wanted to see the real windmills and the tulips . . . and the Queen." The original plan was to go directly to Shell headquarters, demand a meeting with an official, present him with the bags of polluted air and water, and engage him in a dialogue about what Shell might do to rectify the situation. But when she landed in the Netherlands, Larson and others suggested that Richard make the presentation instead at the climate treaty conference, where Shell was giving a presentation

But the timing was very tight: Richard's plane arrived just before the Shell's presentation, their taxi was late, and she had rush to the climate negotiations to make her presentation in front of an international audience. When she finally got to conference her entrance was further delayed because security was shut down due to a visit by the queen. Once inside, Richard's first view of the conference made a big impression on her. "They were all sitting their in their gray and black suits. I said 'Look at these people. They are so sophisticated that they look like little statues,'" she recalled. She should have been scared at the prospect of speaking in this hall but she was not, she said. Instead she reflected the fact that all these doors had been opened to her so that she could bring the suffering of the people of Diamond to the attention of the whole world. She recalled thinking, to herself, "God, look what you have done. You are so awesome."

Then she heard the chairperson say "We will entertain one more questions from the floor." Richard raised her hand and started to wave it around to be recognized, but she was surrounded by taller people. "I had to jump a little bit because I am so short. There was a crowd where I was standing and it hit me: 'God, this is my last chance to be heard.' And I prayed the quickest, shortest, and most sincere prayer I have ever prayed. I said: 'God, you didn't send me this far to fail. . . . It is your will and I am on the right path, let him call me.'" Richard's prayer was answered, and she was designated as the last speaker.

Behind her people were asking "What are you going to say?" She told them to be quiet and asked God to speak through her. The walk up to the speaker's table was a long journey, she remembered. In her mind she heard a voice say "Simplicity and truth from the heart." Then it was Diamond's turn. She started by telling everyone her name and where she came from and that she represented the voice of the people pleading for help. She had been to see all the officials at Shell who would speak with her in the United States but the residents of Diamond were still suffering, she continued. At this point the chairperson of the conference interrupted Richard to ask if she had a question embedded somewhere in her statement.

In response Richard held up the bucket with the polluted air sample from Diamond and said "Sir, would you like to breathe this air?" Whispering started all around her. "I broke the monotony of the setup with that [comment]," she noted with considerable satisfaction. "Would you like to drink this polluted water [from Nigeria]?" she asked. According to one account, a Shell official took the bag, put it up to his face, and asked "Can I breathe it?" The room erupted in laughter.[2] But Richard was not diverted from her point by humor. Denny Larson remembered what she said: "You have been talking about being a Good Neighbor. Here is a bag of polluted air from Diamond and a bag of contaminated water from Nigeria. What I want to know is when are you going to start doing what you say you are going to do? When is your rhetoric going to match your actions? I've come across the world. Please, somebody, send some help our way. . . . Please come down and help us relocate."

After the public scrum was over and a Shell representative had spoken about all the programs Shell had in place to help the residents who lived near its facilities, Richard cornered the Shell official she had just questioned in public for a quick chat in the hallway. "What are you going to do about Diamond?" she asked Robert Kleiburg. "Are you Margie Richard?" he asked. When she confirmed that she was, he said "I've heard about you." Not easily put off, Richard pushed for an answer about the demand for relocating residents on the fenceline in Diamond. "I'm not the one to answer that question," Kleiburg replied. Richard shot back: "Then who is?" Before they parted company, Richard had squeezed a commitment from Kleiburg that he would get back to her with the name of someone to speak with at Shell headquarters and had gotten his cell phone number. Over the next day he called Richard three times to keep her up to date with his efforts to find the right person for her to speak with. "That is when I knew that it [relocation] was going to happen. If God took a little country person like me and opened all these doors I had to be on the right track," Richard recalls thinking.

Robert Kleiburg was "clearly moved" by Richard's statement, Larson reported. "We repeatedly saw that Margie [Richard] and other community residents had a dramatic impact on top Shell officials away from the plants in Norco," he noted. The top officials from Shell in London and in the Netherlands, who were in charge of maintaining and when necessary repairing Shell's image, did not like what they were hearing out of Norco, he added. The strategy of going directly to top management and demanding action was effective, he observed.

Just how effective Richard was at publicizing the plight of Diamond residents in the international arena can be judged by the fact that two weeks after her protest in the Netherlands a top Shell executive from London was knocking on her trailer door in Diamond. "It was as if he had dropped out of the sky," Larson recalled. "Hello. Are you Margie Richard? I just stopped by for a chat," said Titus Moser, a social development manager from Shell

International. Richard remembered the moment vividly: "I will never forget. . . . While we were standing there was some [foul-smelling] air and the guy said 'What is that?' And I almost said 'Praise the Lord.'" Her guest had just received his first whiff of contaminated air from the Shell plants. And now, suddenly, Diamond and Norco were on the map for top Royal Dutch/Shell executives. Clearly, they did not want their problems in Louisiana to turn into the same kind of public-relations black eye they earned in Nigeria, so the company went into full damage-control mode.

In her work as a program officer at the Ford Foundation, Vernice Miller-Travis provided grant money that permitted some of the grassroots activists from communities like Diamond to travel to international gatherings in the Netherlands, India, and South Africa. "I love seeing these people [fenceline activists] in other spaces [such as international environmental gatherings]. . . . I know how articulate they are, I know how passionate they are, and I also know they have a fairly complex understanding of the science of the issues they are dealing with," said Miller-Travis. To hear residents from Norco and other fenceline communities speak at international conferences brings an authentic voice to these gatherings that policy-oriented environmentalists cannot provide, she continued. Taking the Diamond story abroad and interjecting it into the international arena turned out to be a remarkable effective strategy, she added.

Grassroots activists have been so successful in describing their environmental justice struggles in the United States at international conferences that the "EJ paradigm" is spreading abroad, Miller-Travis observed. At a number of international conferences, NGO activists from developing nations wanted copies of The Principles of Environmental Justice and advice about how to launch similar initiatives in their country, she reported. "I had to tell them that it took 700 people four days to come up with these 17 principles and that it was reflective of many years of prior discussion and debate," she continued. "We told them that they would have to evolve their own process but that we would support their efforts."

Back Channel

It was in no way obvious that Michael Lerner would become involved in the campaign for relocation in Diamond. He came from a very different world than the residents who lived on the fenceline with Shell. Lerner, 61, is the founder and president of Commonweal, a health and environmental research institute based in Bolinas, California. Commonweal focuses on what Lerner calls "the emerging environmental health movement." As I mentioned in the preface, he is my brother. I have worked with him, as the director of the Commonweal Research Institute, for 27 years. This report comes out of that collaboration.

For 18 years Lerner has co-led the Commonweal Cancer Health Program, a week-long residential support program for cancer patients. He is president of two small foundations and of the Smith Farm Center for Healing Arts, which offers a similar program in Washington. Lerner is also the author of *Choices in Healing: Integrating the Best of Conventional and Complementary Approaches to Cancer*. In 1983 he received the MacArthur Prize Fellowship for contributions to public health.

A graduate of Harvard and Yale, where he studied political science, Lerner moved to California in 1972 where he founded Full Circle, a residential treatment facility for children with learning and behavior disorders. He started Commonweal in 1975. Since then he has also been instrumental in establishing the Health Care Without Harm campaign, an effort to reduce the burning of plastics and emissions of dioxin from hospital incinerators around the country. He is currently involved in setting up the Collaborative on Health and the Environment, a network that brings together those who suffer from environmentally induced disease, those who care for them, and those who seek to prevent these diseases.

In 1999, Gary Cohen, director of the Environmental Health Fund in Boston, suggested that Lerner come with him on a toxics tour of Louisiana. Lerner, who described Cohen as one of his mentors on toxics organizing, agreed. They were joined in Louisiana by the chemist Wilma Subra and by Monique Harden, then with the EarthJustice Legal Defense Fund. With these two local experts as guides, they visited the Agricultural Street Landfill in New Orleans, the community of Mossville near Lake Charles in southwest Louisiana, and the river parish communities of Convent and Norco/Diamond.

Like others who had made the trip to Norco, Michael Lerner met Margie Richard, then president of Concerned Citizens of Norco. At the time Richard was living in her trailer at 28 Washington Street with her daughter and grandchildren. Her mother's house was next door on the street adjacent to the Shell plant. "As I sat with Margie in her living room you could hear very loudly the Shell plant's loudspeaker blaring orders to workers to move things around in the plant. Then Margie took us out and showed us the place where Leroy Jones and Helen Washington burned to death. At that point I had this really deep instinct that this just wasn't right," Lerner recalled.

The situation in Diamond was different than that of the other sites because Diamond was sandwiched between two Shell plants and it was clear where the pollution came from, Lerner continued. The residents of Diamond had also been struggling for relocation for over a decade, he said. "So it all came together for me at a personal level that this wasn't right and that something should be done about it," he added.

The second time Lerner visited Diamond was with Janet Moses, a pediatrician at MIT who was deeply concerned with health and environmental issues, and her husband, Robert Moses, a civil rights leader. Also on this tour of Diamond were a nurse-practitioner from Texas and Monique Harden of the EarthJustice Legal Defense Fund. Once again Lerner walked with Margie Richard to the spot where the two Diamond residents had died in 1973 when a leak from a Shell pipeline ignited. "I just had a feeling that I was supposed to stay with this until Concerned Citizens of Norco won its fight to relocate. Something happened in me that made this a very important two years of my life. . . . I felt it was important to be a witness [to the situation in Diamond] but I also felt—and this is the strange part—I approached this as if my mother had been living in Diamond. . . . This became deeply personal for me and that gave me the kind of energy and commitment to do this," he said. This commitment came from what struck Lerner as "an impeccably just demand that all the residents of Diamond who wanted to move be given a fair price [by Shell] for their house."

Lerner was deeply moved by the courage of Margie Richard and other Diamond residents who were willing to stand up to Shell and demand relocation. "I was struck by Margie Richard: her grace, her courage, her clarity, and her willingness to put everything she had on the line to win this struggle," he said. He was also impressed by Richard's commitment to take the high road in this campaign. When he joined her on a picket line outside Shell headquarters in New Orleans, he watched Richard's response when a national environmental justice leader suggested that top Shell officials belonged in jail for their misdeeds. He recalled Richard leaning over and saying to a local community activist "You can't go negative. You have to stay on the high road."

Margie Richard was the entry point for many people who came to Diamond to learn about the environmental justice problems there, Lerner continued. There was a constant stream of visitors coming to Norco, and Richard "was kind of like the fisherwoman who stands by the river and catches the fish that were going to help. And I was one of the fish," Lerner observed. Richard's willingness to meet with the ever-changing parade of people coming through her trailer and tell them the same stories about Diamond over and over and still be able to keep it fresh required endless patience, Lerner noted. This was hard work that, over the years, required great perseverance, he added.

As chance would have it, Lerner had discussed the situation in Diamond with an old friend, Peter Warshall, 60, former editor of the *Whole Earth Review*. Shortly thereafter, Warshall was asked to be a judge at an essay contest held in London and sponsored by Royal/Dutch Shell and *The Economist*. One of the other judges was Sir Phillip Watts, then CEO of Shell. Without wasting time, Warshall turned to Watts and said "You might have another Nigeria on your hands in Norco, Louisiana." That got Watts's attention. Warshall then told Watts what he had learned from Lerner about the struggle for relocation in Diamond. The next day, Watts reported that he had made plans to visit Norco and find out for himself what was going on. In this fashion, Warshall opened up a back channel to Shell's management team in London.

Warshall then joined Lerner in Norco to familiarize himself with the situation on the ground there. He spoke with both residents in Diamond and toured the Shell/Motiva refinery with David Brignac. "This is one of the largest refineries in the world," Warshall noted. "I came to look at it as America's crackhouse. We are all addicted to petrochemicals and this is where we come as addicts to get our fix and fill up our cars."

Warshall and Lerner then emailed Watts in London: "I suspect you don't know what is going on at your two facilities in Norco, Louisiana but given the two page color ads you keep running in *The Economist* about how much you care about the environment and the communities where you work I can't believe that you want this situation in Norco to be what it is."

Lerner then called a number of colleagues in the funding and nonprofit community, including Janet Maughan of the Rockefeller Foundation, Pete Meyers of the W. Alton Jones Foundation, Herbert Bedolfe of the Home-land Foundation, and Mil Duncan of the Ford Foundation. He also invited

Peter Warshall, whose contacts with senior Shell officials were to prove valuable, and Rachel Bagby, an attorney and performance artist from Virginia.

One of the funders said to Lerner that she hoped he had "a clear picture of the factual situation on the ground in Norco." That made Lerner realize that he had a lot of research to do. He subsequently compiled a briefing book that included documents put out by Shell, by the media, and by a number of local, state, and national groups. He also met with a group of Shell officials in Norco to get their side of the story. "I was acutely aware that I was responsible for bringing the attention of a group of [foundation] colleagues that I really respected to this situation and I was concerned about whether I had an accurate factual picture of what was going on," he noted.

Through his research and the meetings at Shell, Lerner came to appreciate the complexity of the relationship between the Diamond/Norco community and the adjacent Shell facilities. He discovered, for example, that a majority but not all of the Diamond residents wanted to be relocated. "Even as all the nuances were added, however, my belief in the righteousness of the demands of Concerned Citizens of Norco never wavered," he said. He also came to the conclusion that he had to make a personal distinction between backing a cause—the push for relocation—and searching for the truth about what was going on in Diamond. Though he was sympathetic to the cause, Lerner decided that he would have to pursue what he saw as the truth of the situation wherever it led.

Some members of the foundation community had warned Lerner against becoming involved in Louisiana environmental health and environmental justice issues—there was a lot of contention among these groups, they had told him, and it would be difficult to create sustained statewide networks that would work collaboratively on the issues. But Lerner noted that the foundations themselves may have contributed to that state of affairs. "If the foundations come into the state and simply make grants to a whole range of nonprofits, many of which have never had significant resources before, and then expect those nonprofits to work together effectively, it is not surprising that different people developed different agendas," he observed.

While Lerner said he appreciated the warnings, he found that, while there was friction among some of the environmental groups working in Louisiana, in the end he was struck by how effectively the nonprofit alliance that supported Concerned Citizens of Norco held together despite strong divergences in their perspectives. The key was to structure the work of the nonprofit organizations in a collaborative way and get an agreement on the agenda and on which pivotal players would play what roles. In the end the nonprofit organizations used the struggle in Norco to prove to the funding community that they could work together, and they acquitted themselves well, Lerner said.

Bringing grant officers from the major foundations through Diamond and Norco made Shell nervous, said Anne Rolfes. "Shell officials don't care what I think—some random resident of New Orleans—but they do care what the Rockefellers and Fords of the world think about them, so that was important," she observed.

Bringing in foundation representatives to look at the situation in Diamond did contribute to changing the tenor of discussions between Shell officials and residents of Diamond, Lerner noted. Before that, communications between Shell and Diamond residents had not been effective, he continued. But he recognized that he came to this struggle only in its final stage and that the decade of struggle by Concerned Citizens of Norco and their allies laid the groundwork for arriving at a successful agreement.

Lerner believed that it was critical to the success of the negotiations that the framework focus not on past grievances but rather on creating plausible "win-win" outcomes that could result in a joint declaration of victory by both Concerned Citizens of Norco and Shell. "I had the direct personal experience that there were people of good will who wanted to solve this problem both in CCN and in Shell," he said. It seemed essential to signal to Shell that the Norco struggle was no longer simply a regional embarrassment but had the potential to be a sustained issue at the national and international level with constituencies that mattered deeply to Shell, he said.

"The key to understanding the struggle, I felt, lay in the fact that Shell is an unusual company. It has reached out to solve social and environmental problems in recent years to a far greater extent than, for example, Exxon Mobil. There is no question that a major motivation for this is public-relations concerns, but there are also senior staff officials at Shell who genuinely have a vision of a greener and more community-oriented energy company. So I wanted to be clear with Shell that I thought we had the resources and the commitment to stay with this struggle for another decade if necessary.

At the same time, I wanted to communicate that we thought this problem could only be solved if we saw a way that everybody could win," Lerner concluded.

Deadline

At one critical moment in the negotiations, the Concerned Citizens of Norco and their allies came up with the idea of setting a deadline for Shell to decide whether it would relocate residents on the back two streets of Diamond. The nonprofit allies of the Diamond residents had some leverage with Shell and were willing to use it. Coming up in September 2001 was the World Summit on Sustainable Development (WSSD) in South Africa.

Shell's chairman, Sir Phillip Watts, was scheduled to speak as chairman of the World Council on Sustainable Development. His message would be that "business was good for sustainable development, and sustainable development was good for business." His presence at the meeting was meant to showcase the new, environmentally sensitive Shell, which in 1995 had committed itself, at least on paper, to sustainable practices and human rights. In 1998, to bolster its credentials as an oil company with progressive "green" goals, Shell withdrew from the Global Climate Coalition oil group, which was lobbying against an international climate treaty. Shell officials were determined to demonstrate that theirs was a socially responsible corporation, sensitive to environmental issues and the welfare of communities near its facilities.

"The deadline," Michael Lerner recalled, "grew out of strategizing among the allies of Concerned Citizens of Norco." The idea emerged after Coming Clean, a national coalition that focuses on industrial toxics issues, held a national organizing meeting in New Orleans. After the meeting, these experienced toxics organizers from across the country went out to Diamond and had lunch on the fenceline with the Shell Chemical plant on a day when there was a particularly noxious flare. It was after that lunch, Lerner remembered, that the coalition adopted Norco as the subject of one of its major environmental justice campaigns.

A number of local, state, and national groups, becoming aware of the importance of the environmental justice struggle in Diamond, identified the World Summit on Sustainable Development in Johannesburg as a logical place to focus on that struggle because they would all be sending representatives there. Activists began to talk about organizing an international network of groups that would examine Shell's environmental record and highlight the similarities between the plight of residents living on Shell's fenceline in the Louisiana delta with the predicament of the farmers in the Niger delta who had suffered from their proximity to Shell activities there. These groups would then deploy at the WSSD and protest the considerable distance between Shell's rhetorical commitment to sustainability and its actions. This was precisely what Shell did not want to happen. Shell managers were determined to use the WSSD as a chance to refurbish their company's environmental credentials. They did not want the summit to become a focal point for Shell bashing by a determined group of environmentalists.

"I communicated to Shell that I thought it would be a good thing if this [dispute in Diamond] could be resolved before [the Johannesburg Summit]," Lerner said. It was in this fashion that Shell was presented with a deadline to make its best offer to Concerned Citizens of Norco concerning whether or not it was willing to relocate the residents on the back to streets of Diamond.

"It was brilliant," commented Denny Larson, coordinator of the Refinery Reform Campaign. Shell officials were frightened of the prospect of a campaign devoted to publicizing Norco as Shell's new Nigeria-style fiasco at the WSSD. Furthermore, they did not want such a campaign to connect with protesters in South Africa who were blaming Shell for a huge underground pipeline leak of a million liters of oil in a populated area, Larson continued. The prospect of the two campaigns joining forces at WSSD would be daunting for even Shell's high-powered PR machine to contain.

Credible Threat

Gary Cohen, executive director of the Environmental Health Fund, said he played the role of "credible threat" in presenting the deadline to Shell officials. He had the connections to put together groups of anti-Shell activists who would show up at international gatherings. If Shell failed to come up with a reasonable solution to the problem in Diamond before the deadline, it was understood that Cohen and other toxics activists would expose Shell's environmental shortcomings in Durban.

As activists began to talk about a "Nigeria to Norco" campaign, Shell officials smelled a disaster in the making—something akin to the problems they had with the Brent Spar and with Nigeria. "We told them that the campaign in Diamond was just going to keep building and that Shell would become a poster child for environmental injustice," Cohen recalled. In view of the huge amount of money Shell had spent trying to improve its image and "rebrand" itself as a company that cared about sustainable development and the welfare of people in adjacent communities, none of this sounded good. So they decided to settle, he noted.

As the former co-director of the National Toxics Campaign, Cohen had connections that permitted him to funnel activists and resources into the struggle in Diamond. He and Judy Robinson, his partner at the Environmental Health Fund, also joined in weekly telephone conferences calls with a growing number of activists interested in the plight of Diamond residents.

That Cohen has devoted his career to working on toxics issues is not surprising. He had grown up in New Jersey, a state permeated with odoriferous chemicals. But the impact of toxic chemicals on human health had not always been his first interest.

After college, Cohen spent several years in India, studied Hindi and Indian philosophy, then moved to Europe, where he wrote guides to London and Paris. Subsequently he became involved in environmental health organizing as a result of a friendship with John O'Connor, who was involved in assembling a coalition of groups of residents of areas adjacent to toxic dump sites. In the years 1984–1986, the coalition O'Connor organized (which eventually became the National Toxics Campaign) successfully lobbied Congress on behalf of the Superfund legislation. It was during that period that O'Connor asked Cohen to write a guidebook to toxics organizing that would help a mother in Pittsburgh living next to a Dow Chemical factory figure out how she could become involved in protecting herself and her family from exposure to hazardous chemicals. The guide would help her figure out how to organize her neighbors, deal with the media, and access government data bases that had crucial information about what chemicals the plant was emitting. Further, the guide should tell her what laws were on the books that could help protect the community. Cohen leapt right in.

After the Superfund legislation was passed, in 1986, a number of the groups in the coalition felt that they had achieved their goal and were ready to declare victory and disband. O'Connor, however, argued that cleaning up the largest and worst toxic waste disposal dumps was just one aspect of the toxics issue and that the coalition should continue to build power to begin to address the other problems posed by the large-scale production and use of toxic chemicals. To address these broader issues, the National Toxics Campaign refocused its efforts. Cohen was brought on as its co-director, working there from 1986 to 1993. During that period the NTC focused on problems associated with the incineration of toxic chemicals and operated its own laboratory so that citizens could test their soil and water for toxic chemicals. He subsequently helped put together the Military Toxics Project. Currently he directs Health Care Without Harm, an international coalition that has as its goal the reduction and ultimately the elimination of toxic chemicals emitted by the health care industry.

It was this considerable background in organizing around toxic chemicals that Cohen brought to the struggle in Diamond. He had the further advantage of already having worked in Louisiana in the 1980s, when NTC set up a joint project with the Oil Chemical and Atomic Workers Union. Together they established a position for a paid staffer who worked on what they called the "Labor/Neighbor" project that looked at chemical exposures of both industrial workers and residents living in neighborhoods adjacent to chemical plants.

More recently, after the Bill Moyers's "Trade Secrets" documentary, which exposed deceptive practices used by the chemical industry to downplay the impact of toxic chemicals on worker health, a number of toxics groups decided to focus on the health impact of the chemical industry as a whole. The group, calling itself Coming Clean, held a conference in Louisiana where the chemical industry was heavily concentrated and chose Norco as a focal point for some local activity.

The Coming Clean conference in New Orleans brought together environmental health activists from around the nation to talk about working on a variety of projects including one on PVC, one on chemical policy, and one focusing on a "body burden" strategy in which testing would be done to see how many toxic chemicals people were carrying around with them in their body. After their meeting they held a picnic in Diamond, saw the conditions there, and decided to focus on the struggle there as a potentially high-profile campaign that could put a face on what it was like living next to chemical plants.

Potential Lawsuit

Gary Cohen's promise to help assemble anti-Shell protesters in South Africa was not the only consequence that Shell faced if it refused to relocate residents on the back two streets of Diamond. There were other legal issues in Norco that Shell executives had to consider.

"I like to think we created a credible threat" that if the negotiations broke down members of Concerned Citizens of Norco had alternative legal actions they could take, said Adam Babich, director of the Tulane Environmental Law Clinic since May 2000. While the negotiations were underway between Shell officials and CCN, Diamond residents were exploring the possibility of bringing a lawsuit against Shell with lawyers from the clinic.

While Babich was unwilling to be specific about what legal action the Environmental Law Clinic researched for its clients in Diamond, he did present a hypothetical case having to do with permit violations. If they are being candid, compliance officers at facilities as large as the Norco Complex will admit that it is impossible to run a facility that is in compliance with all the regulations that govern it at all times, Babich pointed out. The best they can do is ensure that a system is in place that brings permit violations to their attention as early as possible so that they can report the problem to the appropriate regulatory official and ensure that they are fixed as soon as possible. This leaves a facility such as the Norco Complex vulnerable to lawsuits by residents who charge that it is not living up to its permit requirements. In fact, there were already a number of regulatory concerns about some of the facilities at the Norco Complex: for example, the interpretation of the New Source Review regulations by Shell and Motiva officials was already on the Environmental Protection Agency's radar screen, Babich observed.

It is a matter of public record that the Environmental Law Clinic requested Shell documents while the negotiations between CCN and the company were underway, Babich noted. "Most companies would prefer not to have a citizen group with sophisticated legal counsel actively going through their files to ensure that they are in compliance," he continued. The fact that Environmental Law Clinic lawyers were involved in a lawsuit against Orion, the refinery adjacent to Shell, might also have made the threat of legal action by Diamond residents seem even more tangible, he added.

But Babich is quick to put this "credible legal threat" in context. There are important constraints in Louisiana that limit the legal remedy available to residents in fenceline communities adjacent to highly polluting industries. In the case of Diamond residents, the community had already lost a lawsuit over relocation, he pointed out. Second, Louisiana abolished the ability of plaintiffs to seek punitive damages making suits by groups like Concerned Citizens of Norco less appealing to the best toxic tort lawyers in the country because it limited the amount they could collect. Diamond residents could still seek compensatory damages but not punitive damages, Babich explained.

Hypothetically, in addition to suing Shell over failure to fully comply with its permit to operate, Diamond residents could have sued Shell for damage to their health caused by emissions from the Shell plant and sought compensatory damages, Babich continued, but these are tough cases to prove. To begin with most chemicals have never been tested on humans and thus one has to extrapolate from animal laboratory testing. Further, proving that any one chemical caused a specific health effect is difficult in view of how many chemicals we are all exposed to and their potential synergistic effects. Proving that cancer clusters are caused by a chemical release is also hard in view of the large percentage of Americans who contract cancer during their lifetime. Industries can also argue that fenceline residents became ill not from exposure to industrial chemicals but rather because they smoked cigarettes or ate an unhealthy diet. Finally, there is very little reliable air monitoring data which one can use to prove that residents have been exposed to a given chemical. As a result, one is often left with trials at which dueling experts leave juries with room for reasonable doubt about a case. All of this does not make it impossible to win a class-action lawsuit that aggregates a number of cases of residents who claim to have been hurt by chemical emissions from a plant, but it does make it arduous, Babich conceded.

15

Finding Agreement

On March 4, 2002, Shell agreed to engage in face-to-face negotiations with the leaders of Concerned Citizens of Norco over the issue of relocation. The combined efforts of Diamond community activists and their allies—a disparate coalition that included grassroots activists, environmental justice advocates, environmentalists, social justice organizations, members of Congress, celebrities, and foundation officers—finally convinced Shell officials that it was in their best interests to reach a negotiated settlement with the residents of Diamond. The increasingly critical media coverage of this environmental justice/fenceline community story no doubt also played an important role in Shell's decision to negotiate.

Shell might have decided not to negotiate. The press coverage of the dispute in Diamond had been damaging, but Shell is a big company and can absorb a good deal of carping. Shell executives could have stonewalled the activists, as they had in the past, and hoped that eventually Diamond residents and their allies would tire. They could have pursued their strategy of buying out some of the most vociferous activists. They could have continued to make the argument, which resonated well in the local white community, that if some people did not like living near the Shell plants then they could jolly well move.

One of the reasons Shell probably agreed to negotiate a settlement was that there came to be a tacit understanding between the parties involved in the dispute that Shell would be permitted to decouple the relocation issue from the health issue. This was possible because some of those who had been hammering on Shell for relocation understood that it would not happen unless they could fashion a win-win scenario in which community residents could achieve what they wanted and the company could back down gracefully from its "no relocation" stance without losing face or exposing itself to lawsuits.

The core of this strategy permitted Shell to say that it was moving people to create a buffer zone and that it was doing so because of "unique historical considerations" rather than because its plants were causing any health problems in the community. Shell was willing to deal on relocation as long as the settlement was not attached to the health issue. So the Concerned Citizens of Norco and their allies concentrated on relocation and tabled the health question until some later date. Once they had a deal about relocating those people who wanted to leave, they reasoned, they could revisit the health problems.

At the outset of the negotiations, it looked as if Shell officials were using the meetings just as proof that they were "engaged" with the community and that they brought nothing to the table other than a willingness to work on their "Good Neighbor Initiative," which was a hodgepodge of giveaways for the community, Wilma Subra recalled. Skirmishes between the two sides continued. Though Shell officials had made it clear that they would not relocate residents on the back two streets of Diamond, they had indicated that they might institute an "exceptions policy" whereby some residents of the back two streets (those who had relatives on the front two streets) might qualify for relocation. This softening of Shell's no-relocation policy was explored by activists who thought they saw an opportunity. What, they asked, were Shell's criteria for this exception policy? When Shell remained vague about it, residents offered their own generous version. This prompted Shell officials to respond that what the activists proposed was not an exception policy but rather a new relocation program—one they refused to fund or implement. Peter Warshall, who helped open up the back channel with Shell management, attended one of the negotiating sessions involving Concerned Citizens of Norco, some of their allies in the Environmental Justice movement, and Shell officials. While Warshall was sitting toward the back of the room and listening to Wayne Pearce (Shell's Norco manager) parry residents' demands for relocation, it occurred to him that no one was addressing the fact that this dialogue was taking place in the context of racism. As an outsider, Warshall felt free to point out the obvious. He stood up and addressed his comments to Pearce, a man with a distinctly Scottish brogue. Warshall told Pearce that he didn't know how much Pearce knew about the history of the state, but that it was important to understand the residents' demands for relocation as part of a long legacy of racism and corrupt politics in Louisiana. Bringing race up explicitly may later have given Shell a new opening to justify relocating Diamond residents, Warshall conjectured. Now they could claim that they were relocating Diamond residents because of the unique history of the community and the past injustices it had suffered.

Meetings between Shell officials and Diamond residents and their allies continued for a number of months, but as time dragged on it became clear that the activists were just waiting for Shell to make its final offer. Then, at one negotiating session, when there was no indication if Shell would ever offer relocation, the facilitator asked each participant to sum up in a word how he or she felt about the prospects for agreement. Some activists were depressed and others were angry, but community organizer Anne Rolfes described herself as "determined." What Shell had failed to take into account was the tenacity of the groups involved in the struggle, said Rolfes. "I guess they thought we would go away . . . but I knew that I wasn't going to go away. I was going to be 80 years old out there [on the picket line]."

By late May, Shell was signaling that it was preparing to make an offer to landowners in Diamond. Peter Warshall suspected that the breakthrough came after Shell's CEO Sir Phillip Watts visited Norco and recognized that the struggle for relocation had the potential to cause his company serious international embarrassment. With this in mind, Watts decided to cut a deal. From what Warshall gathered while talking with Shell officials, Watts realized he had to do an end run around Shell's management teams in both Norco and Houston, which had been unwilling to negotiate about relocation. To break the deadlock, Watts set up a small committee to come up with a solution. The new committee was based at the Shell Foundation in London. Executives in the London office then exerted pressure on managers in Houston and Norco to broker a deal. "As a result," Warshall recalled, "managers in Norco were getting pressure from two sides to agree to relocation: they were feeling the heat from the environmental justice groups and from their own bosses in London."

Unaware of this behind-the-scenes activity, Diamond residents were unconvinced that the signals coming from Shell officials would lead to a relocation deal. They had been disappointed too many times. They were not convinced that Shell would make an offer, and they were quite disconsolate, Denny Larson recalled. To pump up the pressure on Shell, Concerned Citizens of Norco decided to take their fight to Shell's U.S. corporate headquarters in Houston. Their strategy was "bulletproof," said

Larson with admiration: they would go to Houston and engage in a pray-in at corporate headquarters, praying that Shell would listen to its neighbors in Diamond and hear their appeal to be relocated. Anne Rolfes helped plan the Houston trip, printed up a big banner that read "Let My People Go," and invited the media to attend the protest. A reporter from the *Houston Chronicle* picked up on the pray-in story and wrote a follow-up feature about how Shell's previous offer to move only half the residents of Diamond was tearing the community apart. Now Shell officials in Texas were starting to feel the heat.

With a deadline of June 5 for Shell to make its offer, the negotiating parties met again on May 30. Everything started out cordially enough. Then Wayne Pearce, Shell Chemical's plant manager, said that the pray-in in Houston had boxed him into a corner and that he had to get a settlement within the next hour. "There was no more Mr. Nice Guy," Larson noted. Diamond residents had gone over Pearce's head to his bosses in Houston and in the process had shot themselves in the foot. Now they had to make an on-the-spot decision.

Pearce then laid out Shell's offer, which came to be known as the Shell Options Program. Basically, the offer agreed to buy out any Diamond residents who owned properties on the back two streets of Diamond; or, if they chose to stay, agreed to give them a home-improvement loan that would be forgiven over a five-year period. The dual program offered residents a choice, Pearce emphasized. There was a financial incentive for them to stay in the form of a forgivable home-improvement loan, or they could chose to sell their home to Shell and move elsewhere. Any way one looked at it, this was a breakthrough deal and a tremendous victory for Concerned Citizens of Norco. After decades of lobbying there was now an offer on the table that would provide all landowners in Diamond the option to accept a buyout.

But there was a hitch. The leaders of Concerned Citizens of Norco were asked to either take the deal or reject it in the next hour. Their pray-in had clearly touched a nerve at Shell headquarters in Houston, and this was their punishment.

After going over the offer in some detail, CCN and its allies praised Shell for what look like a good offer on its face. They refused, however, to accept or reject the deal in the next hour, arguing that they were obliged to take the proposal to a meeting of the residents of the community to see if they wanted to accept or reject it. Without the consent of the community's residents they were not empowered to act: that was not the way they did business. Instead they wrote up a statement saying that they were "encouraged with the progress" of the negotiation and would present Shell's offer to the community two days later. Pearce finally agreed to let the offer be submitted to the community.

A few days later, the community gathered at a small church in Diamond. The leaders of Concerned Citizens of Norco reviewed the relocation-and-home-improvement offer in detail. The community accepted the offer. Shell officials were relieved that the meeting had gone so well, Larson recalled. It looked as if a win-win solution in which both the residents and Shell could claim victory was within sight.

But then Shell began to engage in a negotiating tactic known as "nibbling at the end." This well-tested strategy calls on the party that has just made an offer that the other party wants to accept to begin asking for little concessions right at the end of the negotiation. In this instance, Shell asked the nonprofit organizations that had supported the relocation effort to remove all mentions of Norco from their websites. In essence, Shell wanted to rewrite history by removing from the Internet all references to the protracted struggle in Diamond that had led up to their current offer. Shell officials asked the leaders of Concerned Citizens of Norco to make this request of their allies. This was the first salvo in an endgame battle to drive a wedge between Concerned Citizens of Norco and their allies in the environmental justice movement, Larson observed.

The environmental justice activists were understandably reluctant to accede to this demand to purge all their websites of all mentions of the struggle in Norco. They were willing to excise any rhetoric urging readers to put pressure on Shell to come up with a relocation offer for the residents of Diamond now that one was on the table, but they were not willing to erase from their archives the numerous stories about the struggle for relocation. By asking CCN to request of their allies something they were unwilling to do, Shell had created tension between the grassroots activists in Diamond and their allies in nonprofit organizations.

Shell also pressed the leaders of CCN to join them immediately in making a joint press statement on Friday evening, June 7, which would emphasize the options Shell was offering to residents of Diamond. CCN and its allies argued for putting the press statement off for a few days until Tuesday, June 11, so there would be time to prepare a statement and so the media could be properly alerted that a joint statement was going to be made. Shell eventually agreed to this with the proviso that there be no leaks to the media.

On Monday, June 10, Shell officials told the leaders of CCN that the press embargo had been broken and that they were getting calls from an Associated Press reporter advising them that a media advisory about a settlement had been issued by CCN. One account of this delicate moment also suggests that a reporter asked Shell officials to comment on a statement by an environmental justice activist that an agreement had been reached between Shell and Diamond residents. Instead of just telling the reporter that they would make no comment until the next day, Denny Larson contended, Shell officials used this as evidence that the press embargo had been broken.

Unbeknownst to the allies of CCN, Shell officials then met with the leaders of CCN and told them that press embargo had been broken and that the deal was in jeopardy unless CCN agreed to make a joint statement with them immediately. "The substance of the Joint Statement of Success was far more important to CCN and Shell than any kind of public ceremony," one Shell official noted. So CCN agreed to issue the joint statement.

The Shell officials brought a video crew with them so that the statement could be taped for the media. Here Shell was further hammering in the wedge between the local activists and their allies, making sure that the people who helped the residents over the years were not present when the final press statement about the agreement was shaped, Larson noted. The tactic worked. CCN and Shell released a "Joint Statement on Success Between Concerned Citizens of Norco and Shell Chemical LP," which read as follows:

As a result of Shell's discussions with the CCN and other members of the Diamond neighborhood, Shell has developed its Diamond Options Program that consists of a Property Purchase Component and a Home Improvement Loan Component. Under the Home Improvement Loan Component, Diamond residents have the choice to stay in the Diamond neighborhood and take advantage of the Good Neighbor Initiative and other programs that Shell and Motiva offer. This component is designed to improve the lives of Diamond residents, contribute to a vibrant and growing Norco, and preserve the historic Diamond neighborhood. Under the Property Purchase Component, Diamond residents have the choice to sell their properties to Shell at a fair price and leave Norco. This component provides residents the opportunity to relocate to areas they believe are best for their families.

• CCN declares that these options demonstrate Shell's commitment to the Diamond neighborhood.
• Shell and CCN believe that both have acted in good faith in listening to each other and addressing their respective concerns.

• CCN appreciates the generous support of the following organizations, Commonweal, Deep South Center for Environmental Justice, Earthjustice, Environmental Health Fund, LA Bucket Brigade, Refinery Reform Campaign, and the Subra Company, which have contributed to achieving successful resolution.

• Shell and CCN jointly declare that their discussions and the resulting Diamond Options Program have successfully resolved their differences. In addition, both Shell and CCN are committed to continuing dialogue to ensure successful implementation of the Diamond Options Program.

The statement was signed by representatives of Concerned Citizens of Norco and Shell Chemical LLP.

"Shell pulled a lot of divide-and-conquer stuff during this period, and frankly some of it worked," Larson conceded. The leaders of CCN became convinced that their allies had jeopardized the deal they desperately wanted to make with Shell, Larson continued, and what hurt the members of the nonprofit organizations most was that the leaders of CCN, after working with their allies for years, never called any of them up and said "This is what Shell is saying about you guys. Is it true?" But Shell's last-minute tactical maneuvers produced only a temporary advantage. Within a few days, Larson reported, the leaders of CCN and the allies were sorting out what had happened, and residents of Diamond were hugging the people who had been in their corner and helped them in their struggle.

The Real Deal

Shell, reversing its position, offered to purchase the property of anyone in the community of Diamond who wanted to relocate. In essence the company extended its initial buyout from the first two streets of Diamond to include the back two streets, which encompassed about 160 houses and mobile homes, 30 vacant lots, and 350–400 residents. Shell also offered generous incentives to those who chose to stay.

Shell had previously argued that it could not possibly buy out all four streets of Diamond because to do so would be unfair to the white community in Norco, where Shell was offering to buy out only two streets. The reversal of this position required some explanation. This ticklish task was assigned to David Brignac, Shell's Sustainable Development Manager in Norco, who for the previous year and a half had been the company's point man in Diamond.

"In talking with residents of Diamond especially over the last couple of months we listened and learned and came to the conclusion that Diamond is unique in the sense that it has special needs," Brignac explained. Residents in Diamond are more dependent on each other for their care than are residents in other communities, he continued. The community is made up of multiple generations of families who have lived close to each other over generations. As a result, there is a network of mutually helpful relationships. Shell's first buyout program in Diamond, the Voluntary Purchase Program, which offered relocation for only half the community, had severed some of these close ties and disrupted the operation of this tight-knit community, Brignac conceded. "The situation [in Diamond] was unique in the sense that as a company we helped create some of the problems, " Brignac noted. Diamond was also a "unique" case because there were numerous people in the community who wanted to leave but could not because they found it impossible to find buyers for their homes. The same was not true on the white side of Norco, where there was an active real estate market, Brignac continued.

Wayne Pearce, Shell's site manager in Norco, echoed this "uniqueness" rationale: "We have come to recognize that the Diamond community is truly unique. . . . The community is like an extended family and we realize now that our previous efforts to create a greenbelt around our facilities may have created difficulties for some families and caregivers in the Diamond neighborhood. . . . While our first preference is to preserve the historic fabric of the Diamond neighborhood, we believe it is important to give residents the choice of determining what is best for their families."[1]

The deal Shell made with the residents of Diamond was presented to the media as a "win-win" arrangement whereby residents would have the option of moving out or could accept generous incentives to stay. Shell, for its part, gained by resolving a long struggle with its immediate neighbors and securing maneuvering room to pursue its vision of establishing a community of people who wanted to be there along its fenceline. The company could also now say that it had demonstrated a willingness to enter into dialogue with its neighbors and address their concerns.

Anne Rolfes had a different perspective on Shell's decision to offer to buyout all the homes in Diamond. This was "a significant victory for the residents," she noted. Shell did not want to extend the program to all four streets but had been forced to do so by the tenacity of Diamond residents, she continued. Some of them had been fighting for relocation since the 1970s. Shell did not want the relocation program to be seen as a program to relocate people away from a place that was environmentally harmful, Rolfes added. "That is fine. . . . Whatever makes them happy, as long as we get the people out who want to get out," she said.

The program offered to residents on the back two streets of Diamond was different than the one in effect on the front two streets, Brignac explained. The new Diamond Options Program offered homeowners on the back two streets who wanted to relocate a minimum of $80,000 for properties with homes, $50,000 for lots with a trailer, or the assessed value of their property.[2] The $80,000 minimum buyout figure was arrived at by looking at the local real estate market and determining that some homes in the area outside Diamond were available for that amount, Brignac said. Residents eligible under the program would be shown photos of homes for sale in that price range so they would have a concrete idea of what kind of property they might be able to purchase elsewhere, he added.

Assessments for all homes in Diamond were to be based on the values of comparably sized homes in central Norco, where home values were higher than near the fenceline in Diamond. However, the two programs did differ in that those homeowners on the front two streets were offered the assessed value of their home plus 30 percent under the Voluntary Property Purchase Program, while those on the back two streets were offered the $80,000 minimum or their assessed value. Overall, the two programs were quite similar in total compensation offered, although homeowners with properties appraised at more than $73,000 did slightly better under the Voluntary Purchase Program, while those with homes assessed under that amount did better under the more recent Diamond Options program, Brignac said.

To sweeten the new Diamond Options relocation offer, residents of the back two streets of Diamond were also eligible for $15,000 to cover miscellaneous relocation expenses, $5,000 to cover moving expenses ($4,000 for renters), and $5,000–$10,000 to cover demolition of their house and clearing of the site. Owners of mobile homes on rented sites were offered a $7,500 relocation fee. Shell offered to buy vacant lots for $17,500.

Residents of the back two streets could also choose take advantage of Shell's incentives to stay in the community. For those who were not set on relocation, Shell offered a $25,000 home-improvement loan that was forgivable over five years. Eligible residents could even get this loan from Shell, fix up their home, and then sell it five years later, and they would not owe Shell a penny, Brignac noted, although he hoped that by then they would decide to stay.

The beauty of the Diamond Options Program, Brignac continued, was that it offered residents a real choice: "We wanted to design something that offered a choice so that people who wanted to stay could feel like there was something in it for them . . . that they could stay and improve the quality of their life; and there was something for people who wanted to leave." This required striking a balance by devising a program in which the financial incentives to leave were not overwhelming, Brignac added.

Though the agreement between Concerned Citizens of Norco and Shell worked to the advantage of most homeowners in Diamond, it left some renters in very difficult circumstances. Just weeks after the deal was announced, a number of Diamond residents I spoke with were worried about how it would affect their future. Two sisters, for example, who lived in trailers with their children on land owned by their mother-in-law, said the deal would leave them homeless. Their trailers had become so broken down that they would disintegrate if anyone tried to move them. And since they were not homeowners, they were eligible for very little relocation money. With their mother-in-law selling her home and land to Shell, they would both soon be without a home.

"The downside of this deal I can't change . . . and I hurt over it," said Margie Richard. It would have been better if all of Diamond's landlords had given their renters warning that they planned to sell their properties to Shell so that they would have had time to make arrangements, Richard continued. Furthermore, she noted, there were multiple generations living on some of the Diamond properties. Richard advised a number of Diamond families to share the proceeds from family property with their relatives, just as their ancestors had done when forced to move from Belltown to Diamond.

The relocation deal did not adequately take into account the complex web of informal relationships that had grown up over generations. Over the years, people who needed a place to stay were often permitted to park a trailer on a relative's land, or to move into a vacant home for very little money. When parents moved away, children or grandchildren were permitted to move into their houses for nominal rent. Thus, when the buyout took place and the owners of the land were paid off, people who had lived on the land (sometimes for decades) were suddenly out in the street.

"There is no perfect program that will meet everyone's needs," observed David Brignac. In most communities where buyouts occur, about 10 percent of the residences have complicated ownership and clouded title issues. In Diamond the percentage is reversed: about 90 percent of the homes have multi-generational ownership problems. Recognizing this, Shell has provided residents with more legal aid to work out some of these problems and has delayed moving forward on many of the sales.

Despite these complications, Brignac expected that the majority of Diamond residents would sell their properties and relocate, leaving only a small number of residents on the land. As of May 2003, about 99 percent of the residents on the back two streets of Diamond had chosen to participate in the program, Brignac reported. Of the owners of the 159 eligible properties, he added, 123 had said they want to be bought out so they could relocate; 30 were considering either moving or taking the forgivable, interest-free home-improvement loan; only six had indicated that they definitely wanted to stay. One could already see a transformation of the community in progress. Twenty-five homes had been demolished. Others were up on blocks, ready to be moved. Others were being taken apart carefully, one piece at a time, so that the materials could be used elsewhere. Shell's goal in this process was to ensure that "the people who leave feel they have been treated fairly and to build a relationship with those who decide to stay," said Brignac. After it becomes clear who is staying, Shell plans to meet with the remaining homeowners and talk about how to improve the quality of life in Diamond, Brignac said.

"Our premise," said Brignac, "is that Norco as a community can exist where it is between two large petrochemical plants and [it can] grow and thrive. . . . It is our belief that Norco can become a preferred place for a lot of people to live. We want to see Diamond become a place where people want to live instead of having it be a place where people live who can't get out." Diamond has a first-class educational system, he added, and green space along the perimeter with the Shell plants and in the Gaspard Line property will appeal to many home buyers. There is also a plan to build a high earthen berm that will block the residents' view of the plant. "People who own [homes] in this place will hardly know the plant is there."

The fate of Shell's facilities in Norco is intimately linked to the fate of the community, Brignac stated, clearly articulating the strategic thinking of the Shell's leadership. "We feel that for us [at Shell] to grow and prosper, the community of Norco has to grow and prosper," he continued. Shell is dependent on its permits to operate, which are a privilege and not a right, he noted. "So we know that if Norco is not happy our long-term future is at stake as a company."

To ensure the long-term well-being of the local community, Shell is taking a two-pronged approach: it will devote substantial resources to upgrading the equipment at its plants in order to reduce emissions, and it will provide generous support for community development activities. The first of these initiatives entails $200 million in capital improvements over seven years. The funds will be largely used to reduce emissions and flaring by modernizing the plants' instrumentation, Brignac said. This will give plant operators more control of the chemical processes, thus reducing "upsets" that lead to releases and flaring. There are a number of paybacks to the company that can be anticipated from this investment in upgrading the plants infrastructure, Brignac added. While none of the money is devoted to increasing production at the plant, reducing flaring will mean the waste of less product and increased energy efficiency will reduce operating costs, he noted.

To improve the quality of life in Norco, Shell will also give $5 million for the establishment of a community development district in Norco that will be run by local residents, independent of Shell. The goals of this new organization will be to improve the infrastructure of the town, to promote small business, to create programs for the elderly, and to open job training programs that will prepare local residents for jobs in petrochemical plants. Shell Oil also made a grant of $350,000 to the Norco Community Education Initiative.

Where Credit Is Due

Credit is due to Shell's managers for finally understanding that the only way they could satisfy the demands of the residents of Diamond was by offering them the option of selling Shell their homes and making enough money from the transactions to move elsewhere, observed Denny Larson, coordinator of the Refinery Reform Campaign. Shell would have much preferred to meet residents' demands by making technical improvements in its plants that would result in lower emissions and by offering to upgrade living conditions in the surrounding residential community, Larson continued. But this would not have satisfied local residents.

Shell should also be given credit for entering into negotiations with Concerned Citizens of Norco without the threat of a lawsuit, Larson added.

Most oil companies negotiate only if they are forced to either because of a lawsuit or because of their need to get a permit application approved. Shell negotiated without these threats hanging over the company. Instead, it was the combined pressure from local activists and their allies, in concert with bad press and the threat of international protest, that ultimately brought Shell to the bargaining table.

Having been party to some 25 different agreements signed between officials of large petrochemical plants and the residents of neighboring communities, Larson saw the settlement between Shell and the Diamond community as breaking new ground. "It is unique because it offers a choice to residents. In most relocation programs everybody is relocated or nobody is," he said.[3] Shell also broke with the standard way in which industries handle disputes with fenceline residents, and they probably caught hell for it from the rest of the industry, Larson surmised. They negotiated a deal in the spotlight of the media whereas most companies prefer not to have their negotiations be public. Finally, Larson concluded, they are to be applauded for having done the right thing in Diamond despite the fact that it set a precedent that might cause them problems with other fenceline communities.

"I give them credit," said, Beverly Wright, one of Shell's harshest critics. But the settlement they reached with the community did not come "out of the goodness of their hearts," she observed. "This is a business, so they were looking at their bottom line and public image." That having been said, Wright gives Shell credit for coming to the negotiating table and for the civility with which they conducted themselves during most of the negotiations. There were times when Shell officials were taking a lot of heat from community activists and their allies, she recalled. "All they could do was take the beating, smile, and come back. That is a very hard job," she added.

By the end of the negotiations, Wright continued, Shell had "a pretty decent team" of officials who respected the community leaders and were sensitive to their history. There was a definite evolution in the diplomatic skills of the Shell representatives who were fielded to negotiate with the Diamond residents. "This was a nicer group of human beings," said Wright. The earlier Shell officials stonewalled the community's request for relocation and even refused to come to Diamond to engage in a dialogue with residents, she recalled. This led to meetings that ended with people screaming at each other and walking out. But by the end the process the atmosphere improved, she added.

Others give Shell credit but put it in the context of the human costs that were incurred over the course of the conflict. "Who can be happy that these people [in Diamond] were poisoned for years?" asked Marylee Orr, director of the Louisiana Environmental Action Network. Nevertheless, she continued, "You have to give Shell credit where credit is due. They have done what some other people [in their industry] were not willing to do. They have listened when other people wouldn't . . . and it couldn't have been comfortable. But . . . they are not coming to this dance because they wanted to. They are coming because they have to. . . . It was an incredible victory that local people brought Shell to the table."

A number of other community activists qualified the credit they gave Shell for reaching final agreement with the residents of Diamond. "We have to give them credit now because they did it," said Anne Rolfes. "Change is possible, and you have to recognize that a good step has been taken. . . . So, sure, they deserve credit." But Rolfes does not forget what it took to wrest the right decision from Shell. It took tens of thousands of dollars and a lot of people outside the community coming in and telling Shell that they should listen to the local residents. "I am sitting here," Rolfes continued, "remembering all the awful things that happened with the police patrols in the neighborhoods . . . [police] officers at meetings . . . [Shell's initial] refusal to come into the [Diamond] neighborhood. Sure they deserve credit. They deserve credit because they listened [to residents]. [But] it is a shame. . . . It is a shame that we had to wait for ten to twelve years to give them credit. Now everybody is laughing and smiling; everybody is so friendly and they seem so pleased. . . . And I wonder: Why couldn't they have done this a long time ago? [Why didn't Shell officials recognize earlier that] it would make you happy to do the right thing by listening to the people who are directly affected by their operations? That is shocking to me. Why wouldn't you go and talk to your neighbors? Listen to what the people who live right next door to you are saying. . . . Don't steamroll over people and not listen to them. . . . I'm glad they did something about the situation.'

In view of the difficult political climate in which the relocation struggle in Norco took place, with the state government giving full backing to industrial development in the chemical corridor, credit should also be given to the willingness of residents of Diamond to "fight despite setbacks and the government not listening to them most of the time," said Adam Babich, director of the Tulane Environmental Law Clinic. Many of the residents were people of limited economic resources who had to worry about making a living, Babich pointed out. It would have been a lot easier for them to give up, he continued. What is most impressive is that instead of just trying to get themselves out of Diamond they worked to get the whole community out, he continued. Further, they took a risk holding out for relocation rather than settling for some kind of financial compensation.

Trying to sort out whether Shell officials decided in favor of relocation for altruistic reasons or in order to limit the damage to their reputation is impossible, Michael Lerner observed, because the public-relations function is intertwined in all such corporate decisions. There was a lot of opposition within Shell to settling the dispute with residents of Diamond, Lerner continued; however, looking at the breadth of the support for Concerned Citizens of Norco and the cost of continuing the struggle for years, Shell decided to resolve the dispute because the costs of not settling were outweighing the benefits of resisting the community's demands. Nevertheless, Lerner noted, "there are a lot of companies that would not have settled and Shell could have withstood this opposition for a long period of time. So, yes, they made a risk assessment but it was made in a [corporate] framework in which there were powerful leading forces (who are listened to within the company) who are seeking to move Shell toward sustainability and working effectively with communities where they are based."

Though Lerner gives credit to Shell for having made the right decision in Norco, this credit "should not excuse for a nanosecond Shell's many egregious faults in America and around the world," he said. Shell's pro-sustainability stance is a very powerful public-relations tool that Shell wields skillfully, he observed. But when a company advertises itself as being concerned about sustainability and about the well-being of residents in communities adjacent to its facilities it also gives local residents and environmental justice advocates leverage to hold the company accountable to its publicly stated commitments, he added. Lerner gives Shell credit for taking a strong rhetorical pro-sustainability and pro-community stance despite the fact that the company is far from living up to its publicly stated aspirations.

Asked if he sees Shell's agreement to offer to buy out Diamond homeowners as an important victory for environmental justice, Lerner said that he prefers to look at the agreement as a mutually arrived at win-win for both sides in the dispute. This was really a victory both for the residents and for Shell, he said. "I had to approach this by recognizing that there were really good people on both side of this struggle and that we were trying to solve a problem together," he continued. "There were good people in Shell who were trying to do their best under very trying circumstances . . . and I was deeply comforted that Margie Richard and others in Concerned Citizens of Norco kept referring to the fact that they were praying for the people in Shell. So the fact is that we succeeded collectively in solving this problem." It was a long, bumpy road, and it took a lot of skillful work on both sides of the issue and an impressive mobilization of human resources within Shell to get to a win-win outcome, Lerner concluded.

The relocation deal in Diamond must also be seen in the context of the work of Citizens for Health Environment and Justice under Lois Gibbs and the work of other nonprofit organizations that have effectively used relocations over a number of years to remove residential populations that were suffering intense exposures to industrial pollutants, Lerner observed. The settlement reached in Diamond "contributes to the evolution of the set of tools available to environmental health and justice advocates. . . . I think it will set a benchmark in the American South that will be remembered," he said.

Peter Warshall gives Sir Phillip Watts, former CEO of Shell, credit for having skillfully set the corporate stage so that a relocation deal was possible. In a company as large as Shell, he explained, often one department doesn't know that another is working at cross-purposes. Watts empowered a group of Shell managers who wanted to make the company more sensitive to community and sustainable development issues, to solve the problem in Norco. The fact that this managerial group within Shell pulled off the relocation deal in Norco gave them credibility within Shell and may have strengthened their hand to deal with similar problems in the future, Warshall speculated.

VI

Looking Ahead

16
Lessons Learned

Local Shell officials intimately involved with the Diamond negotiations were proud of the agreement they reached with residents and said they learned a lot from the sometimes tortuous process. Shell learned the importance of being engaged with the community, meeting with them in face-to-face discussions, and getting all the issues out on the table, David Brignac noted. "Keep in mind that it is incredibly difficult. It sounds easy but it is really not because I can tell you the last few months the conversations have been strained sometimes and emotional," Brignac said. Despite the discomfort, the willingness to talk with residents face to face proved critically important and eventually helped lead to resolution of many of the problems that had festered for years between residents and the neighboring industry, he continued. Having Shell officials attend meetings in Diamond was critical to arriving at an agreement. But the relocation deal would never have been possible had people on both sides of the fence not been willing to listen, Brignac observed. Once the issues had been aired it was then up to Shell to try to design programs that would serve both the company and the community, he said. Brignac is enthusiastic about the deal he helped broker.

Shell corporate officials are trying to draw some lessons from their experience in Norco that will help them avoid similar problems with adjacent communities at other facilities, said Brignac. They have commissioned a report on "lessons learned" in Diamond, which drew the following conclusions.

First, Shell officials should be aware that the history they have with a community near their facility will be an important factor in how local residents relate to them. It is not enough just to be sincere today because there may be a history of problems that cause local residents to be angry with Shell and distrust its officials.

Second, Shell officials should not assume that they know what local people are thinking. Instead they should actively engage the adjacent community in dialogue and carefully listen to local concerns. To this end, they should go into neighboring communities to speak with people on their own turf rather than simply invite them to the plant for discussions.

Shell officials should also think about how they can hire more local people. This is difficult. In 2002, when Shell advertised openings for 15 new operators at the facilities in Norco, 2,100 people applied, many of them more qualified than local residents. Nevertheless, Shell should devise ways to hire more people locally and should ensure that its subcontractors hire a certain percentage of local people.

Gary Cohen of the Environmental Health Fund drew quite different conclusions from the struggle in Norco: "I think the Diamond struggle will be seen as a watershed event where the toxics and environmental health movement learned that bringing international pressure to bear could yield an environmental justice win and help leverage a larger engagement with one of the largest corporations in the world." To win in Diamond required bringing in outside forces, Cohen explained. There just was not enough power in the grassroots group in Diamond or for that matter among toxics activists in Louisiana to force Shell to relocate the residents of Diamond so national and international activists had to be mobilized to catch Shell's attention, he added.

One of the lessons that residents of fenceline communities should take from the struggle in Norco is that relocation campaigns can work, said Marlee Orr of the Louisiana Environmental Action Network. "I think, in some instances, it has made other people think about relocation," she said. The successful outcome for Diamond residents in Norco provided further ammunition for groups demanding that large industries in the chemical corridor engage their adjacent communities in meaningful dialogue with a goal of reducing the negative impact of these plants on their neighbors, Orr suggested. It also "sends a message to industry to move people out of harms way who want to move."

But other observers were cautious about the implications of the Diamond relocation on other communities. Wilma Subra noted that some fenceline communities were moved in the mid 1980s, and that some observers thought this would catch on, but it did not. The Morrisonville community along the fenceline with Dow was moved en masse to another location and named New Morrisonville, Subra recalled. Another residential neighborhood near a Georgia Gulf facility was also moved, she said. One could argue that the Diamond relocation program might set a precedent locally and be used as a model for dealing with the problems experienced by the residents of New Sarpy, located on the fenceline with the Orion Refinery about half a mile from Diamond, but Orion does not have the deep pockets that Shell has and that may make relocation harder to win, Subra speculated.

Despite these words of caution, some environmental justice advocates look at the successful relocation campaign in Diamond as providing leverage for progress in other similarly afflicted communities. The environmental justice victory in Diamond is a great platform from which to talk about needed changes in policies and regulations that govern the relationship between big petrochemical plants and their residential neighbors, argued Denny Larson of the Refinery Reform Campaign. Shell officials were worried about the precedent that cutting a relocation deal with Diamond residents would set for other sites around the country, and they had reason to worry, continued Larson, who promises that he will use the Diamond precedent wherever applicable.

But ask Shell officials if the Diamond relocation deal set a precedent that will be hard to live up to at other sites and you will get a hedged answer. It could be precedent setting, but one has to keep in mind that the situation in Diamond was unique not only historically but also because Shell had had a negative impact of the community when it offered to move only half the residents, said Brignac. Circumstances might be different with other fenceline communities, and therefore remedies would differ, Brignac implied. This is the famous "Diamond is unique" arguments, Larson observed. "But . . . every one of these fenceline communities is unique." They are just not all unique in the same way, Larson added. You may not find another place where a bunch of sharecroppers had a chemical plant built on top of where they used to live and they were forced off the land onto a site that was sandwiched between a refinery and a chemical plant. But each fenceline community has its own unique history. What they have in common is that they are all disproportionately burdened with pollution from the adjacent plant and with the danger of being killed by a release or an explosion.

"Everybody learns from these situations," observed Adam Babich. "The companies get a better idea about what may be an appropriate settlement [with a fenceline community]. . . . And companies learn that people aren't just going to go away if you ignore them." For their part, citizen groups "get a better idea about what they can achieve . . . and these agreements certainly look more doable once somebody has already done it."

Perhaps the most significant lesson to come out of the agreement was the fact that Concerned Citizens of Norco finally got a huge multinational corporation—Royal Dutch/Shell—to acknowledge that the residents of Diamond had a legitimate place at the negotiating table, Babich said. There is a chance that other companies will look at this and say "Well, Shell officials talked with their neighbors . . . maybe we should talk to ours." They can also look at the agreement and see that it was not hugely expensive for Shell. "One doesn't read about this agreement and think 'Wow, Shell really got its clock cleaned financially,'" Babich observed. (One estimate puts the cost to Shell of buying and razing 250 houses in Diamond/Norco at $30 million.[1]) This was a pretty efficient, coherent, and cost-effective solution to the problem of a residential community being too close to an industrial operation, he added.

Finally, the agreement between Diamond residents and Shell officials broke important ground in the way it dealt squarely with the problem of compensating homeowners in Diamond for their properties that had been devalued by their proximity to the Shell and Motiva facilities. Setting minimum values on properties regardless of their assessed values permitted Diamond residents to be compensated at a level that permitted them to move elsewhere, Babich noted. This was an important step forward, he added.

"Isn't there a more efficient solution than to fight these things out one at a time?" Babich asked. "I don't have a better idea. . . . I think the only way to deal with them is one at a time." There may come a time when a political solution becomes possible but none is on the horizon currently, Babich continued. "I'm impressed by the people in Norco who were in for the long haul. Instead of saying that this will take too long they just got to work . . . and frankly that is what I think we have to do across the country . . . just work on it. Who knows how long the process will take, but ten years from now we will wish we started ten years ago."

Buffer Zones

Common sense and the precautionary principle suggest that people should not live close to an industry that handles large volumes of highly toxic, flammable, and explosive products. In view of the huge loss of life at the Union

Carbide plant in Bhopal, India and the long history of industrial accidents and illness in communities adjacent to oil and chemical plants, it just doesn't make sense to have people living cheek by jowl with heavy industry. The inevitable leaks and explosions that occur at plants such as these make it only logical that there be a broad buffer zone of several miles around these plants. The buffer could be zoned for light industries that feed off the products generated by the big plants.

What is needed is new legislation that will protect residents of settlements adjacent to highly toxic and explosive industrial facilities. Europe is already involved in a review of this issue. European regulators are studying the creation of buffer zones where the extent of protection is based on how different areas are used. In zones where people live and where schools and hospitals are located, construction of heavy industry would be prohibited. Places where people worked would be in a secondary zone of only moderate exposure to industrial toxins. In areas where people were infrequently present, there would be a lower level of protection and more industry. Europeans are also factoring in "worst-case scenarios" for explosions or releases of toxic chemicals when considering where to site industrial facilities.

In the United States, however, there seems less of a sense of urgency about facing this problem. Some Diamond residents live just 12 feet from the fenceline with Shell. They are "grandfathered in" under regulations that today would prohibit their construction this close to heavy industry. This proximity seems patently unwise. The unwillingness of U.S. lawmakers and regulators to grapple with the question of what constitutes a safe buffer zone between residential neighborhoods and toxic industries is doubly unfortunate insofar as homes continue to be built close to industries, thus expanding the problem and creating future confrontations and the need for costly relocation schemes. In fact, we have two problems facing us. First, residential communities continue to be built too close to industry. Second, numerous existing residential communities (such as Diamond) are located too close to toxic plants.

The Environmental Protection Agency is still arguing over the science of how to determine what constitutes a safe zone, noted Beverly Wright of the Deep South Center for Environmental Justice. Some regulators are pushing for a three mile buffer zone for new construction, she said. But even if they agree on it the question still remains what will be done about communities that were built too close to industry built before the buffer zone was established.

Since it has been difficult to prove that pollution from large industries damages the health of residents in adjacent communities, some experts lobby for the creation of buffer zones based on the possibility of an explosion or a one-time release of a highly toxic gas. "We have been arguing for a long time for buffer zones that give people time to react," said the chemist Wilma Subra. Local emergency planning commissions typically used a 10-mile planning radius to prepare and prevent accidents, but when regulatory agencies and insurance companies began to look at "worst-case scenarios" the computer program they used recommended 25-mile buffer zones around large industrial complexes such as one at Norco. A buffer zone of that size, Subra noted, would extend from Norco to New Orleans.

There was some hope that insurance companies would push for larger buffer zones to protect themselves from excessive liabilities. But the heavy industries involved successfully argued that each facility should be judged case by case because they dealt with different chemicals and had different safety systems in place. This approach, which came to be called the "planning case" approach, maps "vulnerable zones" in relatively close proximity to industry. Holding up a "planning case" diagram of Norco, Subra showed that the entire community of Norco is covered by at least one "vulnerable zone" and that the community of Diamond is covered by several overlapping vulnerable zones. "So they are saying that people should not live here," Subra concluded.

The discussion about worst-case scenarios and vulnerable zones was cut short after commercial airliners were crashed into the Pentagon and the World Trade Center on September 11, 2001. Security officials contended that access to data about the vulnerability of petrochemical industries should be limited to those with a legitimate need to know. "They said that terrorists were going to use this information" and the lid was slammed shut, Wilma Subra noted. Reading rooms were established where the planning diagrams and maps were kept, and strict rules were applied that made it illegal to photocopy the data or to look at more than three files at a time. The publication by Greenpeace of a map that showed "worst-case" scenarios threatening New Orleans threw fuel on the fire, Subra noted. According to Subra, Shell's own maps indicating that everyone in Norco was in a vulnerable zone were no longer made available to the public.

These are early days for the push for safe buffer zones between residential areas and heavy industries. The political forces have yet to be mobilized to advance this issue on the regulatory and legislative agenda. And yet the stories of what the people of Diamond suffered for decades because there was no safe buffer zone between them and the Shell and Motiva plants suggest that this is a national debate that is urgently needed.

Systemic Remedies

Mounting a Diamond-style campaign in every fenceline community in the United States is not feasible; there simply are not sufficient human or financial resources to pull it off. So what is to be done? Clearly there should be more stringent regulations and better enforcement of regulations that protect fenceline residents from exposure to high levels of industrial pollutants. But as a practical matter, regulatory relief is unlikely to ride to the rescue any time soon.

Ideas for broader remedies abound. Those who have thought deeply about how to detoxify industrial processes have argued for limiting the amount of toxic materials stored in and around facilities near residential populations and for re-engineering the production processes so that they use the least toxic and least explosive alternative materials. This could reduce the need for impracticably large buffer zones.

Further, the tax system could be altered to tax the use of hazardous materials, thus providing a financial incentive for companies to use less toxic materials in their production processes. The substitution of more benign chemicals for toxic ones would not only make life on the fenceline with industry less dangerous; it would also benefit consumers.

Short of the establishment of a nationwide system of buffer zones, there are a number of practical steps that can be taken to begin to protect fenceline residents, observed Denny Larson. First, large industries should be required to establish and pay for a comprehensive program of air monitoring in neighborhoods adjacent to their plants. These industries are permitted to emit huge volumes of toxic chemicals, but they are not required to prove that the air in the adjacent community is safe to breathe. This should change, Larson contended. Second, Larson plans to looks at the quality of air in schools near refineries and petrochemical plants. In Houston there are about 140 schools within 2 miles of refineries, he noted. Public housing projects near refineries would also be worth checking.

Furthermore, when a home is purchased, the buyer should, by law, be told about the proximity of the house to a significant source of pollution as documented in the Toxic Release Inventory, Larson argued. Often buyers do not know what is happening in big industrial buildings, and they certainly do not associate them with silent poisons or dangers of explosion. Potential home buyers should be warned if they are buying into a highly polluted neighborhood, Larson contended.

Royal Dutch/Shell and other energy companies should also start applying the stringent regulations under which they operate in Holland to their operations in the United States and elsewhere around the world, Michael Lerner said. Demanding that Shell implement the best practices that it uses in Holland to its operations all over the world is a logical next step, he continued. However, in view of the huge expense involved in this kind of transformation, achieving this unified standard of corporate behavior is likely to be an uphill struggle, he added.

There are signs that the ways toxics are perceived and controlled in the United States are gradually changing, Lerner noted. For example, a number of communities are considering banning or limiting the use of long-lasting bio-accumulative toxins. There is also a maturing movement that is pushing for buffer-zone laws, for more effective and stringent emissions laws, and for the recycling of industrial wastes in a closed loop system. According to Lerner, these strategies, though unlike to succeed anytime soon, are leading toward a better resolution of the problems faced by fence-line communities.

Americans are becoming increasingly aware of the dangers of ignoring the spread of environmental contamination and the diseases it causes. "Polling data show that people are very concerned about the effects of toxics on their health," Lerner said. As science continues to move forward and make clear the relationship between environmental pollution and disease this public concern will grow ever more focused. Furthermore, as it becomes clear that the "body burden" that Americans carry around in their blood and tissue is rising, political pressure to do something about this worrisome development is likely to mount. One early sign of this is the fact that the breast milk of many American women is already substantially contaminated with chemicals that have the potential to cause developmental harm to their fetus and infant. The emerging science on the contamination of breast milk is likely to spur a campaign that aims at putting in place regulations that make it possible for women to breastfeed toxics free. "So I think we are moving in the right direction but the opposition and the obstacles are tremendous," Lerner observed.

To get environmental contamination under control will require "fundamentally restructuring society on a sustainable basis. That is the vision and it is every bit as compelling as the vision that moved us from monarchy to democracy, from slavery to equal rights, and from women as property to the women's movement of today," Lerner said.

"I do believe," Lerner continued, "that we get to choose what we do in this defining moment in time. And for me it is more interesting to live as a part of the resistance against the forces of death that are destroying life than it is to simply cynically accede to them and say that we can't change them. At a minimum I want to be able to tell my grandchildren, if I am fortunate enough to have them, that I was part of the resistance; and at a maximum I want to tell them that the resistance became a peaceful movement that created a sustainable world."

Community Environmental Monitoring

In the meantime, helping residents of fenceline communities gather data about the quality of their air may hasten some form of interim regulatory relief. The kind of "bucket" air sampling done in Diamond in 1998, which provided hard data about Shell's release of MEK into the community, might "significantly expand democratic participation in environmental regulation," wrote Dara O'Rourke and Gregg Macey of MIT's Department of Urban Studies and Planning in a paper titled "Community Environmental Policing: Assessing New Strategies of Public Participation in Environmental Regulations."[2] Many low-income residents in communities of color adjacent to large industrial plants have long suffered from a lack of access to accurate information about what levels of toxic pollutants are in the air they breathe, O'Rourke and Macey continued. Often, air monitoring in their community is inadequate. Regulatory actions are frequently "ritualistic" in nature and result in obfuscating problems, failure to fix endemic leaks, or inadequate fines.

Air sampling by citizens is a first step toward changing the dismal record of failure to protect the health of residents in fenceline communities. Armed with these buckets, residents of highly impacted areas can make a transition from just being able to report anecdotally that the air smells foul and that they feel sick to having hard data about what is in the air in their back yard. This changes their relationship not only with the industry next door but also with the regulatory agencies responsible for monitoring pollution from these plants and ensuring the healthy safety of the resident population.

Enabling citizens to take air samples along the perimeter of adjacent industries empowers them to transform themselves from impotent victims whose only role is to "shelter in place" when there is an incident to active agents of change. Further, citizen air sampling can call into question whether government agencies are doing a good enough job of monitoring the air and can spur them to take more samples in hot-spot communities and carry out more regulatory inspections and actions. If samples collected by citizen air monitors show significant levels of pollutants in a community, and if this information is made public in the media, the efforts of "bucket brigade" groups can also bring industry to the bargaining table with local residents. This can result in Good Neighbor Agreements, environmental improvements in the operation of plants, and the installation of an appropriate air-monitoring system.

It makes sense for the U.S. Environmental Protection Agency and for state and local regulatory agencies to support and expand the efforts of groups interested in participating in community environmental policing, O'Rourke and Macey contended. For one thing, residents are ideally located to perform first-response monitoring: they see, smell, hear, and are affected by releases sooner than anyone else. Having volunteers take low-cost samples also makes sense in view of the limited resources of many regulatory agencies. Further, regulatory agencies could increase the potential of these groups to do good monitoring by providing them with funds for equipment, training them in the use of the equipment, providing quality-assurance programs, and helping them cross-reference the findings of their sampling with data about releases from the plant and health impacts in their neighborhood.

Citizen environmental policing in residential communities adjacent to industrial plants supported by funding and training from regulatory agencies also has the potential to give communities greater confidence that regulatory agencies are helping to do everything they can to see that they are not exposed to illegal concentrations of chemical pollutants. Greater participation in the regulatory process will also assure residents of highly impacted communities of the accuracy of the data on the quality of the air they breathe. In these respects, "bucket brigade" air sampling points the way to a new era of community environmental policing, O'Rourke and Macey suggested.

In addition to improving air and water monitoring so that fenceline residents will know about their exposure to toxic chemicals, a better system should also be put in place to give heavily impacted communities access to people like Wilma Subra who can help them interpret the regulatory data and navigate the Kafkaesque regulatory process. It should not be left up to the Wilma Subras of the world to donate their time to help these people. Fortunately, there are some instances in which the government does provide this kind of support, such as the EPA grants that enable residents of communities adjacent to Superfund sites to hire their own technical advisers. For most communities, however, there is little support.

The one program that does exist, the EPA's Toxic Substance Research Center, is deeply flawed, Subra contended, because it works through universities that receive large grants from the industries the center is designed to go up against. As a result, the technical consultants hired under this center cannot be advocates for the affected communities, Subra continued. For example, when the Native American community in Grand Bois needed help protesting landfarming of oil wastes, Louisiana State University's *Chevron* Professor of Engineering was dispatched to help them. In view of the clear conflict of interest, this assignment obviously does not inspire confidence, Subra noted. Clearly, changes should be made in the program so that residents can hire experts who are not beholden to an industry that is polluting their neighborhood.

17
Unfinished Business

Gary Cohen of the Environmental Health Fund saw the victory in Norco as a precedent-setting settlement that should be applied to other fenceline communities facing similar problems elsewhere around the world.

The outcome of the relocation struggle in Norco demonstrated that bringing national and international pressure to bear on a large corporation could force it to the negotiating table. But Cohen was determined to take the next step by creating a global coalition so that groups in many different nations can coordinate their protests against companies such as Royal Dutch/Shell and Dow Chemical. Only by broadening the coalition could the environmental health movement become powerful enough to force companies like Shell to change their behavior, he argued.

The big petrochemical corporations will make the transition away from their highly toxic products into more benign alternatives only if they engage in meaningful discussions and negotiations with groups that are focused on ensuring that their operations do not pose a significant threat to public health, Cohen contended. To do this, however, required convincing them that environmental health activists were "serious players" who could not be ignored, he added.

An international campaign was needed to require Shell officials to address some awkward questions, said Cohen. For example, Shell should explain why it did not operate its plants in South Africa and in Louisiana plants as cleanly as its European plants, Cohen said. Furthermore, Cohen asked, if Shell's plants were not causing ill health in neighboring communities, why didn't Shell prove it by erecting appropriately targeted and calibrated air monitors in those communities? And if Shell continued to pump out thousands of pounds of benzene and other hydrocarbons in inhabited areas, why didn't Shell provide health services for those residents who were affected?

Shell claimed to be a socially responsible company while it was "the biggest producer of benzene in the world and its plants [were] raining toxic chemicals down on people," Cohen continued. How could Shell claim to be a "sustainable company" when it was still producing chemicals linked to cancer, birth defects, and other health impacts? Eventually people were going to catch on to the damage Shell was doing to human health, Cohen predicted. When cancer rates increased so that one in every two people were affected (instead of the current incidence of one in three), people were going to look at the chemical industry as the culprit, he continued. What was the industry's contingency plan for dealing with the public outrage that was likely to ensue?

Needless to say, in view of Shell's huge investment in petrochemical production, this was not a conversation in which Shell executives wished to participate. Cohen wanted to engage Shell in a real debate so that company officials could hear the argument that many of its product lines were "fundamentally at odds with life on the planet" and that Shell should begin a transition out of these product lines and into alternative energy and green chemistry.

Furthermore, Shell would soon be facing some real liability issues, Cohen predicted. He argued that Shell should be telling stockholders about its reservoirs of toxic chemicals and about "massive liability issues" related to them. In the process of facing these questions, Shell would be forced to look at the full costs of its commitment to oil extraction and petrochemical production.

Cohen also looked at the chemical industry's production processes from a very personal perspective: "Look, their chemicals are in our bodies. As a father I am deeply outraged that they are chemically trespassing into my daughter's body and I bet there are millions of other people who will also be deeply outraged by this. . . . It is an uncontrolled chemical experiment against our informed consent." The only defense the chemical industry had against this charge was to try to "normalize" the presence of their toxic chemicals in our bodies by convincing us that this is normal. But Cohen did not hold out great hope that this strategy would prove convincing to the American public.

In the long term, Cohen looked forward to an improved regulatory regime that would phase out entire classes of dangerous chemicals and would shift the burden of proof of safety onto industry. He also foresaw the possibility of changes in the liability coverage that would provide financial incentives that would encourage companies to produce fewer toxic chemicals and to clean up reservoirs of existing toxins. There was a real need for a deep transformation of the chemical industry, Cohen asserted. While there was some movement in that direction, the heavy investment by the chemical and petrochemical industries in equipment that turned out large volumes of toxic chemicals prevented any rapid change, he added.

Should Shell be given credit for what it did in Norco? "They sat across the table from their African-American neighbors and negotiated a fair settlement," Cohen said. "They deserve a lot of credit. Most companies in the petrochemical industry wouldn't have done that. . . . We want to say to them 'We did great in Norco. Let's do it again where you have similar problems in Africa.' So, yes, there is an olive branch. I think there are ways in which Shell can resolve environmental health disputes in a number of places."

Ongoing Health Complaints

The concept of "chemical trespass" that Gary Cohen and other toxics activists propounded resonated strongly with residents of Diamond, many whom saw themselves as the victims of corporate poisoning. In conversation, many of them claimed that they had been exposed to toxic chemicals released by neighboring Shell facilities, and they thought it only fair that restitution should be made for the harm they said had been done to them.

These health claims, however, were deliberately set aside because Shell would not negotiate about relocation unless the buyout of Diamond residents was decoupled from the question of whether its facilities impaired the health of Diamond residents. This delinking of two intimately connected issues was strategically effective because it permitted a win-win scenario in which Shell was willing to reach an agreement with Diamond residents on relocation. But the strategy also required that one ignore the obvious.

"The leadership of Concerned Citizens of Norco has always focused on relocating Diamond for the obvious reason that they are affected by pollution," said former EarthJustice attorney Monique Harden. "They all have various kinds of health problems. You go in their houses and you see oxygen tanks and prescription medicines to deal with the various symptoms their families are suffering."

"Shell is holding to this notion that the relocation is not because of environmental racism or environmental health issues," agreed Beverly Wright. Shell hides behind the fig leaf that the relocation is being done because Diamond is a "unique community" with a unique history, she continued. "I say they can call it whatever they like but that there is another unique community down the street. So if they need to use 'unique community' [argument] to get out from under this situation then we will let them but it is a face saving device."

"This was a great victory," Wright continued. Everyone was saying that Shell would not bend on relocation because Diamond residents could not prove that a specific chemical that escaped from the Shell plants had caused a specific disease in a specific person. Petrochemical companies know how hard it is to prove that they are making people sick or killing people and so they can stonewall the demands of fenceline residents, she contended.

Though Shell has chosen to deny that there was a health problem caused by their facilities in Diamond and Norco, the problem is unlikely to go away. Just because Shell finally offered to relocate residents of Diamond does not mean that Shell is no longer liable for the damage that many residents alleged the company did to their health over years of exposure to their pollution.

A report published by a coalition of environmental groups, including Friends of the Earth and the Refinery Reform Campaign, drew these conclusions: "Members of the Diamond community are convinced that the spate of health problems they are suffering is caused by chemicals from the [Shell] plant. They know the generation of people who lived on the land before the plant was built did not experience the health problems of today. Shell is to be credited for engaging directly in talks with its fenceline neighbors that suffer from the impacts of its facilities. The next responsible step is to work with past and present Diamond residents who want Shell to address the health problems they have suffered. They want an accurate and comprehensive health diagnosis and treatment of the problems linked to Shell's industrial pollution."[1]

"Like a lot of people in Norco, I am sick. Who is going to pay for my ongoing health needs?" asked Iris Carter, who attributed her chronic bronchitis and sinus problems to pollutants from Shell. Carter is convinced that the deaths of her mother and her 47-year-old sister were also related to pollution. Similarly, Margie Richard attributes the death of her sister at 43 to the fact that she breathed polluted air in Diamond all her life. "We worked for a fair and just relocation because of our health problems and the impact of industrial pollution. . . . Shell needs to take care of all the health problems that their chemicals caused," said Richard.[2] How Shell handles these claims remains to be seen, but in the past company officials have resolutely fought any suggestion that their facilities are damaging to the health of their neighbors.

There is also the question of what will happen to the people who continue to live near Shell's Norco facilities after the relocation program—those on the white side of Norco, those who choose to remain in Diamond, and those who are just now building new homes in Norco. Will these people eventually demand relocation? One indication that they might do so came after the relocation agreement with the residents of Diamond had been reached. According to *Times-Picayune* reporter Mary Swerczek, a 2002 accident at a hydro-cracking unit in the Motiva refinery "caused it to spray heavy oil onto numerous cars and houses in Norco."[3] At a community meeting called after the accident, Motiva officials assured residents that the release was not harmful to their health, and residents were given a telephone number to call to submit claims for damage to their property. One Diamond resident who attended the meeting observed that a number of white Norco residents were visibly and vociferously upset about the release and angry about the black gunk that had descended on their neighborhood. "You should have relocated all of us," one Norco resident is said to have shouted.

Shell did an excellent job on the white side of Norco of selling the idea that Norco is a safe place to live and work, said Beverly Wright. However, as a result of this false advertising campaign, she noted, people are building new homes in Norco. This makes some Shell officials nervous that the new residents may eventually complain about pollution from the plant and want to be relocated at Shell's expense, Wright said she was told off the record. "I told them that they had done a really good job of lying about how safe their plants are . . . and that if they stopped lying maybe people would stop coming," said Wright.

Many of the white residents of Norco "bought the brainwash" and were in denial about the impact of pollutants from the plant on their health, Wright continued. They thought that because they understood what the different noises and smells were that come from the plant that they were safe, she continued. Wright says she had some serious conversations with white residents in Norco about this issue during which residents asked her to explain why there were so many elderly people living in Norco if conditions were unsafe. She responded by asking if they were counting all the people who were sick or had died. Just because some people escaped illness means nothing; maybe they had good genes that made them less vulnerable to the effects of the pollution. But not everyone is so lucky, Wright noted. At one time people thought that smoking was safe, but now they know better, she continued. In a few years people may come to understand that living close to these plants was not good for their health. "By then I just hope that you are not dying of cancer," she told one resident. "Well, I have survived this far," he responded. "It is not over yet," Wright replied.

Conclusion

"What a difference it is to get up in the morning and to hear the birds sing instead of the roaring of the Shell plant next door," said Margie Richard as she sat in her comfortable home removed from the sounds and smells of the refinery and chemical plant. Against the odds, Richard and Concerned Citizens of Norco won a victory that will be remembered in the annals of the environmental justice movement. "If we would not have spoken up it would have been the same old status quo," she observed. Instead the main goal of Concerned Citizens of Norco has been realized: Diamond homeowners who wanted to sell their homes and leave are now able to do so. "Now those who wanted to move are happy. I can see it in their faces. They are decorating their new houses," said Richard.

Was Diamond a big win? "Very much so," replied community consultant and chemist Wilma Subra. "It was for the betterment of the community not to live on that fenceline." It would have been very hard to raise enough money privately to be able to relocate the Diamond residents who wanted to move. "I think it is a very big win," Subra concluded.

On July 5, 2002, there was a victory celebration for those involved in the Diamond struggle for relocation. Representative Maxine Waters spoke. "You get kind of jaded in Washington," she told the assembled residents of Diamond and their nonprofit allies, "and you begin to believe that you can't win sometimes, that sometimes the corporations are so powerful or the money is just so much, or that it is hard to win for the people. But I want you to know that you inspire me. I came here and I stood in the playground [right near the chemical plant last summer] and I listened to what was going on, and I stood in the shadow of the plant. This is a small victory. This is a little light shining through the tunnel that says it is possible to win if you are committed to the struggle, if you are committed to the fight, if you have no fear, if you won't let them stop you at the front gate, if you keep on going you can win."

Despite Waters's rousing rhetoric and despite a clear sense among Diamond residents that they won a long and hard-fought struggle with Shell, the celebration was muted because many residents see themselves as caught in a double bind: they need to move out to protect their health, but they know that they will never again enjoy the kind of close community they leave behind in Diamond. Anne Rolfes, who worked closely with local activists since 1999, felt this keenly. The victory in Diamond is a bittersweet, she says. "It is a sad day because this beautiful, historic community will soon be a bunch of vacant lots."[1]

One can still hear a plaintive note coming from Diamond residents who wish the problem posed by exposure to Shell's emissions could have been solved without requiring them to move. But in practical terms, residents recognized that demanding that the Shell facilities be relocated rather than the people who lived next to the plants was not feasible economically or politically. They might be able to convince Shell to buy them out, but they could never marshal the backing to get Shell to decamp.

However, a third possibility—moving the *whole* community to another location all at once—was lost in the protracted struggle for relocation. Other communities have been moved wholesale away from plants, and it has worked reasonably well. But this was one step too far for a community with few resources. Residents of Diamond came to believe that it was going to be hard enough to get an agreement on a buyout plan, much less to convince everyone to agree on a plan to move the whole subdivision. That could add years to the process while people were suffering today.

The failure to seriously consider moving the whole subdivision was a significant loss because the close relations among the residents of Diamond were not only of sentimental value, they were also important at a very practical level. The ability of working parents to leave their children in the care of neighbors while they went to work meant they did not have to pay for after-school child care. And the ability of family and friends to pick up groceries for elderly relatives or take them to the doctor made it possible for the elderly to live in a non-institutionalized setting. Now that this intricate web of community relationships has been broken, many Diamond residents find themselves bereft not just of their family and friends but also of the practical support that the neighborhood network provided. While many are thrilled that they will be able to move away from the fumes from the Shell plants, they will nevertheless mourn the destruction of Diamond. With this in mind, Margie Richard is already organizing a fellowship picnic so that former residents of Diamond can come back to their community and share memories of living there. She also wants to build a Diamond museum. She is asking current and former residents to gather their old photographs of what life was like in Belltown and Diamond. "We can still visit Diamond," noted Richard, who goes there frequently. "Most of us have cars and live only about 15 minutes away," she continued. Richard recently went to look at a hundred-year-old oak tree that she is fond of and to pick oranges from a tree her father planted. She also takes students through Diamond and explains to them its history now that Diamond, like a number of other communities overtaken by industrial development, is ceasing to exist.

Homecoming Service

A bulldozer piled up scrap near the smoldering remains of a house that had been demolished on Cathy Street, a few blocks from the Greater Good Hope Baptist Church in Diamond. Here was visible evidence that yet another neighbor had fled to safety. As the bulldozer tore at the wet sod, mourners arrived at the church for a funeral. They picked their way carefully along the street trying not to get their shoes muddy.

It was early February 2002, and the mourners were paying their respects to Margie Eugene Richard's mother, Mabel Smith Eugene, a woman known by everyone in town. Born in Belltown, she had been evicted and displaced to Diamond when Shell decided to build its chemical plant on the land where her father had an extensive farm. After moving from Belltown to Diamond, Eugene worked for years as a cook in a local restaurant that had two entrances: a door for "whites only" and a window for "coloreds only."

Years of living on the fenceline made Eugene so chemically sensitive that she was a virtual shut-in in her house because going outside would trigger an asthma attack, Richard explained. She died only a few months after moving out of Diamond to a house with a beautiful rose garden. Unable to garden in Diamond because of the pollution from the Shell plants, Eugene had a few months to tend her roses in the backyard of her new home. Now she lay in an open coffin inside the Greater Good Hope Baptist Church.

Within months, nearly every home in Diamond was bulldozed, burned, or disassembled as residents took Shell up on its relocation offer and moved to safety. The residents had won their struggle, but their beloved community was transformed into another fenceline ghost town. It was a victory for the residents to have won the relocation offer from Shell, but it was a bittersweet victory that meant the end of their community and the severing of their ties with the land, their neighbors, and their churches.

The Goldman Award

On April 19, 2004, Margie Richard was awarded the Goldman Environmental Prize for the 13 years of work she did in Diamond organizing a grassroots relocation campaign. The $125,000 award is given every year to six "ordinary" people from around the world who make an "extraordinary difference" protecting the environment. The award is widely seen as the Nobel Prize for grassroots environmental activists. First presented in 1990, the award, which is given to environmental heroes from six continental regions, has been bestowed on 101 recipients. Richard is the first African-American woman to receive it.

The day of the award ceremony, Richard found herself far from the trailer on the fenceline with the Shell Chemical Plant. Rather than enduring the toxic fumes that waft into the Diamond community, Richard sat in the front row of the Herbst Theatre at the San Francisco War Memorial Opera House and watched a video of her early days carrying protest signs on the fenceline in Diamond, heard a speech by Jane Goodall about protecting the earth for all species, and listened to Kenny Loggins and the Oakland Youth Chorus. Finally, it was time for Richard to climb up onto the stage, give a short speech about her work in Norco, sing one of her favorite spirituals, and receive a bronze "ouroboros"—a sculpture of a snake with its tail in its mouth—which is a symbol of nature's powers of renewal.

Richard was in good company. Other 2004 Goldman prize recipients included two women from Bhopal, India—Rashida Bee and Champa Devi Shukla—who mounted protests in the wake of the Union Carbide gas disaster that killed thousands of residents; Libia Grueso from Colombia, who secured 5.9 million acres of territorial rights from Afro-Colombian villagers; Rudolf Amenga-Etego from Ghana, who fought the privatization of water and championed access to water as a human right; Manana

Kochladze from Georgia, who struggled to mitigate the damage done to the ecologically fragile valleys endangered by the world's biggest oil export pipeline; and Demetrio Do Amaral de Caravalho, who promoted sustainable development of war-torn East Timor. Richard's relocation campaign in Diamond/Norco was acclaimed as "a landmark environmental justice victory" and "an inspiring example for activists nationwide battling environmental racism in their own backyards."

About her award, Richard said "This is a great victory for every community living along the fenceline of toxic industrial facilities seeking respect and justice." Richard went on to credit prayer for helping her achieve her goals: "I consider myself an environmental evangelist. All my stances on environmental protection and preservation are based on the principle that the Earth is the Lord's." In addition to prayer, Richard said she also sought help from science by contacting experts who could interpret air quality reports and provide facts that could help her win her community's struggle with its industrial neighbor.

Margie Richard's campaign in Diamond "really was a David and Goliath story," said Lorrae Rominger, director of the Goldman Environmental Prize. "Through her persistence and her leadership, she has shown us that environmental victories against great odds can be achieved. . . . She just never gave up. She spent 13 years of her life and she won. It's certainly about the victory but it's also about the struggle."[2]

Rather than resting on her laurels, Richard said she would continue to carry the struggle for environmental justice beyond her home town. To this end, she has become a consultant to other African-American communities, such as the neighborhood of Westside in Port Arthur, Texas, where residents lived next to the giant Premcor refinery. She also planned to press Royal Dutch/Shell officials to "take responsibility for its dirty industrial practices and the medical costs associated with treating environmental illness" at the company's annual meeting in London two weeks after receiving her award.

Richard's environmental prize was no doubt somewhat awkward for Shell officials. The woman who fought them for over a decade and lobbied successfully for Shell to pay for relocating 300 families in her community was suddenly making national headlines. A statement issued by Shell headquarters in Houston tactfully said "Margie [Richard] has served as a leading advocate on environmental and sustainable development issues in

Louisiana and we are pleased she has been recognized for her tireless work in the Norco community." Upon hearing Shell's statement, Richard responded that she had never been the enemy of industry: "I know that industry can operate cleaner, smarter and cheaper."

For the tenacity with which she fought for relocation in Diamond and for her ongoing outreach to other fenceline communities, Margie Richard may well be the Rosa Parks of the environmental justice movement. Picked as the "person of the week" by ABC News, interviewed on National Public Radio, and written up in the *Wall Street Journal* and other newspapers, Richard has come to personify the environmental justice movement. The face of this schoolteacher from Louisiana reminds us of the devastating health problems that result from unwise land use decisions that place people too close to heavy industry.

Notes

Introduction

1. All ages are as of 2004.

2. Robert Bullard, *Dumping in Dixie: Race, Class, and Environmental Quality* (Westview, 1990), p. 36. See also Phaedra Pezzullo, "The Beginnings of a Movement: A Story of Hope," *EJ Times: The Environmental Justice Newsletter of the Sierra Club* 1 (1999), no. 1, p. 4.

3. There is some new evidence that traditional civil rights groups are beginning to appreciate the potential of the environmental justice movement. Environmental justice conflicts are fast becoming an important new battleground in the struggle for civil rights in the U.S., concludes a recent report by the U.S. Commission on Civil Rights titled Not in My Backyard: Executive Order 12,898 and Title VI as Tools for Achieving Environmental Justice. The report, issued on September 11, 2003, found that U.S. agencies failed to fully implement the 1994 regulation requiring that all federal agencies incorporate environmental justice into their programs.

Chapter 1

1. The Shell Oil refinery was reorganized as Motiva Enterprises, a joint venture of Shell, Texaco, and Saudi Aramco.

2. In Louisiana, 'parish' is the word for what is called a county in most parts of the United States.

Chapter 2

1. The Ormand Plantation is still standing. Tourists can visit it.

2. Mary Anne Sternberg, *Along River Road: Past and Present on Louisiana's Historic Byway* (Louisiana University Press, 1996; revised 2001), pp. 123, 130.

3. Albert Thrasher, *On to New Orleans! Louisiana's Heroic 1811 Slave Revolt* (Cypress, 1996), p. 50.

4. Ibid., pp. 54–55.

5. Harnett Kane, *Plantation Parade* (William Morrow, 1945), p. 129, cited in Thrasher, *On to New Orleans*. See also Sternberg, *Along River Road*, p. 130.

6. This information is drawn from an exhibit tucked away on the top floor of the Louisiana State Museum in New Orleans.

7. Thrasher, *On to New Orleans*, pp. 62, 65.

8. Interview with Margie Eugene Richard, February 6, 2002.

9. Jack Doyle, *Riding the Dragon: Royal Dutch/Shell and the Fossil Fire* (Environmental Health Fund, 2002), p. 187.

10. Louisiana Bucket Brigade and Communities for a Better Environment, Shell Games: Divide and Conquer in Norco's Diamond Community (undated), p. 8.

11. Doyle, *Riding the Dragon*, p. 187.

12. Norco Chemical and Motiva Enterprises, Community Progress Report, 1999, p. 1.

Chapter 3

1. Emily Bazelon, "Bad Neighbors," *Legal Affairs*, May-June 2003, p. 54.

2. Shell Games. See also "Bad Neighbors," p. 54.

3. Doyle, *Riding the Dragon*, pp. 69–72.

4. Ibid., p. 197.

5. Mary Swerczek, "Mending Fences," *Times-Picayune* (New Orleans), September 17, 2000.

6. Wilma Subra, *Norco, Louisiana: Environmental Issues* (Subra & Company, 2001), p. 12.

Chapter 4

1. Bazelon, "Bad Neighbors," p. 53.

2. Patricia Meeks and Peter Orris, "Petrochemical Production and Community Health: New Sarpy, Louisiana, USA" (white paper distributed at lecture, November 18, 2002), p. 1.

3. Ibid.

4. William P. Simmons, Community Health Survey: Norco/Old Diamond Plantation. Statistical Analysis Report, Deep South Center for Environmental Justice, Xavier University, 1997.

5. Kim Kennedy, "Balancing oil and the environment," Cable News Network, September 30, 2000.

6. Louisiana Bucket Brigade, "Shell's Great Divide: Lofty Principles v. Low-Down Land Deals" (undated), p. 4.

7. Concerned Citizens of Norco et al., Shell-Norco: Toxic Neighbor: The Case for Relocation, second edition, 1999, p. 2.

8. Wilma Subra, Norco, Louisiana: Environmental Issues (Subra Company, New Iberia, Lousiana, 2001), pp. 9–10.

9. Ibid., p. 5.

10. Shell Oil Company, "Norco: A Success Story," at www.fenceline.com.

11. Subra, Norco, Louisiana, p. 12.

12. Ibid., p. 13.

13. Shell Oil Company, "Norco: A Success Story."

14. "Frequent, Routine Flaring May Cause Excessive, Uncontrolled Sulfur Dioxide Releases," Enforcement Alert 3, no. 9 (2000) (U.S. Environmental Protection Agency, Office of Enforcement and Compliance Assistance, EPA 300-N-00-014), p. 2.

15. Ibid., p. 1.

16. Cynthia M. Mendy, "Reflections of Life in Cancer Alley," Old Diamond News, December 1998, p. 4.

17. As large as this figure of over a million pounds of sulfur dioxide released sounds, it may be grossly underestimated according to a new study of the amount of pollutants that result from flaring and other practices at refineries. A study of flaring in the San Francisco Bay Area found that refineries that were thought to emit 200 pounds of emissions daily were actually emitting 22 tons a day. The local air district found refineries where flares were "routinely used as a gas disposal system." See Mike Taugher, "Flares Spew Pollutants by the Ton," Contra Costa Times, January 6, 2003. Officials at Shell Oil and Valero said that "the reports released to the public overstate the negative effects of emergency flaring on the local environment by almost three times the accurate amount." But Jim Karas of the Bay Area Air Quality Management District, where the study was conducted, stands by his figures. Bay Area refiners were making a case to him that the study was conducted at a time when their emissions were unusually high and that emissions were significantly lower before and after the study but Karas remains unconvinced by their explanation that it was just bad luck as to when the study was conducted. However, he did credit the refineries with making changes since the study that may have reduced emissions somewhat.

18. John Biers, "Fiery Flares Point to Questions About Safety," Times-Picayune, August 13, 2000.

19. Shell Oil Company, "Norco: A Success Story."

20. Dara O'Rourke and Gregg Macey, "Community Environmental Policing: Assessing New Strategies of Public Participation in Environmental Regulation," Journal of Policy Analysis and Management 22 (2003), no. 3, p. 18.

21. Jennifer Lee, "Vowing to Enforce the Clean Air Act, While Also Trying to Change It," New York Times, April 22, 2003.

22. Eric Pianin, "Crackdown Urged on Coal Pollution: Panel Criticizes Administration on Clean Air Rules," Washington Post, April 22, 2003.

23. The only bad news in the study was that there were more brain cancers than expected, but the numbers were so small that it was hard to say whether they were statistically significant, Brignac said.

Chapter 5

1. William Booth, "Study: Pollution May Cause Asthma: Illness Affects 9 Million Children," *Washington Post*, February 1, 2002.

2. Sarcoidosis, a disease of unknown etiology, manifests itself as lesions that are morphologically indistinguishable from those caused by germs, foreign bodies, and chemical insults. In the U.S., a preponderance of the cases occur among rural African-Americans with slightly more women than men affected. If diagnosed early it is usually not fatal. In its later stages it attacks the lymph nodes, lungs, kidneys, and joints. The prognosis is worse for African-Americans than for others.

Chapter 6

1. There is a substantial medical literature to back up Johnson's contention that living next to a chemical plant and refinery could have made her hyper-reactive to chemical exposures. Yale professor and Alcoa consultant Mark Cullen describes this illness as multiple chemical sensitivity (MCS), which some people contract when exposed to the cocktail of chemical emissions from adjacent plants. When cases of MCS appeared near Alcoa's Wagerup refinery in western Australia, "the onus was the company to manage the MCS-related cases which had occurred 'at the plant and on our watch,'" he said. See Nadia Miraudo, "Alcoa Expert Links Illness to Refinery," *Sunday Times*, Western Australia, February 24, 2002.

2. Mark Schleifstein, "New Orleans: A City on the Environmental Edge," Society of Environmental Journalists, September 10, 2003.

3. Bullard, *Dumping in Dixie*, pp. 30–32.

4. Beverly Wright, Voluntary Buy-Outs as an Alternative Damage Claims Arrangement: A Comparative Analysis of Three Impacted Communities (submitted to Institute for Environmental Issues and Policy Assessments in 1994), pp. 6–9.

5. Rick Bragg, "Toxic Water Numbers Days in Trailer Park," *New York Times*, May 5, 2003.

6. Terry Harris, "Baltimore Neighborhood Relocated," *EJ Times: The Sierra Club Environmental Justice Newsletter* 1 (1999), no. 1, p. 7.

Chapter 7

1. See Daniel Yergin, *The Prize: The Epic Quest for Oil, Money, and Power* (Touchstone/Simon & Schuster, 1991).

2. Ibid., p. 128.

3. Doyle, *Riding the Dragon*, p. 24.

4. Ibid., pp. 23–24. See also Nikki Thanos, "Shell Oil and the Norco Community," in D. Dole, A. Fifield, and E. Niemi, *Getting Smarter* (ECONorthwest, 1998).

5. Lisa Rimmer, *Failing the Challenge: The Other Shell Report 2002*, Friends of the Earth et al., www.foei.org. See also Neela Banerjee, "Wall Street Sees Possibility of a New Suitor for Conoco," *New York Times*, November 20, 2001.

6. Bazelon, "Bad Neighbors," p. 53.

7. Doyle, *Riding the Dragon*, p. 51.

8. D. Derezinski, M. Lacy, and P. Stretesky, "Chemical Accidents in the United States, 1990–1996," *Social Science Quarterly* 84, no. 1 (2003): 122–143.

9. Peter Schwartz and Blair Gibb, *When Companies Do Bad Things: Responsibility and Risk in the Age of Globalization* (Wiley, 1999), pp. 26–27.

10. Doyle (*Riding the Dragon*, p. 164) cites U.S. Department of Energy, Energy Information Agency, Nigeria Country Profile, 2000.

11. Doyle, *Riding the Dragon*, p. 174.

12. Andrew Rowell, *Shell Shocked: The Environmental and Social Costs of Living with Shell in Nigeria* (Greenpeace International, 1994), p. 9, cited in Ike Okonta and Oronto Douglas, *Where Vultures Feast: Shell, Human Rights, and Oil in the Niger Delta* (Sierra Club, 2001), p. 45.

13. Doyle, *Riding the Dragon*, p. 165.

14. Statement from Bopp van Dessel on Granada Television documentary "Shell Nigeria," World in Action, May 13, 1996, cited in Steve Kretzmann and Anne Rolfes, *Shell Shocked: Federal Republic of Nigeria* (Project Underground, Berkeley, California, undated), p. 4.

15. Kretzmann and Rolfes, *Shell Shocked*, pp. 4, 5.

16. Shell Media Center, "Case Study: Nigeria," www.shellfacts.com, November 14, 2002.

17. Okonta and Douglas, *Where Vultures Feast:*, pp. 126–127.

18. Kretzmann and Rolfes, *Shell Shocked*, p. 30.

19. Okonta and Douglas, *Where Vultures Feast*, p. 157.

20. Schwartz and Gibb, *When Companies Do Bad Things*, p. 28.

21. Doyle, *Riding the Dragon*, p. ix.

22. Such regulation was proposed in the course of international negotiations on climate change held in Kyoto.

23. Denny Larson, correspondence, November 14, 2002. Larson cites Jack Doyle as his source.

Chapter 8

1. Anne Rolfes, "Shell Games in the Diamond Community—Norco, Louisiana," *Everyone's Back Yard* 19, no. 3 (2001), p. 5.

2. Bazelon, "Bad Neighbors," p. 57.

3. The on-site recreational facilities and employee housing were bulldozed in 1962–63 after a bitter union fight in which employees joined the Oil Chemical and Atomic Workers Union, Webb said.

4. Doyle, *Riding the Dragon*, p. 186.

Chapter 9

1. The EPA sets the maximum achievable control technologies rules by taking as its standard "the average emissions from the cleanest 12 percent of companies in each industry," wrote *Los Angeles Times* reporter Gary Polakovic. The Bush administration was proposing to relax these regulations, he added. See "EPA Plans to Relax Toxic Emission Standards," *Los Angeles Times*, February 11, 2003.

2. John Biers, "Blown Off," *Times-Picayune*, August 13, 2000.

3. O'Rourke and Macey, "Community Environmental Policing," p. 12. The authors cite EPA data from 2001.

Chapter 10

1. The plan to buy out houses on the two streets in Diamond closest to their plant had been in place for 30 years, Brignac claimed. However, when pressed by local residents to show documentation of this 30-year plan, Shell offered none.

2. Louisiana Bucket Brigade and Concerned Citizens of Norco, Shell's Great Divide: Loft Principles v. Low-Down Land Deals (undated), p. 3.

3. Margie Richard points out that the early purchases Shell made of homes in Diamond were for very little money. A wood home would go for about $10,000, she recalls. Brick homes sold for somewhat more. It was only after Concerned Citizens of Norco negotiated with Shell for better prices that the deal became viable enough for the residents of Diamond to sell their homes and move into a house in another community without going into debt.

4. Shell Games: Divide and Conquer in Norco's Diamond Community, co-authored by members of the Louisiana Bucket Brigade, Communities for a Better Environment, and residents of Diamond (undated; circa September 2000).

5. Mary Swerczek, "Mending Fences," *Times-Picayune*, September 17, 2000.

6. The Shell Oil Company runs Royal Dutch/Shell's U.S. operations from Houston.

7. Letter from Rep. Maxine Waters to Steven L. Miller, CEO, Shell Oil Company, November 1, 2001.

8. Blaine Harden, "Born on the Bayou and Barely Feeling Any Urge to Roam," *New York Times*, September 30, 2002. Harden describes the community of Vacherie, Louisiana, where the children and grandchildren of sharecroppers continue to live together much as they did in Diamond.

9. Harden, "Born on the Bayou."

Chapter 11

1. The federal government does not classify oilfield wastes as hazardous wastes.
2. Bazelon, "Bad Neighbors," p. 54.
3. Thanos, "Shell Oil and the Norco Community."
4. Mark Schleifstein, "EPA Inspector Blasts Dallas Arm: Its Oversight of LDEQ Too Slack Report Said," *Times-Picayune*, February 5, 2003.
5. Brett Barrouquere, "DEQ Blasted for Its Rate of Enforcement," *Advocate* (Baton Rough), April 13, 2003.
6. Guy Gugliotta and Eric Pianin, "EPA: Few Fined for Polluting Water," *Washington Post*, June 6, 2003.
7. Jennifer Lee, "Vowing to Enforce the Clean Air Act, While Also Trying to Change It," *New York Times*, April 22, 2003.
8. The office is now closed.
9. The EPA created NEJAC in 1995 to serve as a citizens' advisory board made up of a variety of stakeholders that included elected officials, appointed governmental officials, business leaders, and representatives of community groups, environmental justice groups, and environmental health organizations.

Chapter 12

1. O'Rourke and Macey, "Community Environmental Policing."
2. Ibid., p. 14.
3. John Biers, "Bad Air Day," *Times-Picayune*, September 17, 2000.
4. As of May, 2003, the EPA proposed to drop MEK from its list of 189 Hazardous Air Pollutants. A regulatory battle over the delisting, pitting industrialists against environmentalists, is expected.
5. Toxic Terror Strikes Norco on Tuesday, December 8, 1988 (flyer published by Louisiana Citizens Committee for Participation in NEJAC).
6. National Oil Refinery Action Network, "National Environmental Justice Advisory Council Gets Taste of Chemical Assault in Louisiana's Toxic Corridor," *Oil Rag* 10, winter 1988–89, p. 2.
7. Shell Notice, December 8, 1998.
8. Biers, "Bad Air Day."
9. Thanos, "Shell Oil and the Norco Community."
10. Rolfes, "Shell Games in the Diamond Community," p. 5.
11. Bazelon, "Bad Neighbors," p. 56.
12. Shell would later agree to install monitors outside their fenceline but environmentalists question whether or not the air sampling regime being set up by Shell will take samples frequently enough and be calibrated to detect low level releases of toxic chemicals.

Chapter 13

1. The Louisiana Bucket Brigade has moved its office to 1036 Napoleon Avenue, New Orleans, LA 70115.

2. Kretzmann and Rolfes, *Shell Shocked*.

3. For a detailed account of Shell's alleged involvement in human rights abuses in Nigeria, see Okonta and Douglas, *Where Vultures Feast*.

4. Mike McCloskey, "The New Challenge of the EJ Movement," *EJ Times: The Sierra Club Environmental Justice Newsletter* 1, no. 1 (1999), p. 2.

5. "Sierra Club's National Environmental Justice Grassroots Organizing Project," at www.sierraclub.org.

6. Jenny Coyle, "Growing Justice," *Planet News Letter* (Sierra Club), May 2001.

7. Ibid.

8. Robbie Cox, "Toxic Tours and the Sierra Club," *EJ Times* 2 (2001), no. 1, p. 3.

9. Coyle, "Growing Justice," p. 3.

10. Ibid., p. 4.

11. "Toxic Tours: Challenging Polluters' Business Sense(s)," *EJ Times* 2 (2001), no. 1, p. 4.

12. Annette Hewlett, "Environmental Justice: Stories from around the Country," at www.sierraclub.org.

Chapter 14

1. Oral testimony of Margie Richard, United Nations Commission on Human Rights, Geneva, April 7, 1999, cited in R. Bullard, *Dumping in Dixie* (Westview, 1990, 1994, 2000), pp. 156–158.

2. Bazelon, "Bad Neighbors," p. 57.

Chapter 15

1. Mary Swerczek, "Shell Offers Buyout for All of Diamond," *Times-Picayune* , June 11, 2002.

2. Mary Swerczek, "Diamond Cheers Its Hard-Won Offer," *Times-Picayune*, June 12, 2002.

3. Ibid.

Chapter 16

1. Bazelon, "Bad Neighbors," p. 57.

2. O'Rourke and Macey, "Community Environmental Policing," p. 32.

Chapter 17

1. Lisa Rimmer, Failing the Challenge: The Other Shell Report 2002, at www.foei.org.

2. Ibid.

3. Mary Swerczek, "Motiva Refinery Valve Spews Oily Mess on Norco: Cars and Houses Splattered with Spray," *Times-Picayune*, October 9, 2002.

Conclusion

1. Mary Swerczek, "Diamond Cheers Its Hard-Won Offer," *Times-Picayune*, June 12, 2002.

2. Mary Swerczek, "Activist Took Lead Role in Fight Against Chemical Plant Hazards," *Times-Picayune*, April 19, 2004.

Brian K. Obach, *Labor and the Environmental Movement: The Quest for Common Ground*

Peggy F. Barlett and Geoffrey W. Chase, eds., *Sustainability on Campus: Stories and Strategies for Change*

Steve Lerner, *Diamond: A Struggle for Environmental Justice in Louisiana's Chemical Corridor*

Index